ECONOMICS HANDBOOK SERIES

SEYMOUR E. HARRIS, EDITOR

Socialism

ECONOMICS HANDBOOK SERIES

SEYMOUR E. HARRIS, Editor

ADVISORY COMMITTEE: Edward H. Chamberlin, Gottfried Haberler, Alvin H. Hansen, Edward S. Mason, Joseph A. Schumpeter, and John H. Williams. *All of Harvard University.*

Hoover • THE LOCATION OF ECONOMIC ACTIVITY
Hansen • MONETARY THEORY AND FISCAL POLICY
Sweezy • SOCIALISM

Socialism

by Paul M. Sweezy, Ph.D.

FIRST EDITION

NEW YORK   TORONTO   LONDON

McGRAW-HILL BOOK COMPANY, INC.

1949

SOCIALISM

TO MY MOTHER

Preface

THIS BOOK is written from the standpoint of a socialist as the term is defined in Chapter 1. The purpose of the book, however, is to instruct, not to persuade. I hope that it will help all readers, whatever their personal attitude toward socialism, to understand a form of society and a political movement which have been and are still among the most important forces shaping the world of the twentieth century.

A few sections of Part One, Socialism in the World Today, deal with rapidly changing events and will inevitably be somewhat out of date by the time the book appears in print. The reader will be better able to make allowances and adjustments for subsequent developments if he bears in mind that the book was written during the last half of 1947 and the first two months of 1948.

I want to thank the following persons for reading parts of the manuscript and making valuable suggestions for improvements: Otto Nathan, Leo Huberman, Paul Baran, Ruth Glass, Norman MacKenzie, Lewis Feuer, and Richard Schlatter. My greatest obligation is to John Rackliffe, who has gone over the whole manuscript with great care and has done his best to help me say what I wanted to say in straightforward, readable language. Needless to say, the responsibility for opinions expressed is entirely my own.

For permission to quote copyrighted material I am indebted to Harcourt, Brace & Company for a quotation from R. H. Tawney, *The Acquisitive Society;* to Harper & Brothers for quotations from J. A. Schumpeter, *Capitalism, Socialism, and Democracy;* to Longmans, Green & Co., Inc. for a quotation from Sidney and Beatrice Webb, *Soviet Communism;* to the University of Minnesota Press for quotations from Benjamin Lippincott (ed.), *On the Economic Theory of Socialism;* to Oxford University Press for a quotation from Ernest Barker (ed.), *The Politics of Aristotle,* and for a quotation from H. D. Dickinson, *Economics of Socialism;* to The Macmillan Company for a quotation from Lionel Robbins, *The Great Depression,* and for a quotation from A. C. Pigou, *Socialism vs. Capitalism;* to the University of Chicago Press for a quotation from F. A. Hayek, *The Road to Serfdom;* and to Little, Brown & Company for a quotation from Walter Lippmann, *The Good Society.*

PAUL M. SWEEZY

WILTON, N. H.
January, 1949

Contents

Editor's Introduction

FOR YEARS many teachers of economics and other professional economists have felt the need of a series of books on economic subjects that is not filled by the usual textbook or by the highly technical treatise.

This present series, published under the general title The Economics Handbook Series, was planned with this need in mind. Designed first of all for students, the volumes are useful in the ever-growing field of adult education and also are of interest to the informed general reader.

The volumes are not long—they give the essentials of the subject matter within the limits of a few hundred pages; they present a distillate of accepted theory and practice, without the detailed approach of the technical treatise. Each volume is a unit, standing on its own.

The authors are scholars, each writing on an economic subject in which he is an authority. In this series the author's first task was not to make important contributions to knowledge—although many of them do—but so to present his subject matter that his work as a scholar will carry its maximum influence outside as well as inside the classroom. The time has come to redress the balance between the energies spent on the creation of new ideas and on their dissemination. Economic ideas are unproductive if they do not spread beyond the world of scholars. Popularizers without technical competence, unqualified textbook writers, and sometimes even charlatans control too large a part of the market for economic ideas.

In the classroom the Economics Handbook Series will serve, it is hoped, as brief surveys in one-semester courses, as supplementary reading in introductory courses and in other courses in which the subject is related.

In this volume, the third to be issued in the Economics Handbook Series, Dr. Paul M. Sweezy writes on *socialism qua socialist*. As anyone in the least familiar with it must know, socialism is itself a subject of much dispute. Socialists, as defined by Dr. Sweezy, are full of disagreements among themselves. Many groups which regard themselves as socialists do not even recognize as socialists others who deem themselves socialists. It goes without saying, therefore, that Dr. Sweezy's volume will not fully please or adequately represent all the different bodies of thought usually considered as socialist. For example, it leans more closely to the Marxian than to the Fabian approach. Its viewpoint is nearer that of the group which determines Soviet policy than the one which now holds the reins of government in Britain. The volume in some regards differs from the fully stated position of any single organized socialist or communist political body. Yet in many regards it expresses a great deal which is common to all socialist thought. The result is a major contribution to the literature of socialism. The author is eminently qualified to write this volume. Dr. Sweezy in the Marxian tradition knows classical economics, having studied it at Harvard, London, and Vienna, all centers of orthodox economics. For many years he taught economics at Harvard.

In recent years he had the opportunity to study European socialism and politics at first hand, and in a previous work, *The Theory of Capitalist Development,* he showed a comprehensive grasp of Marxian economics unusual among English-speaking economists. His first book, *Monopoly and Capitalism in the English Coal Trade, 1550–1850,* reflected his ability to deal with historical problems. The present volume, the result of years of study and reflection, deals with the historical, theoretical, and practical aspects of socialism. It is fair to say, the editor submits, that it is by the leading Marxian in the United States—one with a rare faculty of expressing himself tersely and lucidly.

It is important that we should know more about socialism and planning—even we who have faith in private enterprise. Those of us who want to preserve capitalism had better at least learn about socialism. As the socialists have taken over what they consider worth preserving in capitalism (*e.g.,* certain kinds of incentives), so the defenders of private enterprise might be able to strengthen our system by borrowing from socialism.

Three successive parts of Dr. Sweezy's book include a discussion of socialism today, a broad historical survey, and finally the pros and cons of socialism. Among the many features of the book are an examination of the meaning of socialism and communism; an appraisal of socialism in the Soviet Union, the United Kingdom, and Poland; the Marxian philosophy and history; Marxian views on capitalism, on value and surplus value, on the relation of over-saving and crises, and on imperialism; the growth of the socialist movement, particularly over the last 100 years; the case for *democratic* socialism, and notably its effective use of incentives, its capacity to utilize resources rationally, and its compatibility with freedom; and throughout an analysis and evaluation of planning.

Many will not agree with some of Dr. Sweezy's conclusions. Those who fear undue influence of the present volume may be cheered by a forthcoming companion volume on capitalism in this series written by one as devoted to private enterprise as Dr. Sweezy is to socialism.

The Editor welcomes Dr. Sweezy's contribution to the Economics Handbook Series.

SEYMOUR E. HARRIS

Part One

Socialism in the World Today

CHAPTER 1

Socialism and Communism

Concerning the Definition of Socialism

In its primary usage the term "socialism" means a social system which is differentiated from other social systems by the character of its property relations. Thus socialism properly belongs to the same species as capitalism and feudalism, to name the social systems which are most familiar to people living in countries with a western European historical background. We shall attempt to bring out the essential nature of socialism by contrasting it with capitalism, the social system under which we in the United States live at the present time.

Capitalism and socialism are alike in that each guarantees to the individual a wide latitude in the ownership and disposal of the means of consumption. In this sense it can be said that both systems recognize the principle of private property. They differ, however, in their treatment of the means of production. Capitalism recognizes a relatively unrestricted right of private ownership in the means of production, while socialism denies this right and reserves such ownership to public bodies. It goes without saying that we are here speaking of "pure" capitalist and socialist systems. In any actual capitalist system there is likely to be a considerable amount of public and cooperative ownership of the means of production; while in the Soviet Union, which is so far the only unquestionable example of socialism in practice, collective farmers who own their land and most of their means of production cooperatively are nevertheless permitted to own privately a certain amount of livestock and other necessities of agricultural production.

The property systems of capitalism and socialism are of crucial

3

importance not only because they affect the lives of individuals differently, but also because they reflect and condition radically different social structures, each of which has its own laws and developmental tendencies.

Under capitalism ownership of the means of production is typically confined to a relatively small percentage of the total population; the rest are obliged to sell their labor power in order to earn a livelihood. The property system is thus a legal expression of the basic social structure of capitalism, the division of society into two fundamentally antagonistic classes of employers and wage earners. In such a system production is organized through the market, with each owner or associated group of owners producing for sale the types and quantities of goods which will yield a maximum profit over the cost of materials and labor power. Hence, capitalism operates according to the laws of the market. Finally, it must be noted that the ownership of the means of production and the profits which are derived therefrom are not only a source of consumable income, they also confer the freedom from labor and the command over the labor of others which, taken together, add up to social power and prestige. It follows that the road to advancement in capitalist society lies through the accumulation of ever more property, and this endless striving to expand the means of production as an end in itself becomes the motive force of capitalist development.

The social structure, laws, and tendencies which are associated with the property system of socialism are different from those of capitalism. Since under socialism there are no private owners of the means of production, it follows that there is no class of employers and no separate class of workers; in principle everyone is a worker, and the only employer is society itself acting through various governmental and cooperative organs. This does not mean, of course, that there are no social differentiations under socialism, but it does mean that there are none corresponding to the chief social differentiation of capitalist society. In a system without private employers, production for profit, and hence also the organization of production through the market, loses its rationale and must be replaced by production in accordance with a plan. This necessarily implies that the economic laws of capitalism are no longer applicable to socialism. Finally, since private ownership and private profit are nonexistent under socialism, it follows that the driving force of accumulation, the means of advancement in a capitalist society, must also be absent. In its place we have the conscious striving to reach general social goals, which planners in a socialist society must set in order to be able to regulate and evaluate their activities. It is these social goals which become the motive force of socialist development.

In later chapters we shall inquire further into the structure and functioning of socialism. For the present we are concerned only with establishing the fact that when we talk about socialism we are talking about a social *system* and not simply about a certain set of property relations. Only if this is clearly recognized can the subject be discussed realistically, that is, in its historical setting and in its proper relation to other social systems.

A number of secondary meanings have become attached to the term "socialism," as well as to the derivative term "socialist" (both noun and adjective). Some of these are quite logical and legitimate; others are a hindrance to clear thinking.

The idea of a socialist society came into existence long before the reality, and in the meantime it was natural for anyone who believed in socialism or advocated it to be called a socialist. Similarly, the movement aiming toward the achievement of socialism was called the socialist movement. The next step was for the socialist movement to take on the name of socialism. The term thus acquired two quite distinct meanings: on the one hand a new form of society and on the other a movement striving to substitute this new form for the existing social order. These two meanings, however, are closely and logically related to one another, and in any given context it is usually easy to determine which is intended. Thus, for example, if one speaks of American socialism it is clear that one means a movement looking to the achievement of socialism in America; while if one speaks of Soviet socialism it is equally clear that one is referring to the social system of the Soviet Union.

In other contexts the problem of interpretation is more complicated. For example, in Russia before 1917 the term "socialism" clearly referred to a movement, and at the present time it refers just as clearly to a social system. But this difference inevitably raises the question of when the Russian socialist movement succeeded in establishing a socialist system. Similar questions can be asked with respect to several countries today. British socialism, in the sense of the British socialist movement, is in power today and is striving to change Britain into a socialist country. Has it succeeded in doing so? What meaning or meanings can be legitimately attached to the expression "British socialism" today? When we are faced with questions of this sort—and they will recur in the course of this book—we must be cautious and critical in the use of terms. It must be emphasized, however, that the essential difficulty in dealing with these problems is not solely—or even primarily—verbal, as some of our more fashionable semanticists would have us believe; the difficulty lies instead in the extraordinary complexity of the real world, and it can be overcome only by a painstaking and clearheaded analysis of the facts.

So far we have mentioned only such meanings of socialism and socialist as are legitimately and usefully derived from the primary meaning. As already noted, however, there are others which are confusing and misleading. There has been a widespread tendency —unfortunately not least among socialists themselves—to attach the socialist label to every measure of reform that happens to have the support of socialists. And this practice has been all too easily extended to include the identification as "socialist" of almost any sort of reform, whether or not it has the support of socialists. Consider, for example, the following definitions of socialism, both by eminent social scientists.

According to William Graham Sumner, "Socialism is any device or doctrine whose aim is to save individuals from any of the difficulties or hardships of the struggle for existence and the competition of life by the intervention of 'the State.' " [1]

And according to James Bonar, "Socialism is that policy or theory which aims at securing by the action of the central democratic authority a better distribution, and in due subordination thereunto a better production, of wealth than now prevails." [2]

It will be noted that the Sumner definition would classify any sort of Poor Law as socialism, while the Bonar definition would put even a mildly progressive income tax in the same category. Needless to say, such measures (and many others which could be more plausibly called socialist) have been not only advocated but actually put into operation by people ranging all the way from those who never heard of socialism to those who regard socialism as the mortal enemy of civilization. In short, definitions of such a loose and general nature have lost all connection with the primary meaning of the term and for this reason are worse than valueless.

The foregoing discussion is intended to give the reader an idea of how the terms "socialism" and "socialist" are and are not used in this book. At the risk of oversimplification, the following summary gloss is appended for convenience:

Socialism. In its primary meaning, socialism is a complete social system which differs from capitalism not only in the absence of private ownership of the means of production but also in its basic structure and mode of functioning. By extension, socialism is also any movement under capitalism which sets as its goal the attainment of socialism in the sense just indicated.

Socialist (noun). A socialist is one who believes in socialism or attempts to practice its principles.

Socialist (adjective). Something is said to be socialist if it is specifically associated with socialism in either of the above-

[1] As quoted by C. H. Page in *Class and American Sociology: From Ward to Ross,* p. 103.

[2] "Socialism," *Encyclopaedia Britannica,* 13th ed.

mentioned meanings of the term. Thus, for example, socialist economics has two possible meanings: either it is concerned with the functioning of a socialist economy, or it is the body of economic doctrines produced by the socialist movement. It is to be noted that this is a rather narrow definition; it excludes nearly all isolated reforms (*e.g.*, the nationalization of a given industry) from the category of socialist measures since they can be adopted by a capitalist society without altering its basic structure or mode of functioning.

Communism

Much confusion exists, even in the minds of well-informed people, as to the meaning of communism and its relation to socialism. Since these questions are unavoidably involved at nearly every stage of the subsequent analysis, it is necessary to discuss them with some care at the outset.

"Communism" is a much older term than "socialism." The latter seems not to have been used at all before 1800 or in its present-day sense before the late 1820's. Communism, on the other hand, dates back to classical antiquity, though at that time its meaning was not what we usually understand by the word today. Originally and for many centuries communism referred not to an entire social system but rather to the pooling of property, usually only in consumption goods, by a group of people acting within a given social system. For example, the communism attributed to ancient Sparta was not a social system; the social system of Sparta was fundamentally one of slavery. To the extent that communism existed, it concerned only a part of the ruling class and was primarily a device for strengthening the military power of the Spartan state. It was not until the dawn of the modern era—to be exact, not until 1516, the year in which Thomas More's *Utopia* was published—that the idea of communism as a community of property for all, and hence as an entire social system, came into the world. From this time on, the two concepts of communism have continued to exist side by side, and different writers have used the term to denote either one or the other and not infrequently a confused mixture of the two.

It is against this background that we must trace the development of the present-day usage of the term. The 1830's and 1840's produced an extensive literature of social reform and reconstruction in western Europe. The first "socialists," so called, were the followers of Robert Owen, but after 1835 the name began to be applied more generally; and when it was introduced into Germany about 1840, it was soon appropriated by various writers and sects whose wordy muddleheadedness threatened to discredit the entire radical movement of the day. Hence, when Marx and Engels, along with a handful of associates, set out to organize a political movement in the later 1840's they avoided the term "socialist" and used "communist" as an uncompromised and at the same time understandable substitute. This explains why the Communist League (founded in 1847) and the *Communist Manifesto* (published in 1848) were named as they were.

In the quarter century following the publication of the *Manifesto* Marxism forged ahead of all rival left-wing schools. In the course of this process the old reasons for shunning the term "socialist" lost their force, and the Marxists gradually took it over as their own, without modifying their aims or doctrines. As a consequence the terms "communist" and "socialist" came to be used more or less interchangeably, with the latter in time supplanting the former in common usage. The *Communist Manifesto* became the recognized and authoritative statement of the aims and methods of the *socialist* movement.

This was roughly the situation in the years immediately before the First World War. One development of the nineteenth century, however, must be noted, since it was to become an important influence in the new period which opened in 1914. Before 1875 the German socialist movement had been divided into two parties. In that year the two parties merged at a congress held in the town of Gotha and adopted a unified program, which has come down in history as the Gotha Program. Marx thought poorly of the Gotha Program and wrote a long memorandum from his home in London to his German followers criticizing its most important points. This was finally published in 1891 and has since become (under the title *Critique of the Gotha Programme*) one of the classic documents of Marxian thought.

From our present point of view the importance of the *Critique* lies in the fact that here for the first time Marx distinguished between two phases of communist society. The "first phase," which he also calls "socialist" in various passages, is the form of society that will immediately succeed capitalism. This phase will bear the marks of its origin: the workers as the new ruling class will need their own state (the dictatorship of the proletariat) to protect them against their enemies; man's mental and spiritual horizon will still be colored by bourgeois ideas and values; incomes, though no longer paid out on the basis of property ownership, will have to be calculated according to work done rather than according to need. Nevertheless, society's productive forces will develop rapidly under this new order, and in the course of time the limitations imposed by the capitalist past will be transcended. Society will then enter what Marx called the "higher phase of communist society," under which the state will wither away, a totally different attitude toward work will prevail, and society will be able to inscribe on its banner the motto "From each according to his ability, to each according to his need."

It cannot be said that the *Critique* exercised a great influence when it was written or even when it was first published. In fact, neither the analysis nor the terminology of the *Critique* seems to have attracted particular notice until they were revived and emphatically restated by Lenin in his famous booklet *State and Revolution*, written on the eve of the October Revolution in Russia. For the sake of clarity Lenin dropped Marx's "first" and "higher" phases of communism and used the terms "socialism" and "communism" in a corresponding sense. From that time on, this usage has been followed not only in the Soviet Union but also in all branches of the world Communist movement. To the loyal Communist, communism (written with a small *c*) means the form of society, lying beyond socialism, to which mankind will ultimately attain when the inheritance of classes and class conflicts has finally been overcome.

The reader may now be asking what is the relation between communism in this sense and the name Communist (written with a capital *C*) as it is used in the two preceding sentences. The answer is that the relation is at most a very indirect one. During the First World War Lenin became convinced that most of the world's socialist parties had betrayed the cause of socialism by abandoning internationalism and backing their respective governments in what he regarded as a purely imperialist conflict. He therefore decided that it would be necessary to break decisively with the past and to build a new international movement of parties which had been purged of all association with "traitors." To emphasize the break he wanted a new name. Under the circumstances, it was quite natural for Lenin, who regarded himself as above all else a faithful disciple of Marx, to seek guidance in the history of the socialist movement. Moreover, it was not hard to find an instructive parallel from the past. As already pointed out, in the 1840's Marx and Engels felt the need to avoid "socialism" and "socialist" in order not to be confused with those who were then calling themselves socialists. Hence they chose the name "Communist." Lenin, faced with a very similar problem, quite deliberately adopted the same solution. Thus we see that the relation of the Communist parties of our day to socialism is the same as that of the Communist League and the *Communist Manifesto* to socialism in the mid-nineteenth century. They are socialist parties in the sense that they believe in, and work for, the attainment of socialism; they do not (except in a few special cases) bear the name "Socialist" for reasons which can be understood only in terms of the history of the movement.

The usage of terms in the Soviet Union illustrates this situation very clearly. The leadership of the Soviet Union is organized in the Communist Party; yet the social system of the Soviet Union is always referred to as socialism, and the full official name of the Union is the Union of Soviet Socialist Republics. Moreover, Soviet theorists retain the distinction between socialism and communism made by Lenin in *State and Revolution:* in their view the present socialist system will eventually evolve into full-fledged communism.

Social Democrats and Communists

We have one final distinction, or set of distinctions, yet to make before we shall be in a position to handle our material without unnecessary ambiguity. This is the distinction between the terms "Communist" and "Social Democrat" as applied to the two great branches of the world socialist movement of the present day. We have already sketched the background of the term "Communist" in this context, and it remains to explain the origin and meaning of the term "Social Democrat."

Before the First World War most of the socialist parties of the world were loosely united in the so-called Second International.[3] These parties had a variety of official names. For example, there were two American parties affiliated to the International, one called the Socialist Labor Party (founded in 1877) and the other called the Socialist Party (founded in 1901). Similarly, there were several British parties, which, of course, had different names. By far the largest and most influential socialist party of this period was the German party, which was called the Social Democratic Party of Germany (*Sozialdemokratische Partei Deutschlands*). The fact that the German party occupied such an outstanding position led to the frequent use of its name to refer to the movement as a whole, or to some particular branch of it, even though the latter might have a specific name of its own. It came about in this way that before 1914 the terms "socialism" and "social democracy" were often used more or less interchangeably.

[3] See Chap. 8.

After the breakup of the Second International and the found-
·ing of the Communist, or Third, International [4] the situation
became considerably more complicated. Many socialist parties
split in two, with one section forming a Communist party and
joining the Communist International, while the other remained
under the leadership of men who were satisfied with the traditional ideas and methods of the prewar period. The latter revived
the Second International in the early twenties, and henceforth
the division of the world socialist movement was both ideologically and organizationally clear-cut.

The reader must note, however, that whatever official names
they might adopt, all parties on both sides regarded themselves
as socialist parties. Hence there was an obvious need for some
sort of generally recognized terminology which would take account of this fact and at the same time not slur over the vital
differences dividing the two branches of the socialist movement.
The Communists had given themselves a name and insisted that
every one in their camp should use it; but what should the others
be called? It was essentially in answer to this question that the
term "Social Democrat" acquired its now widely accepted meaning. As it happened, the name was applied to the adherents of
the revived Second International by both sides, though for opposite reasons. The Communists regarded it as a term of derogation,
smacking of what they considered the treachery of the war period.
Their rivals, on the other hand, tended to blame the Communists
for much of what had gone wrong since the war and were proud
of their intellectual and spiritual affinity to the prewar movement.
Hence it came to pass that socialists who might be at odds on
practically everything else were at least willing to agree that their
once-united movement had split into two factions, which should
properly be called Communist and Social Democratic.

It should be noted that the new connotation of the term "Social
Democratic" is narrower than its usual pre-1914 meaning. It had
then been virtually synonymous with "socialist," while since the

[4] See Chap. 9.

First World War it has referred to a part of the socialist movement. It is in this narrower sense that the term is used throughout .
the present work.

The World Socialist Movement Today

Socialism today is, in the true sense of the word, a world-wide
movement. In later chapters we shall trace its growth and spread
from small beginnings in England and France to central and
eastern Europe, to America and Australia, and finally to Asia and
Africa. We shall not attempt to give a quantitative estimate of the
present strength of the movement as a whole or of either of its
major branches, partly because reliable statistics exist only for
certain countries and certain dates, and partly because conditions
are changing so rapidly in many parts of the world that such an
attempt would probably be more misleading than helpful. We
are, however, reasonably safe in saying that the main centers of
Communist strength are in the Soviet Union, eastern Europe,
France, Italy, and China; that the main centers of Social Democratic strength are in Great Britain, the smaller countries of western Europe, and the British Dominions; and that in colonial and
economically backward areas the foundations of a socialist movement are being laid by small but rapidly growing Communist
parties.

In the remainder of Part One we shall analyze more closely
certain of these regions which may be considered to be of crucial
importance to the future of socialism. The Soviet Union and
Great Britain have been chosen as the major strongholds of Communism and Social Democracy, respectively. The countries of
eastern Europe (with special attention to the largest, Poland) are
treated for two reasons: because both branches of the socialist
movement are playing a role there, and because recent developments in these countries enable us to bring into sharp focus many
of the most important problems of the transition from capitalism
to socialism.

CHAPTER 2

Socialism in the Soviet Union

THE SOVIET UNION is as yet the only country in the world which nearly everyone agrees lives under a socialist system of society. The purpose of this chapter is to explain the origin and nature of the Soviet system and to indicate the main accomplishments of socialism in its first homeland.[1]

The Origin of Socialism in the Soviet Union

There is a widespread opinion that Russia before the Revolution was composed of an all-powerful autocracy on the one hand and a vast stagnant mass of ignorant peasantry on the other. This is a picture of the *ancien régime* in Russia which leaves out what is most important to an understanding of the Revolution and the subsequent development of the Soviet state. The peasantry, far from being stagnant, was in a state of almost continuous ferment during the years before 1914; at the same time a swift process of industrialization was bringing into existence a highly exploited factory working class in the urban centers. Large-scale participation of foreign capital and technical personnel accelerated the pace of these changes but at the same time prevented anything like a corresponding growth of an indigenous middle class.

The result was that though the antiquated rule of Czarist and landlord aristocracy was being irrevocably undermined, the Russian *bourgeoisie,* unlike its French counterpart in the eighteenth

[1] A separate volume in this series by Abram Bergson on Soviet economics, tentatively scheduled for publication in 1949, will analyze the institutions and mode of operation of the Soviet economy.

century, was not strong enough to carry through a revolution and to maintain its grip on state power. When Czarism collapsed under the strain of war, the *bourgeoisie* took over the reins but proved incapable of consolidating its newly won position; revolutionary initiative quickly passed to the peasant masses and the urban working class. Under these conditions the Communist Party, thanks in large part to the genius of Lenin, was able to seize power and organize popular support behind a victorious four-year war against counterrevolutionary and foreign interventionist armies.

The new Soviet regime was committed to the principles of socialism, but during the period 1917–1921—usually referred to as the period of War Communism—its energy was so absorbed in meeting the overwhelming problems of survival that there was little to spare for the task of beginning to shape a new social order. Neither in industry nor in agriculture was it possible to pursue a consistent socialist policy, and the measures which were actually adopted were for the most part improvisations to meet a series of immediate crises.

It is not surprising, therefore, that by the end of the Civil War Russia was in a state bordering on chaos. The resistance of employers had forced the government again and again to extend its nationalization decrees until all but the smallest plants and workshops had been taken over by the state. But the government was as yet incapable of managing such a vast and heterogeneous collection of enterprises, and by 1920 industrial production had fallen to about one-fifth the prewar level. Agriculture suffered less severely, but production of foodstuffs was still far from adequate for the needs of the country. All land had been formally nationalized in 1918; this was necessary to satisfy the peasants' twofold demand for distribution of large estates and for the abolition of mortgages and similar encumbrances on their own property. But the right of the government to control the distribution and use of the land remained on paper, and what in fact happened was a vast multiplication of small holdings. Millions of peasants, who now had land to work and could buy almost no industrial products, naturally tended to consume or hoard their crops and animals. The result was a sharp decline in marketable surpluses. In order to feed the cities, the government was obliged to requisition grain by force; this naturally led to peasant resistance and thus contributed to the seriousness of the underlying crisis. Gross crop yields in 1920 were little more than half the prewar average, while the severe drought of 1921 reduced them still further and produced a disastrous famine.

Thus, while Russia emerged from the Civil War under a socialist government and with a property system which theoretically conformed to the traditional principles of socialism, the country was in fact exhausted, and the social order was in a state of disintegration. It was under these circumstances that Lenin introduced the New Economic Policy (NEP), which made far-reaching concessions to private enterprise in both industry and agriculture.

Under NEP the government retained in its own hands what were called the "commanding heights"—banks, the transport system, and large industrial establishments. (The latter constituted only about 10 per cent of all industrial establishments, but they employed more than four-fifths of the total number of workers.) The remaining small enterprises were either denationalized and returned to their former owners or leased to private individuals or cooperatives. In agriculture NEP relied on the recuperative powers of a relatively unfettered small peasant husbandry. The title to the land remained with the state, but the right of use was guaranteed to the occupiers, and even a limited amount of leasing of land and hiring of labor was permitted. As far as the vast majority of the peasants was concerned, the system under which they lived during the period of the NEP differed but little from the prewar system.

Considered as a whole, the Soviet Union under NEP was a peculiar mixture of socialism, capitalism, and what Marx called simple commodity production.[2] The government was socialist, the means of production were at least nominally publicly owned, and heavy industry was actually publicly managed, but still it would be incorrect to describe the entire system as socialist. The government was not really in a position to shape its development, and the relative weight of agriculture, which had practically no socialist features, was too great. As a result, attempts at economic planning during this period were all limited to a relatively small sector of the economy, and over-all plans remained in the theoretical stage. On the other hand, although capitalism was important in agriculture and became more so as the richer peasants (commonly called kulaks) expanded their production and played an increasingly important role in buying up and marketing the crops of their poorer neighbors, it would be equally incorrect to describe the system as a whole as capitalist, since by far the major part of industry and finance was in the hands of the state.

This mixed system worked effectively enough as long as the main problems to be solved were those of recovery from the devastation and exhaustion of the war and Civil-war periods. But by the middle twenties, when these problems had been practically solved, it became clear that the mixed system was fundamentally unstable and incapable of providing the necessary base for long-term expansion. It is important to understand the reason for this, because it provides the key to the future development of the Soviet social system.

In industry (and also in trade) state enterprise had little dif-

[2] Simple commodity production is characterized by a society composed of independent artisans and farmers each owning his own means of production and producing articles both for direct use and for exchange. In such a society there is division of labor but no employers and no wage laborers. There probably has never been a pure case of simple commodity production, but every civilized society of which we have a record has contained significant elements of simple commodity production; and in some—for example, certain parts of western Europe during the later Middle Ages—simple commodity production was the predominant social system.

ficulty in overcoming and gradually absorbing its private competitors. In this respect, therefore, NEP fulfilled the expectations
of its authors and led to a strengthening of the socialist sector of
the Soviet economy. This was undoubtedly an important achievement, but it must be remembered that Russia was still an overwhelmingly agricultural country. What was needed was not only
the socialization of existing industry but, even more, an extensive
program of industrialization which would bring the country up
to something like the economic level of the leading capitalist
countries. The government recognized that only through such a
program would it be possible to raise the low living standards of
the Russian masses and at the same time ensure the defence of
the country against increasingly dangerous threats of renewed
foreign intervention. Moreover, the Soviet regime was anxious
to expand the working-class base on which its own power rested.
But it was precisely such a program of industrialization that the
existing mixed system could not support.

The essential difficulty lay in the field of agriculture. Here, as
already noted, recovery was accompanied by a steady growth in
the number and importance of the kulaks, who quite naturally
favored private enterprise and hated the Soviet regime and all
it stood for. Their possession of capital made it possible for them
to buy up the surpluses of the poorer peasants, who were forced
by a perennial lack of cash to sell their crops immediately after
harvest time. Already the parceling of landholdings, which had
characterized the first phase of the Revolution, had reduced total
marketable surpluses of agricultural products; before the end of
NEP such surpluses as there were had come largely under the
control of the kulaks. This meant that the government's plans for
industrial expansion, which of course required a steadily increasing flow of agricultural products to the cities, were practically
at the mercy of the rural enemies of socialism. By the middle
twenties the situation had reached an acute stage, and the government was faced with the necessity of making a choice which could
not but have decisive consequences for the whole future course

of Soviet development. At bottom there were two, and only two, possible courses.

The government might bow to the strength of the kulaks' position and in effect meet their terms. This would mean the continued encouragement of private enterprise in agriculture, the limitation of industrial expansion, and the redirection of state industry to provide an increased supply of those commodities which would induce the kulaks to expand and sell their surpluses for distribution to the cities. If this course had been pursued, two consequences would almost certainly have followed. First, the kulaks would have grown steadily stronger. And second, the government would have had to renounce the hope of building up defence industries sufficiently powerful to guarantee freedom from foreign intervention. In other words, the socialist regime would have been subjected to growing pressures both from within and from without. Knowing what we do today about the international forces which were already at work in the twenties, we are justified in concluding that the Soviet regime could not have survived under such conditions. Either it would have been forced to capitulate, or it would have been decisively beaten in battle.

The second course which the government might pursue was to meet the challenge of the kulaks head on, and it was this course which was actually adopted. This meant emergency measures to force the delivery of grain, followed by a thoroughgoing reorganization of agriculture to bring it under state control, eliminate the kulak influence, and raise productivity sufficiently to supply the needs of both the countryside and the cities. But such a reorganization of agriculture could be undertaken only in conjunction with a great industrialization drive to supply the necessary agricultural machinery, to drain off surplus rural manpower, and to prepare the defences of the country against any emergency. Hence, the Soviet Government in 1928 embarked upon a vast combined collectivization and industrialization program, which has quite rightly been called the "Second Revolution." The next few years were a period of tremendous effort and tension, of heroism and suffering. By the mid-thirties it was apparent that the Second Revolution had been successful. Table 1 shows how the basic dilemma of the NEP period was finally solved.

It will be seen from these figures that before the First World War Russia had a relatively large marketable surplus of grain, much of which was at that time exported. As a result of the First

Table 1. Production and Marketing of Grain in the U.S.S.R.*
(In million tons)

Type of producer	Prewar		1926–1927		1934	
	Pro-duced	Mar-keted	Pro-duced	Mar-keted	Pro-duced	Mar-keted
Landlords................	9.6	4.5				
Kulaks..................	30.4	10.4	9.6	2.0		
Small and middle peasants..	40.0	5.9	64.0	7.5	10.6	2.0
State and collective farms...	....	....	1.3	0.6	76.8	22.4
Total..................	80.0	20.8	75.3	10.1	87.4	24.4

* Adapted from a similar table in Rudolf Schlesinger, *Soviet Legal Theory*, p. 169.

Revolution and the NEP, total production recovered to very nearly the prewar level, but the marketable surplus fell by more than half; there was no margin either for export or to support a program of industrialization. As a result of the Second Revolution and collectivization, both total production and the marketable surplus surpassed prewar levels; not only was there enough grain for the countryside but also the margin necessary for industrialization was assured.

The Second Revolution accomplished its goals of making possible industrialization and the building up of the defences of the country by introducing socialism into the agricultural sector of the economy. It thereby rooted out the last stronghold of private enterprise and transformed the social system of the Soviet Union into one of genuine socialism.

The Main Characteristics of Socialism in the Soviet Union

It was pointed out in the previous chapter that socialism has been traditionally defined as a social order which recognizes private property in the means of consumption but disallows private property in the means of production. The Soviet property system certainly meets these general tests. Ownership of ordinary consumers' goods, like clothes, household equipment, books, and so on, enjoys very much the same guarantees in the Soviet Union as in, say, the United States or Great Britain. This question, therefore, requires no further comment, and we need add only that both socialist theory and Soviet practice refute the widespread misapprehension that socialism is in principle opposed to any and every kind of private property. With regard to the means of production it is true that certain types of private ownership are still recognized in the Soviet Union; but these are strictly limited by law, their quantitative importance is not so great as to affect the character of the property system as a whole,[3] and they are officially regarded as a transitional, rather than a permanent, feature of the Soviet system. There can thus be no doubt that property relations in the Soviet Union conform to the classical definition of socialism.

From our present point of view the most significant thing about the Soviet property system is that it permits us to do something which previously had been impossible, namely, to study the actual character and functioning of socialist property relations. In par-

---

[3] The most important type of private property in the means of production is that used in the subsidiary farming operations of the collective farmers. In 1938 the personal homesteads of collective farmers accounted for just over one-fifth the gross agricultural production. Most of this was used for the immediate needs of the producing families.

ticular, two points of the utmost importance for an understanding of socialism may now be regarded as established beyond dispute. First, ownership of the means of production under socialism can assume a variety of forms. The two major categories are state ownership and cooperative ownership, and within each there are subcategories. For example, in the Soviet Union state ownership includes ownership by the federal Union, by the constituent Republics, and by all the subordinate units of local government down to the municipality; while cooperative ownership includes ownership by collective farms and by a variety of different kinds of consumers' and producers' cooperatives in the nonagricultural sectors of the economy. Second, ownership of the means of production under socialism does not mean—as it does in the classical Roman conception dominating the theory and practice of capitalist countries—that the owner has the right to do what he likes with his property. Not only are the rights of nonuse and abuse abolished under socialism, the right of use itself is limited by the interests of society as expressed concretely in the directives of the economic plan.

The reader may be inclined to assume that the second point nullifies the first, that if the use of property must conform to the directives of the plan, then all property is, in fact, state property, and the apparent multiformity of ownership has no substantive significance. This, however, is not the case. There is a very important difference, for example, between the ownership exercised by the Soviet state over a steel mill and the ownership exercised by a collective farm over its land, agricultural equipment, and livestock. Both must be used in accordance with the directives of the plan; but in the case of the steel mill all decisions as to how these directives are to be met are taken directly by the state, while in the case of the collective farm they fall within the province of the collective farmers organized as a cooperative body. In other words, the collective farm enjoys a higher degree of autonomy vis-à-vis the state than the steel mill. Other forms of property fall between these two examples, while still others have even greater autonomy than collective farms. The real problem is thus one of the degree of autonomy in the administration of property enjoyed by different types of owners. That this is a problem of substance and not merely of form will be readily admitted by everyone who has had practical experience of business or governmental affairs.

The socialist property system exemplified in the Soviet Union can be described in somewhat different terms; and since such a description may prove illuminating, it seems worth while. One could say that all means of production are owned by society through the medium of its highest organ, the state. A part of the means of production is administered directly by the state, while the remainder is handed over to various trustees in the shape of local governments and cooperative bodies. The terms of trusteeship differ from one case to another, but in every instance they include the obligation to administer the state's property in accordance with the over-all economic plan. This is a mode of expression which is quite familiar to Anglo-American legal thinking, and there is no doubt that it accurately describes the reality of the Soviet property system.

Let us now turn our attention to the economic system of Soviet socialism.

The essence of any economic system is the method which it uses to determine the types and quantities of goods and services to be produced. Under capitalism this is done by a multitude of independent units—individuals, partnerships, corporations—each attempting to maximize its profits. No one exercises control over the general pattern of production; it emerges as a by-product of the profit-seeking activity of all these separate units. In the Soviet Union during the period of NEP, as we have already seen, this method continued to operate in the quantitatively dominant field of agriculture. Since the Second Revolution, however, it has been almost entirely eliminated, and its place has been taken by the method of centralized planning, which is now widely recognized as an essential feature of any socialist economy.

There are certain requirements for successful economic planning which may be said to hold quite generally. We shall list those which appear to be most important and then examine the extent to which they are met in the Soviet system.

First, there must be a central planning authority with at least the following two attributes: (1) a clear conception of social goals and the ability at any time to arrange them in a definite order of priority and (2) a knowledge of the resources and capabilities of the economy.

Second, the planning authority must have effective control (direct or indirect) over the individual units of the economy.

Third, the individual units of the system must be so administered and coordinated as to be responsive to complex directives.

Fourth, the planning authority must be in a position to check and enforce plan fulfillment.

None of these conditions of successful planning existed in Russia at the time the Soviet regime came to power, and the whole subsequent history of the Union could be written around the struggle to create them. The decisive steps were taken during the period of the first Five-year Plan (1928–1932); it was at this time that the planning system first came into operation. Since then there has been a continuous process of extending and improving the planning system, a process which is still under way and will doubtless continue indefinitely into the future.

The central planning authority in the Soviet Union is the Soviet Government itself. The State Planning Commission (*Gosplan*) is simply the government's technical planning arm and has no independent authority to determine the goals or the methods of the plan. After Lenin's death, in 1924, it was not until Stalin won undisputed control of the government four years later that a unified conception of the goals of planning was reached; nor could it be said with assurance that prior to this time the information which had been collected concerning the resources and capabilities of the Soviet economy was adequate for the purposes of over-all planning. Thus even the first prerequisite of successful planning was not realized until a good decade after the October Revolution.

The situation was similar with regard to the government's control over the individual units of the economy. As we have already seen, such control was effectively established in the fields of industry and trade during the NEP period, when the national-ized sector expanded and gradually absorbed the bulk of the private sector. But in the field of agriculture such control was established only as a consequence of the Second Revolution, which consolidated more than 20 million individual peasant households into fewer than a quarter of a million collective farms serviced by some 7,000 machine and tractor stations.

Regarding the administration and coordination of the indi-vidual units of the economy, Soviet experience has been a con-tinuous effort to create a mechanism which would be responsive to centralized controls and at the same time would be character-ized by efficiency, initiative, and flexibility in its parts. This is well illustrated in the field of industrial organization. Under War Communism extreme centralization under the Supreme Economic Council (SEC) prevailed. During the period of NEP, however, the SEC lost much of its authority to the individual enterprises and trusts. With the coming of the first Five-year Plan the author-ity of the SEC was once again strengthened, and the trust was largely supplanted by a new form, the combine. These original combines, however, were too large and unwieldy, and as they were broken up they lost powers to the SEC and gradually merged into the old trusts again. In 1932 the SEC itself was replaced by three People's Commissariats (now called Ministries). These in turn proved to be too large, and by 1940 they had been divided and subdivided into 24 industrial Commissariats. Meanwhile, in 1934, establishments of purely local significance (numerically the great majority of the total) were turned over to the direction of Commissariats of the constituent Republics, thus leaving the Union Commissariats free to concentrate on problems of national concern. Throughout all these changes one can discern not only adaptation to changing circumstances but also a search—unquestionably still in progress—for the right combination of centralization and decentralization.

Finally, we have pointed out that the planning authority must be able to check and enforce plan fulfillment. (If fulfillment should prove to be impossible, the authority must be in a position to make the necessary alterations in the plan. In fact, the need for continuous adjustments in the plan itself is one of the most important reasons for accurate checking of plan fulfillment.) It is probably in this sphere that the Soviet planning system has been slowest to develop. It was not until 1932 that Gosplan was equipped with sections for checking the fulfillment of the plan, and even then the real work of inspection and control rested with other organs of the Soviet Government, which were not properly coordinated with the planning arm. During the later thirties, however, the subject received increasing attention, and Gosplan gradually acquired increasing power and capacity to keep track of economic developments and to initiate measures designed to correct deviations from the plan. By 1940 these were generally recognized to be among the most important of Gosplan's functions.

We cannot attempt to describe here the manner in which plans are drawn up and put into operation in the Soviet Union.[4] One aspect of the problem, however, requires mention. There is a widespread belief that centralized planning is incompatible with freedom of the individual to choose his own occupation.[5] According to this view, the planning authority must have the power to direct the flow of labor as well as the flow of goods. Soviet experience, however, demonstrates that this is not the case.

[4] In this connection the reader is again referred to the forthcoming book by Professor Bergson in the present series.

[5] This problem is treated in theoretical terms in Chap. 12.

Between the end of War Communism and 1940 there was no compulsory direction of labor, and it was during this period that the planning system was conceived and put into operation. The two chief methods of allocating labor were the method of differential rewards and working conditions and the method of adjusting the educational and training system to the anticipated needs of the labor market. It is true that in 1940, as the Soviet Union moved onto a war footing in expectation of the Nazi attack, compulsory labor direction was reintroduced, but similar emergency measures were adopted in Britain and other countries during the war; they are not to be regarded as peculiar to the socialist system as such.[6]

In describing the origins and aims of the Second Revolution, we have already touched upon the goals which have guided Soviet planning since 1928. There can be little doubt that the fundamental goal, to which all others have been subordinated, has been to secure the defences of the country against any combination of potential attackers. This in turn required the speediest possible building up of heavy industry, with the twofold purpose of ensuring an adequate supply of arms and of making the country economically self-sufficient. Soviet planning has never lost sight of the value and desirability of raising mass living standards, but this objective has been deliberately subordinated to the needs of defence. Moreover, as long as the international situation remains as tense and uncertain as it is today, there seems to be no reason to anticipate any important changes in the goals of Soviet planning.

[6] A word should perhaps be added about the much-publicized question of "forced" or "slave" labor in the Soviet Union. What is usually meant by these terms is convict labor, which, of course, exists in other countries besides the Soviet Union, including the United States. No statistics are available on the extent of penal labor camps in the Soviet Union, but it is certain that they are not a decisive factor in the functioning of the Soviet *economic* system. For a sober discussion of this issue, see F. L. Schuman, *Soviet Politics* (1946), pp. 340*ff*.

The Achievements of Socialism in the Soviet Union

The outstanding achievement of socialism in the Soviet Union has been the victory in the war against Nazi Germany. Making all allowances for the importance of American and British aid, the fact remains that the Soviet Union stood up to and finally turned back the armed might of Germany during a period when the Nazis were not only largely free of attack from other quarters but also controlled the manpower and resources of almost the whole of non-Soviet Europe. We have already presented reasons for believing that this could not have been accomplished if the Second Revolution, which made Russia into a socialist country, had not been carried through. It is the Soviet Union's military success in the war against Germany which more than anything else has convinced the world that socialism really works. This is a fact which historians of the future may well rank in importance along with the October Revolution itself.

Behind this military success lie the profound social and economic changes which socialism brought to the Soviet Union in the years between the inauguration of the first Five-year Plan and the Nazi attack of 1941. The remainder of this chapter will be devoted to a brief summary of the most important of these changes.

All aspects of Soviet development have, of course, been dominated by the expansion of industry on the one hand and the collectivization of agriculture on the other. The consequences of these related processes can be seen in an increase of production as well as in alterations in the social structure of the country. The growth of production in certain representative industries is indicated in Table 2. The figures show clearly the tremendous increase which occurred during the 1930's and illustrate the concentration of the Soviet Government on the development of basic industries, as opposed to industries producing consumers' goods.

Tables 3 and 4 present comparable data from the field of agri-

culture. Here, as would be expected, the over-all changes are much
less striking than in industry. This is partly to be explained by
the difficulties and losses which attended the actual process of

Table 2. Production of Representative Industries in the U.S.S.R.*

(Quantities and quantity indexes)

Industry and unit	1913		1929		1938	
	Quantity	Index	Quantity	Index	Quantity	Index
Engineering and metal industries, billions of 1926–1927 roubles............	1,446	100	3,045	211	22,613	2,325
Trucks, thousands.........	14.8	100	15.9	107	49.1	332
Electric power, billions of kw-h...................	1.9	100	6.2	326	39.6	2,084
Coal, millions of tons.......	29.1	100	40.1	138	132.9	457
Oil, millions of tons........	9.2	100	13.8	150	32.2	350
Pig iron, millions of tons....	4.2	100	4.0	95	14.6	348
Steel, millions of tons.......	4.2	100	4.9	117	18.0	429
Cement, millions of tons....	1.5	100	2.2	147	5.7	380
Cotton cloth, millions of meters..................	2,227	100	3,068	138	3,491	157
Woolen cloth, millions of meters..................	95.0	100	100.6	106	114.0	120
Raw sugar, thousands of tons...................	1,290	100	1,283	100	2,519	195

* Derived from a table in A. Baykov, The Development of the Soviet Economic
System, p. 307.

collectivization, especially in the livestock economy. But a more
fundamental reason is that the purpose of collectivization was not
so much to increase aggregate agricultural production as to bring
agriculture under control and to raise its productivity in such a
way as to release large quantities of manpower for industrializa-

Table 3. Gross Production of Chief Crops in the U.S.S.R.*

(Quantities and quantity indexes)
(Unit = millions of quintals)

Crop	1913		1929		1938	
	Quantity	Index	Quantity	Index	Quantity	Index
Grain.......	816	100	717	88	949	116
Flax fiber...	5.1	100	3.6	71	5.5	108
Cotton.....	6.8	100	8.6	126	26.9	396
Sugar beet..	99.2	100	101.4 †	102	166.8	168

* Derived from a table in A. Baykov, *The Development of the Soviet Economic System*, p. 325.
† Average for the three years 1928, 1929, and 1930.

Table 4. Livestock Population in the U.S.S.R.*

(Numbers in millions and indexes)

Type of livestock	1913		1929		1938	
	Number	Index	Number	Index	Number	Index
Horses............	35.8	100	34.6	97	17.5	49
Cattle............	60.6	100	67.1	111	63.2	104
Sheep and goats.....	121.2	100	147.0	121	102.5	85
Pigs..............	20.9	100	20.7	99	30.6	146

* Derived from a table in A. Baykov, *The Development of the Soviet Economic System*, p. 325.

tion. Hence the change in the pattern of agricultural output, as exemplified on the one hand by the very rapid development of such industrial crops as cotton and sugar beet and on the other hand by the dwindling of the number of horses as a consequence of mechanization. The release of manpower, however, is even more significant; neither the industrial nor the agricultural output figures can be properly understood except in conjunction with

Table 5. Distribution of Population in the U.S.S.R.,
*1926 and 1939 ***

(In millions)

	1926		1939	
	Number	*Percentage*	*Number*	*Percentage*
Total population.............	147.0	100.0	170.4	100.0
Rural population.............	120.7	82.1	114.5	67.2
Urban population............	26.3	17.9	55.9	32.8

* B. H. Sumner, *A Short History of Russia*, p. 375.

the population figures given in Table 5. From this it appears that the cities, under the spur of industrialization, absorbed not only the entire natural increase of the Soviet population between 1926 and 1939 but also gained an additional 6 million at the expense of the countryside. That Soviet agriculture could afford this loss of manpower and at the same time increase production was one of the most important achievements of collectivization.

Let us now look at the changes in the social structure of the Soviet population which have been brought about by socialism. Table 6 gives the basic figures.

The main change resulting from the First Revolution was the destruction of the old ruling classes (with the exception of the kulaks). The Second Revolution completed this process, doubled the proportion of workers, turned the individual peasant into a collective farmer, and almost doubled the proportion of students and soldiers. It is impossible to exaggerate the significance of these figures; they demonstrate more adequately than volumes of description that socialism has had a profoundly revolutionary effect on the structure of Russian society.

Table 6. Social Structure of the Soviet Union *
(In percentages)

	1913	1928	1937
Workers and employees..........................	16.7	17.3	34.7
Members of collective farms and other cooperatives..	....	2.9	55.5
Individual peasants and craftsmen................	65.1	72.9	5.6
Landowners, capitalists, kulaks, and shopkeepers.....	15.9	4.5	
Miscellaneous (students, pensioners, military, etc.)...	2.3	2.4	4.2

* Derived from a table in A. Baykov, *The Development of the Soviet Economic System*, p. 357.

One more set of figures will help to make clear the scope of the changes which socialism has brought to the Soviet Union. Not only has illiteracy (which approached a rate of 80 per cent in prerevolutionary Russia) been largely wiped out, but there has also been a great alteration in the size and composition of what Soviet spokesmen call the "intelligentsia." The data in Table 7 are taken from a report made to the Eighteenth Congress of the Communist Party of the Soviet Union in 1939. They relate to virtually the same area, the Kursk Province in 1913 and the Kursk Region in 1937, and may be taken as illustrative of developments throughout the country.

Finally, unemployment, the economic scourge of capitalist society, has disappeared in socialist Russia. During the NEP period registered unemployment averaged over a million; but following the adoption of the First Five-year Plan, it fell sharply. Unemployment benefits were discontinued in 1930, and since then there has been a continuous shortage of labor. The disappearance of unemployment was not the result of a conscious full-employment policy; rather it was the natural by-product of comprehensive economic planning. It is always possible for the planning author-

Table 7. Some Changes in the Soviet Intelligentsia *

	1913 (Kursk Province)	1937 (Kursk Region)
Elementary- and secondary- school teachers	3,000	24,000
Physicians.............................	274	941
Intermediate medical personnel...........	636	2,357
Agronomists............................	70	2,279
Clergymen.............................	3,189	859

* *The Land of Socialism Today and Tomorrow* (Moscow, 1939), p. 150.

ity to aim at a higher level of production than the existing labor force is capable of reaching; and this would seem to be the obvious aim to pursue, at least until average living standards have been raised far beyond the highest levels yet achieved even in the richest of countries. If at some time in the future it should be thought wise to reduce production or to expand it less rapidly than the growth of the labor force, this decision could be easily translated by the planning authority into a reduction of hours and an increase of holidays. Again it is hard to see why any other course should be adopted. What this means is that unemployment is simply not a problem in a socialist society. It follows that there is no reason for a special policy to deal with it.

CHAPTER 3

Socialism in Great Britain

MOST OF THE PEOPLE who took part in founding the British Labor Party in 1900 were convinced socialists, but for many years the party itself was little more than a political alliance of trade unions. It was not until immediately after the First World War that the Labor Party adopted definitely socialist aims and began to accept individual members on the basis of their support for these aims. The constitution of 1918, which, with subsequent amendments, is still the basis of the Labor Party, stated the Party's objectives in part as follows:

> To secure for the producers by hand or by brain the full fruits of their industry, and the most equitable distribution thereof that may be possible, upon the basis of the common ownership of the means of production and the best obtainable system of popular administration and control of each industry and service.

Ever since the adoption of this constitution the party has been generally known, by friend and foe alike, as a socialist party. "The Labour Party," says *Let Us Face the Future,* the program on which the General Election of 1946 was contested, "is a Socialist Party, and proud of it."

Labor's Rise to Power

Twice during the interwar period the Labor Party took office. The General Election of 1923 returned a House of Commons in which Conservatives, though the largest single party with 260 seats, were in a minority compared with the combined Labor

35

(191) and Liberal (158) representation. Under these circumstances the Liberals decided to support a Labor Government under the premiership of Ramsay MacDonald. After less than a year in office, however, the Laborites fell out with the Liberals, and the Government was forced to resign. In the ensuing General Election the Tories were returned to power with an absolute majority.

The second Labor Government, also under the leadership of MacDonald, came into office following the General Election of 1929. For the first time Labor was the largest single party, with 289 seats, followed by the Tories with 260 and the Liberals with 58. Nevertheless, the second Labor Government, like the first, was a minority government dependent on Liberal support; and this support would have been immediately withdrawn if an attempt had been made to put into practice the socialist aspects of Labor's program. The two years during which Labor held office were years of deepening economic depression, climaxed by the acute international financial crisis of 1931. Shaken and lacking a plan to meet the crisis, the Labor Government collapsed. The three leading members of the Cabinet, MacDonald, Snowden, and Thomas, joined the Tories and a group of Liberals in forming a so-called National Government, while the rest of the Labor ministers retired in defeat and confusion. The subsequent General Election cut Labor's parliamentary representation to a mere 58 seats, while the Tories came back 471 strong. Thus, after two years in office, the Labor Party was deserted by its leaders and reduced to a state of virtual impotence.

These two experiences, particularly the second, made a profound impression on the British labor movement. But those who predicted that the British worker would turn his back on the Labor Party, and perhaps even renounce socialism, were grievously mistaken. There were of course defections, but for the most part they were temporary. The British worker, after recovering from the shock of 1931 and having experienced Tory rule again, came to the conclusion (in the words of J. R. Clynes, a prominent member of both Labor Governments) that "socialism had not

failed; we had never yet begun to try even a little part of it."
The trouble, in other words, was not in the structure or program
of the Labor Party but in the betrayal of the Party by trusted
leaders and in their erroneous strategy of taking office without
having secured the substance of parliamentary power. Hence it
came to pass that the Party regained the confidence of the working class and soon rallied from the rout of 1931. Moreover, the
Labor Party of the thirties and forties has been less dependent
upon the personal leadership of particular individuals and more
conscious of its socialist aims.

During the Second World War party politics were virtually
suspended in Britain: a coalition Government took over in 1940,
and the life of the existing Parliament, which would normally
have expired in that year, was prolonged until the end of the war.
The coalition broke up immediately after the surrender of Germany. The first General Election in 10 years, held during the
early summer of 1945, produced an absolute Labor majority for
the first time in British history. The final count gave Labor 393
seats and the Tories 189, the remaining 58 being distributed
among a variety of small parties and independents. The third
Labor Government, under the premiership of Clement Attlee,
thus took office under conditions very different from those of
1924 or 1929. The Party for the first time had the parliamentary
power to carry out its election pledges, which were set forth in a
document entitled *Let Us Face the Future,* adopted by the Annual
Party Conference on the eve of the General Election. It is important that we should examine these pledges with some care.

Let Us Face the Future consists of 11 sections. The first two are
devoted primarily to the existing situation and the general problems created by the war. Here we find a clear statement of a
theme which runs through almost all subsequent Party literature:

> Labour will plan from the ground up—giving an appropri-
> ate place to constructive enterprise and private endeavour
> in the national plan, but dealing decisively with those inter-

ests which would use high-sounding talk about economic freedom to cloak their determination to put themselves and their wishes above those of the whole nation.

Section 3 sets forth Labor's program for full employment, which consists essentially of three points: (1) maintenance of purchasing power through appropriate wage, social security, and tax policies; (2) "planned investment in essential industries and on houses, schools, hospitals and civic centers," with a national Investment Board determining priorities and promoting appropriate timing of private investment; and (3) "the Bank of England with its financial powers must be brought under public ownership, and the operations of the other banks harmonised with industrial needs."

Section 4, entitled "Industry in the Service of the Nation," contains the most explicit statement on socialism in the whole program and is worth quoting at some length:

> The Labour Party is a Socialist Party, and proud of it. Its ultimate purpose at home is the establishment of the Socialist Commonwealth of Great Britain—free, democratic, efficient, progressive, public-spirited, its material resources organized in the service of the British people.
>
> But socialism cannot come overnight as the product of a week-end revolution. The members of the Labour Party, like the British people, are practical-minded men and women.
>
> There are basic industries ripe and over-ripe for public ownership and management in the direct service of the nation. There are many smaller businesses rendering good service which can be left to go on with their useful work.
>
> There are big industries not yet ripe for public ownership which must nevertheless be required by constructive supervision to further the nation's needs and not to prejudice national interests by restrictive and anti-social monopoly or cartel agreements—caring for their own capital structures and profits at the cost of a lower standard of living for all.

On the basis of these principles the Party proposes to national-ize the following industries: fuel and power, inland transport, and iron and steel—"these socialised industries, taken over on a basis of fair compensation, to be conducted efficiently in the interests of consumers, coupled with proper status and conditions for the workers employed in them." In addition, the Party pledges itself to supervise monopolies and cartels, to give state assistance to the export trade, and to retain needed price and priority con-trols "in the transition from war to peace."

Section 5 promises a continuation of something very like the wartime system of controlling agricultural production. If a land-lord fails to make proper use of his land, the state will be em-powered to take it over at a fair valuation.

Sections 6 and 7 pledge the Party to an extensive housing and community planning program. "Labour believes in land nation-alisation and will work towards it, but as a first step the State and the local authorities must have wider and speedier powers to acquire land for public purposes wherever the public interest so requires."

Sections 8, 9, and 10 state Labor's program for improved edu-cation, a national health service available to all, and higher stand-ards of social insurance.

Finally, Section 11 consists of a rather generalized statement on international affairs, which can hardly be regarded as containing any specific pledges.

Clearly, *Let Us Face the Future,* though reaffirming the Labor Party's socialist aims, is not a program for transforming Britain into a socialist society. Many of the proposed reforms are of the New Deal type and have no necessary connection with socialism. We must keep this fact in mind if we are to avoid judging the accomplishments of the Labor Government by irrelevant standards.

Nevertheless, some of the proposals of *Let Us Face the Future* would certainly find a place in a program for transforming Britain into a socialist society. In this sense, they may be regarded (and there is no doubt that the Labor Party intended they should be) as a first installment of socialism, to be followed by further installments, which the British electorate will be called upon to approve at future general elections. Judgments may vary as to precisely how much of *Let Us Face the Future* should be so interpreted, but there would probably be no serious objection to including the various proposals for public ownership of banking and industry and the proposals to expand the state's powers to control and plan the use of the land. In addition, the promise to "plan from the ground up" is of great importance in this connection. It would be unreasonable to look for full-scale socialist planning as a part of the first installment of socialism, but it can hardly be denied that even the first installment ought to include a measure of planning as well as realistic preparations for future extensions of the planning system. (It may be recalled, for example, that the Soviet State Planning Commission was set up as early as 1921 and worked intensively on the problems of economic planning for seven years before a comprehensive plan was finally put into operation.)

In the next section we shall examine what the Labor Government has done in its first two and a half years of office (just half the life of the present Parliament) to carry out those parts of *Let Us Face the Future* which promise the first installment of socialism. We shall then attempt to characterize the present British system as a whole.

Labor in Power

In the course of the first two sessions of Parliament following the General Election of 1945, most of the nationalization measures proposed in *Let Us Face the Future* were enacted into law. During the first session (1945–1946) the Bank of England, civil aviation, coal mining, and overseas wireless and cable services were taken over by the state.[1] During the second session (1946–1947), inland transport (by rail, road, and canal) and electricity were also taken over by the state. In laying down its program for the third session (1947–1948), the Government marked the gas industry for transference to public ownership, and there is every reason to believe that this will have been carried through before this book is in print. For all practical purposes, only iron and steel still remain on the list of industries to be nationalized. The significance of the case of iron and steel will be considered below.

In the fields of agriculture and community planning the Government has already honored the pledges of *Let Us Face the Future.* It is now roughly accurate to say that the traditional rights of nonuse and abuse, as far as landed property is concerned, have been abolished; and the Ministry of Town and Country Planning has been equipped with adequate powers to control the future development of urban communities, even to the point of building entirely new towns in unpopulated or sparsely populated areas.

If we turn our attention from land utilization and nationalization of industry to general economic planning, we find that the record of the Labor Government has been less impressive. Government and Party spokesmen have repeatedly laid claim to great achievements in this field, but the facts provide little support for their claims. For example, Herbert Morrison, one of the top Party leaders, who was until recently cabinet minister responsible for coordinating Government activities concerned with domestic economic affairs, told the 1946 Annual Labor Party Conference that "we have established an overall planning machine." But when he went on to describe this machine, it turned out to consist of the Cabinet Secretariat and the Central Statistical Office. These bodies are concerned respectively with departmental liaison and

[1] Domestic telecommunications, including radio broadcasting, had been nationalized before the war.

fact finding. Both functions are no doubt essential to planning, but to identify them with planning would be fully as misleading as to identify getting into an automobile with taking a trip. Subsequently (in the spring of 1947) an Economic Planning Staff was set up under a civil-service chief, but its purpose seems to have been merely to assist the economic ministries to coordinate their work. The need for proper coordination was further emphasized with the creation of a Ministry of Economics under Sir Stafford Cripps later in 1947; and what may well be the final step in this direction was taken when Cripps became Chancellor of the Exchequer as well as Minister of Economics. It is now probably safe to say that Cripps is in a position to control and coordinate the Government's economic policies, but whether planning is or is not among those policies is evidently an entirely different question.

To find enlightenment on this question, we may consult the White Paper entitled *Economic Survey for 1947*, presented to Parliament in February, 1947.[2] Approximately one-fifth of this document is devoted to a section headed "Economic Planning," which can be taken as an authoritative statement of the views and policies of the Government in this field. The following paragraphs give a condensed summary of the system of planning which is said to be in operation in Britain.

The basis of the plan consists of two so-called economic budgets:

> The man-power budget compares the estimated future working population with the number of workers required, industry by industry. The national income and expenditure budget compares the estimated value of the national production of goods and services with the value of all the goods and services required. [These budgets are then examined in connection with analyses of certain special problems, for example the foreign exchange position.] At the present time,

[2] *Economic Survey for 1947* appears in full in the *Federal Reserve Bulletin*, April, 1947.

a first comparison always shows a large excess of requirements over resources. This means that unless action is taken to increase resources or to curtail requirements, there will be a scramble for labour and goods.

Here, then, is the essential problem of planning as the Labor Government sees it:

> Planning the allocation of resources between the various national requirements is at present a task of deciding which of a number of claimants must go short—in other words, which are the more important national priorities. [And how is this done?] After full examination of possible means of attaining a balance, the Official Committee [which supervises the drawing up of the budgets] submits to Ministers a report on the whole position. Ministers then decide what measures should be taken, and their decisions form the basis of subsequent action.

The question now arises: what means are at the Government's disposal to secure the desired results? The White Paper lists a large number of controls:

> Over an important part of the national economy, the Government can exercise direct influence. The level of Government expenditure approved by Parliament, and the expenditure of other public authorities, determines the amount of production of a wide range of goods and services . . . ; the policies of the socialised industries and services have a substantial effect on the whole economy, and are ultimately subject to Government control. The Government's fiscal policy can exert indirect influence over the course of production. There are now a large number of direct controls . . . —rationing, raw material controls, building licensing, production controls, import licensing, capital issues control, etc. Other controls again, such as price control, influence the course of production by limiting profit margins.

All these methods are useful, but the White Paper concedes that

> . . . they cannot by themselves bring about very rapid
> changes or make very fine adjustments in the economic struc-
> ture. To do this, they would have to be much more detailed
> in their application and drastic in their scope. Indeed, the
> task of directing by democratic methods an economic system
> as large and complex as ours is far beyond the power of any
> Governmental machine working by itself, no matter how
> efficient it may be. [And from this the conclusion is drawn
> that] events can be directed in the way that is desired in the
> national interest only if the Government, both sides of indus-
> try and the people accept the objectives and then work
> together to achieve the end.

The chief points which emerge from this summary of the British planning system are the following: (1) The basic task of planning is the essentially negative one of trimming demands down
to fit foreseeable supplies; (2) decisions as to what form Government action should assume are taken by individual ministers in
their respective fields of responsibility; (3) there are many diverse
methods which the Government can adopt to secure the desired
results; (4) even taken altogether, however, these methods are not
adequate to the task; (5) in the final analysis, therefore, success
depends upon the voluntary cooperation of employers, trade
unions, and the public generally.

The Labor Party is, of course, at liberty to call such a system
"planning," but clearly it cannot be maintained that there is any
necessary connection between this kind of planning and socialism.
A Conservative Government doubtless would not agree with
Labor's conception of "national priorities," and it would probably
also use a different combination of controls to secure its ends—
for example, the Tories would probably make much freer use
of a deflationary fiscal policy than Labor has done. But *in principle* there is hardly anything in the Labor Government's statement
on "economic planning" which the Conservative Party could not

accept. Capitalism long ago ceased to be synonymous with *laissez faire,* except perhaps in the minds of a few die-hard Tories; and the kind of "planning" which the Labor Government is engaging in has become familiar in many capitalist countries since 1914.

The first installment of British socialism, then, consists on the one hand in certain nationalization measures (the Bank of England, coal mining, inland transport, telecommunications, electricity, and gas) and on the other hand in the assumption by the state of extensive powers over the utilization of the land. No significant innovations have been introduced in the field of general economic planning; and as far as one can judge from published statements, there has as yet been no "planning to plan" in the socialist sense of the term.[3]

Let us now attempt to characterize the British social system as a whole, as it exists after two and a half years of Labor rule. A breakdown of total employment between public and private sectors is given in Table 8, derived from data presented in the White Paper cited above. No claim to strict accuracy can be made for these figures. For example, an element of private employment undoubtedly remains in the transport industry, since the merchant marine has not been nationalized. On the other hand, in the private sector there are approximately 300,000 workers in cooperative shops and factories which might more appropriately be classified as belonging to the public sector.[4] Further, the table takes no account of Labor's pledge to nationalize iron and steel. Quantitatively, however, this is not very significant. Even if the pledge is redeemed—and, as we shall see, this is by no means certain—the increase in the size of the public sector would be small.

[3] For further discussion of planning, and especially of the relation between planning and socialism, see pp. 24–28, 232–239, and 241–248.

[4] The figure of 300,000 is based on estimates of G. D. N. Worswick that there are nearly 10 million members of cooperative societies and that the societies employ in their own enterprises about 3 per cent of their membership. N. Barou (ed.), *The Co-operative Movement in Labour Britain* (1948), pp. 7 and 9.

(The exact size of the increase would depend, of course, on the definition of the industry, and on this question the Labor Party has at no time made a specific commitment. It may be noted that

*Table 8. Manpower * Employed in Public and Private Sectors of the British Economy, December, 1946 †*

	Thousands	Per cent ‡
Grand Total........................		18,122	100
Public Sector.......................		4,491	25
Public service §....................	2,130		12
Coal industry.....................	730		4
Public utilities....................	258		1
Transport........................	1,373		8
Private Sector......................		13,631	75
Agriculture and fishing..............	1,081		6
Building and civil engineering........	1,250		7
Building materials and equipment.....	628		3
Metals and engineering.............	2,811		16
Textiles and clothing...............	1,405		8
Food, drink, and tobacco...........	597		3
Chemicals........................	324		2
Other manufacturing...............	1,265		7
Distribution......................	2,304		13
Other consumers' services...........	1,966		11

* Males 14–64; females 14–59. Includes employers and self-employed as well as employees. Two part-time workers counted as one. Excludes private domestic servants, members of the armed forces, and unemployed.

† Source: *Federal Reserve Bulletin*, April, 1947, p. 389.

‡ To nearest percentage point.

§ National and local.

at the end of 1947, according to official statistics, there were approximately 200,000 workers employed in blast furnaces, steel melting and iron puddling, iron and steel rolling, and related branches of the ferrous-metal-producing industry.)

But when all allowances have been made for possible errors of classification and for changes which might occur in the near future, the table still remains a reliable indicator of the general orders of magnitude with which we have to deal. It shows that the public sector, interpreted in the broadest sense to include Government as well as business, accounts for about one-fourth of total British employment. If Government is excluded, as for most purposes it should be, the British economy in the usual sense of the term is approximately one-seventh public and six-sevenths private. Clearly, from a purely quantitative point of view, the first installment of British socialism is not large.

Let us now look a little more closely at the private sector. When we were examining the Soviet Union under NEP, we noted that the private sector of the economy, which was also quantitatively preponderant, consisted largely of simple commodity production: in other words, most of the workers in the private sector were self-employed. And when we analyze present-day Poland in the next chapter, we shall find that a similar situation prevails. Matters are very different in the case of Britain. No recent breakdown of employment statistics into categories of employers, employees, and self-employed is available. Estimates for the prewar period have been made, however, and it is highly unlikely that supervening changes have been large enough to render them misleading. According to John Strachey, Minister of Food in the present Labor Cabinet, there were some one and a quarter million employers and approximately the same number of self-employed (small farmers, handicraftsmen, shopkeepers, professionals, and so forth) in Britain before the war.[5] This would leave somewhat more than 11 million wage earners in private industry. In percentage terms, this means that the whole private sector can be divided as follows: employers, 9 per cent; employees, 82 per cent; and self-employed, 9 per cent. Obviously, simple commodity production is a relatively minor factor in Britain; the predominant private sector of the economy is overwhelmingly

[5] John Strachey, *Socialism Looks Forward* (1945), p. 21.

capitalist in character. And this, of course, is what we should expect in the country where capitalism first developed and the country which for many decades was known as the workshop of the world.

On the basis of the foregoing facts and figures, how should we describe the present British social system? Is it still a capitalist system, or are we justified in calling it, as we did the Soviet system under NEP, a mixed system? There is no hard and fast rule to guide us in answering this question. But if we recall that many staunch supporters of capitalism advocate a considerable degree of public ownership—especially in the fields of transport and public utilities, where the British nationalization program has been concentrated—we shall be cautious about the kind of conclusions we draw on the basis of the relatively small changes which the Labor Government has so far introduced. Probably the safest course is to describe Britain as still capitalist. This is really only another way of saying that the first installment of socialism, if it is not supplemented in due course by further installments, can be swallowed and digested by British capitalism without serious difficulty. The best evidence that this is true is afforded by the Conservative Party's *Industrial Charter,* published in May, 1947, as an official statement of economic policy. The Tories do not propose to undo the basic acts of nationalization which Labor has carried through. They would restore road transport and civil aviation to private ownership, but these are relatively minor matters. On the whole, the Conservative statement, for all its criticisms of Labor policy, is an implicit confirmation of the view that British capitalism is still intact.

But we cannot leave the problem here. The crucial question is whether further installments of socialism can be expected, assuming a continuation of present trends affecting Britain's domestic and international position. For if further installments can be expected, our conclusion that Britain is still capitalist will have a very limited significance; while if further installments cannot be expected, our conclusion will evidently take on heightened importance. In the next section, therefore, we shall review the most important obstacles to further measures of socialization; and in the final section, we shall analyze what now seem to be the possible courses of development.

Obstacles to Further Socialization

The obstacles to further measures of socialization in Britain fall into two major categories, which may be called respectively internal and external. The two are in fact closely related but for the sake of clarity they must be analyzed separately.

The internal obstacles are all connected in one way or another with the great strength, experience, and resourcefulness of British capitalism. Britain is the homeland of capitalism; throughout the nineteenth century she was, economically and militarily, the most powerful nation in the world; even now she is still the possessor of the world's largest colonial empire. The ruling class which has grown up under these conditions, and to a considerable extent molded them to its own interests, is at once tough, flexible, and skilled; as an opponent of socialism it is incomparably more formidable than the pre-1917 Russian ruling classes, which consisted of a demoralized aristocracy and an undeveloped *bourgeoisie*.

The most powerful weapon in the hands of the British capitalists, of course, is their control over the major segments of the nation's economy. The problem of the Labor Party is how to take this control from the capitalists without its first being used to produce a crisis which might be as disastrous to the labor movement as to the country as a whole. The traditional answer of so-called gradualist socialists—and the Labor Party has always adhered to a gradualist philosophy—is that the capitalists' control over the economy will be taken away bit by bit. No single step will be important enough to provoke a showdown, and at a certain stage of the process it will be too late for countermeasures to be effective. Can the success of Labor's nationalization program in the last two and a half years be cited in support of this theory?

The answer is no. As we have already seen, the Conservatives do not feel that British capitalism is seriously threatened by the nationalization measures which have so far been adopted. But this does not mean that they have the same attitude with regard to any and every proposed act of nationalization. In fact, we know that such is not the case. The Conservative *Industrial Charter,* cited above, takes a very different position on iron and steel. As the *New Statesman and Nation* put it in summarizing the relevant portion of the *Charter:* "Iron and Steel—key points in the capitalist citadel—are to be stoutly defended against nationalisation." [6] Since, on the other hand, Labor has promised to nationalize iron and steel within the lifetime of the present Parliament, it seems that here the issue is fairly joined. The nationalization of iron and steel is a crucial test for the Labor Party no less than for British capitalism.

At the time of writing it is impossible to predict how the iron and steel problem will be resolved. We know only that the Government has shied away from action, while reassuring its supporters that the pledges of *Let Us Face the Future* would be fully met. Evidently there is disagreement in the Party itself as to the wisest course to follow, and no outsider is in a position to know the line-up of forces or the probable outcome of such an inner Party debate. It seems fairly safe to say, however, that if Labor does decide to go ahead and nationalize iron and steel—by a legislative act similar in content to those which have already been passed for coal, transport, and public utilities [7]—it will really

[6] *New Statesman and Nation,* May 17, 1947, p. 345.

[7] It is necessary to add this proviso, since it is not inconceivable that the Labor Government might attempt to escape from its present dilemma by what could be called a sham nationalization of the iron and steel industry. For example, a majority of the shares of certain selected companies might be purchased by the state without changing anything essential in the structure and functioning of the industry. There would be a good precedent for this in the giant Anglo-Iranian Oil Company, a majority of the shares of which have been owned by the British Government since before the First World

come to grips with British capitalism, and the outcome of the struggle should go far toward settling the question of whether socialism can be achieved through a step-by-step process. On the other hand, it is probably equally safe to say that unless or until Labor tackles iron and steel, there will be no significant further advance toward socialism.

The external obstacles to further socialization of the British social order arise from Britain's present extreme economic dependence on the United States. The origins of this dependence during the Second World War are well known and require no detailed review here. It is necessary only to emphasize that Britain's international economic difficulties are not due solely to the impoverishment and devastation of war, though these are of course important contributory causes.

The British population grew to its present size of approximately 48 million and achieved a relatively high standard of living on the basis of exchange of manufactured goods for the rest of the world's food and raw materials. In addition, from about the middle of the nineteenth century, Britain received a large and steady income from overseas investments, which in effect constituted a draft on the labor and resources of other countries. For the greater part of the present century, however, both these sources of British economic strength have been drying up. Though British industry was first in the field and was for many decades by far the most efficient in the world, this head start eventually proved to be a disadvantage, in the sense that vested interests were created which resisted rationalization and neglected the problems of technological improvement. Gradually new industrial countries, like Germany and the United States, surpassed Britain and cut into her foreign markets, while other countries began increasingly to supply their own requirements for manufactured goods. Superimposed on these trends—both of which threatened the foundations of British prosperity—came the two world wars. The first war

---

War. It is significant that even under a Labor Government no one ever thinks of classifying Anglo-Iranian as a socialist enterprise.

checked the growth of British investments abroad; the second used up at least half of the outstanding total and ran up heavy debts which more than offset the remainder. Naturally, the result has been a sharp decline in British income from overseas investments.

Thus Britain's position in the world economy has undergone a profound change. The conditions permitting her population to expand and prosper have largely ceased to exist. Moreover, her income is no longer sufficient to allow her to play the role of a great power and still maintain living standards at even their present level. Clearly, Britain must have large-scale foreign assistance or she must make the necessary readjustments to changed circumstances—readjustments which would affect in varying degrees her military commitments, her living standards, the utilization of productive resources domestically, and the methods and direction of her foreign trade.

Until now foreign assistance, mainly from the United States, has been forthcoming in sufficient volume to enable Britain to avoid the drastic measures which would otherwise have to be taken. It would take us far beyond the scope of this book to examine the form these measures might assume, and fortunately such an analysis is not essential for our present purposes. We need only note that as long as Britain relies on American aid to balance her international accounts, it is inevitable that she will have to accommodate her foreign policy and, to some extent at any rate, her domestic policies to the wishes of the United States Government. This is not a question, as some naïve commentators on both sides of the Atlantic seem to assume, of London's being dictated to by Washington. The British are familiar with the implied obligations of a debtor, through having themselves been for so long the world's leading creditor; and if they now assume the role of debtor, they can be expected to play it without the need of constant prompting.

It is a matter of common knowledge that the United States Government is strongly opposed to socialism both at home and abroad, and any government which is likely to succeed it in the near future will probably have a similar attitude. The British obviously have to take this fact into account in shaping their policies. This does not mean necessarily that any further measures of socialization would lead to the withholding of American financial aid, but it can hardly be questioned that such measures would complicate relations between the two countries and might easily lead the United States to attach more burdensome conditions to further grants.

There is thus a sharp conflict between a policy of socialization and a policy of dependence on American aid. Sooner or later one or the other will have to be abandoned—unless in the meantime the United States moves considerably to the left. Since at present there are no signs that the British are preparing to do with less American aid, we must assume that there are strong pressures inside both the Government and the Labor Party against any further measures of socialization. These pressures complement and reinforce the internal pressures which, as we have already seen, arise from capitalist control over the greater part of the British economy.

The Outlook for Socialism in Great Britain

The last section set forth the main obstacles to the further development of socialism in Britain. The actual future course of events will be determined largely by the way the Labor Party reacts to these obstacles. At the risk of some overschematization, we can divide the Party into Right, Center, and Left, each tendency having its own distinctive approach to these critical issues. By examining these tendencies and estimating their relative strength, we should be able to get a general idea of the outlook for socialism in Britain.

The Right wing of the Labor Party favors putting aside long-term considerations and concentrating on what it feels to be the overwhelmingly urgent problems arising from Britain's chronic balance-of-payments crisis. Laborites of this persuasion naturally advocate policies designed to attract the maximum of American aid on the easiest terms and to enlist the full cooperation of the capitalists, who control most of the economy, including the major export industries. Since, as we have seen, both these aims are in direct conflict with further measures of socialization, it follows that this school of thought is willing to postpone important social reforms until a more auspicious time.

All available evidence—Government actions and pronouncements, as well as statements of leading Party and trade-union spokesmen—indicates that the Right enjoys the official backing of the trade-union movement and is in firm control of the Party machine. If there is no important change in this respect, we clearly cannot expect further moves in the direction of socialism until Britain's international economic position has been greatly improved and rendered reasonably secure. Since, however, the causes of Britain's international economic difficulties are neither temporary nor superficial and since they could be removed only by the kind of drastic readjustments which the Government now seems most anxious to avoid, it is hard to escape the conclusion that the policy of the present dominant group in the Labor Party amounts to accepting economic dependence on the United States and renouncing socialism for an indefinite period.

The Center tendency in the Labor Party comprises diverse elements, among which perhaps the most important are intellectuals of the type represented by the *New Statesman and Nation,* some constituency Labor Parties, and elements from the cooperative movement. What distinguishes the Center from the Right is primarily a greater consciousness of, and attachment to, the Party's socialist aims. The Center is therefore critical of the Government's holding back on such issues as nationalization of iron and steel and continuously calls for a greater degree of economic planning. Similarly, the Center is uneasy about the implications of American aid and complains rather more than the Right about the terms on which it is granted. Nevertheless, the Center is not prepared to advocate that Britain do without American aid and for this reason has no consistent policy to propose in place of that which the dominant group in the party is actually putting into operation. The upshot is that the Center opposes the Right verbally and supports it practically.

The Left tendency in the Labor Party is not strong in terms of leadership, but it has considerable support in the lower echelons of the trade-union movement, especially in certain of the larger unions, such as the miners', the engineers', and the electricians'. In practice the Left is closely allied to the Communists, a substantial part of its leadership in the trade unions being Communist Party members.[8] The Left advocates an integrated program covering both domestic and foreign affairs. On the domestic side this program calls for a bold advance toward socialism, and on the foreign side for greatly expanded economic relations with the planned-economy countries. For the moment, of course, the only planned-economy countries are the Soviet Union and the eastern European states; [9] but the Left believes that if Britain were to take the lead, most of the countries of western Europe would soon fall in line. Such a policy might lead to the cessation of American aid and even to positive American countermeasures in the economic field, but the Left believes that this threat must be faced sooner or later if Britain is not to abandon hope of achieving socialism.

The period immediately after the cessation of American aid would admittedly be very difficult; the British people would be forced to take further cuts in their living standards. But the Left

[8] The peculiar relation existing in Britain between the trade unions and the Labor Party—a relation which is not found in any of the countries of continental Europe—allows the Communist Party to play a role in the British Labor movement as a whole which is out of proportion to its membership and its representation in Parliament. If the structure of the Labor Party were similar to that of the continental Social Democratic Parties, it is probable that the British Communist Party would be considerably larger than it actually is.

[9] On planning in eastern Europe see Chap. 4.

argues that the working class, at any rate, would accept these privations cheerfully if it knew that it was at last working for socialism. Moreover, the Left believes that economic planning would raise British productivity so that, taking account of the possibilities for increased trade in an expanding planned-economy area, the period of extra-short rations could be relatively brief. The more optimistic spokesmen of the Left even go so far as to anticipate that, once the United States becomes accustomed to the idea of a socialist Europe, it will be seen on both sides of the Atlantic that a resumption of normal business relations, including American lending, would be in the interests of everyone concerned.

No one can now say with assurance whether or not this Left program is based on a realistic appraisal of existing trends and forces. But it is at least consistent and integrated and for this reason stands out as the only practically possible alternative course to that which the Government has been following.

Let us summarize our conclusions with respect to the three tendencies within the Labor Party. The Right, in firm control of the Party machinery, follows a policy of not "rocking the boat" by further measures of socialization. If and when Britain has fully recovered, and American aid is no longer needed, it would theoretically be possible to resume the advance toward socialism. In practice this of course amounts to a policy of renouncing socialism for an indefinite period. The Center, more conscious of the Party's socialist aims, is critical of the Right but has no consistent alternative policy to propose. The Left, with considerable working-class backing but relatively weak political power, believes in an uncompromising advance to socialism. The program of the Left is consistent and could be tried, but at present there is no chance of its becoming official Labor Party policy.

What, then, is the outlook for socialism in Britain as the first Labor Parliament in British history completes the initial half of its five-year tenure of office? If our analysis is correct and if there are no far-reaching changes in the balance of political forces in

Britain, we are justified in concluding that the process of social-ization has already come to a halt. A conditional statement of this kind, however, is very different from a prediction. In a world as unsettled as the world we live in any number of things might operate to change the balance of political forces, in Britain as elsewhere. For example, American aid might be cut off and thus cease to be a decisive issue in British calculations. There might then take place a rapid swing to the left within the Labor Party, which would put the question of further socialization measures in an entirely different perspective.

At the time of writing, such a development seems unlikely, but it cannot be ruled out as impossible. Where such major uncer-tainties exist, the social scientist can provide the framework of analysis. The analysis itself, however, must be made and remade in the light of changing circumstances.

CHAPTER 4

Socialism in Eastern Europe

THE AREA BETWEEN Germany, Austria, and Italy on the west and the Soviet Union on the east was the first zone of Nazi economic and military penetration. Subsequently it was a battlefield between German and Russian armies as the latter drove westward to Berlin and Vienna. And in the postwar period it has been the scene of deep social change, which is unmistakably moving in the direction of socialism. In this chapter we shall survey briefly what has been happening in the region as a whole and then proceed to a more detailed examination of the case of Poland.

The Postwar Revolution in Eastern Europe

From an economic and social standpoint eastern Europe was ripe for revolution long before the Second World War. In 1939 the region as a whole had approximately a quarter of the inhabitants of Europe west of the Soviet Union, and the population trend was strongly upward. Nevertheless, the economy of the region was backward, and the living standards generally low and even declining. Agriculture, by far the major occupation, was primitive and overcrowded; except in parts of Czechoslovakia, Poland, and Hungary there was little industry; and a semifeudal ruling class consumed or wasted its income, with the result that capital investment was largely left to foreigners who sought maximum immediate profits and cared little for the welfare of the people. What was needed above all was a combined program of industrialization and agricultural modernization, but such a program lay altogether outside both the capacity and the intentions

59

of the ruling elements. Consequently, and in spite of harsh repressive measures, sizable revolutionary movements, under socialist leadership, grew up in all the countries concerned.

This was the condition of eastern Europe when it fell under the domination of Nazi Germany. During the next few years existing institutional patterns were thoroughly upset by German exploitation and by the human and material destruction of the war. Germans acquired control of most of the larger business concerns; the upper classes generally were tarred with the brush of collaborationism; and national liberation became increasingly identified with radical social reform. The predominant role of the Red Army in the actual process of liberation added further to the prestige of the left-wing forces and frightened many conservatives into flight or inaction.

The new regimes which came to power in the wake of the German retreat were naturally very different from their prewar predecessors. This was true whether, as in the case of Czechoslovakia, legal continuity with the past was preserved or whether, as in the case of Hungary, the new regime openly repudiated the old. Political parties which were free of the taint of collaboration with the enemy joined together to form coalition governments. Communists and Social Democrats, partly seasoned revolutionaries and partly new men from the resistance movements, occupied key positions, always with the tacit approval and sometimes with the overt backing of the Soviet authorities. Purges of native fascists and collaborators removed many supporters of the old order from positions of potential influence. Everywhere—except in Greece, which, because it was occupied by British troops, did not conform to the general pattern of the region—liberation from German domination brought with it a genuine political revolution.

One of the first problems faced by the new regimes was that of consolidating their popular support; and in an agricultural area like eastern Europe this meant above all securing a firm political foothold among the peasantry. Consequently one of the earliest acts of the new regimes was land reform: distribution of large estates to landless peasants and so-called dwarfholders. The scope for this reform was greatest in Hungary, parts of Poland, and Albania; smaller in Yugoslavia, Rumania, and Slovakia; and almost nonexistent in Bulgaria, Bohemia, and Moravia.[1] Land reform served a double purpose: not only did it improve the lot of the poorest peasants, it also undercut the position of the previously dominant class of landlords and gentry.

The problem of what to do about industry and trade was hardly less pressing. Immediately following liberation the various governments had no choice but to assume responsibility for a large number of enterprises, including not only those which had belonged to Germans and collaborators but also many which had been left ownerless or managerless by the accidents of war. In addition they had in their hands a considerable number of business concerns which before the war had been the property of the state. (Such state ownership in eastern Europe was quite common, chiefly because private interests were either unable or unwilling to supply the capital needed in certain important fields of economic activity.) It thus came to pass that the new regimes found themselves in control of a large part (in some cases probably amounting to well over half) of the industrial and commercial wealth of their countries. Should this wealth be turned over to private owners, or should it be retained as public property?

Everything favored the public-ownership solution. The dominant left-wing political parties supported it as a matter of principle; the Germans had so scrambled property relations that in many cases it would have been impossible to discover the rightful owners; Jews, who had played a very important part in the economic life of the region before the war, had been almost entirely wiped out by the Nazis and hence could not reassume possession of their properties; the Soviet Union, the most important force in the international relations of the region, would naturally feel

[1] Bohemia and Moravia are the Czech provinces of Czechoslovakia.

sympathetic to reforms of a socialist character. These factors operated in different degrees in the different countries, but the outcome has everywhere been similar: a large proportion of non-agricultural business, including banking and most of what can plausibly be called large-scale industry, has been nationalized. Smaller enterprises held by the state have generally been turned back to private ownership. In some fields, such as the marketing and processing of foodstuffs, assets have been handed over to cooperatives, which have likewise received various other forms of state aid and encouragement.

With basic property questions settled in such a way as to leave small individual farms dominant in agriculture and state enterprise dominant in industry, the new regimes still had to tackle the difficult and complicated problems involved in getting their disorganized and damaged economies back into operation. Since the beginning of the war it has been widely accepted, not only in eastern Europe but in western Europe as well, that reconstruction would require a large measure of economic planning. The eastern European governments now proceeded to act on this principle as rapidly as circumstances would permit. During 1946 Czechoslovakia adopted a two-year plan and Poland a three-year plan. During 1947 Yugoslavia adopted a five-year plan and Hungary a three-year plan. For economic purposes Albania has been practically incorporated into the federal structure of Yugoslavia. Rumania and Bulgaria have moved more slowly, but both are plainly heading in the direction of economic planning.

All the plans that have been formulated to date place primary emphasis upon reconstruction and rehabilitation, with goals generally stated in terms of restoring and then moderately surpassing prewar living standards. It is emphasized, however, that the attainment of these goals is to be regarded merely as a first step; existing plans will be followed by longer range projects with much more ambitious objectives. It would therefore be wrong to look upon planning in eastern Europe as merely an emergency measure designed to deal with problems inherited from German occupation and war. It has become the fundamental organizing principle of the economies of the region. Here again, as in the case of nationalization of industry, the requirements of the immediate situation fitted in with the ideological preferences of the political parties dominating the new regimes.

One more aspect of the postwar revolution in eastern Europe remains to be noted. In the past the region has been notorious for national hatreds and international quarrels. The various countries erected trade barriers against each other and shunned economic relations with the Soviet Union. This absence of political and economic cooperation reflected both the history and the social structure of the region; its chief effects were to accentuate economic backwardness and to increase dependence on the more highly industrialized countries of central and western Europe. Only the forces in opposition to the existing regimes—and this meant primarily the socialists—were in favor of policies of political conciliation and economic collaboration.

When these forces came to power in the new postwar regimes, they quickly discovered that mutual cooperation was as desirable from a business point of view as it was from an ideological point of view. The disruption of east-west communications in the days immediately after the war made trade with the Soviet Union essential to the national existence of all the countries of eastern Europe; and while the flow of trade to and from the Soviet Union has declined relatively with the restoration of communications with the west, it has continued to grow absolutely and seems certain to remain much more important than it ever was in the past. Furthermore, though the countries of the region are all (with the exception of Czechoslovakia) predominantly agricultural, the possibilities of mutually beneficial trade are extensive and can easily be expanded. Poland has enough coal for the whole region

and a potentially important center of heavy industry in the territory taken from Germany; Czechoslovakia has engineering industries; Yugoslavia has a variety of nonferrous metals; Rumania has
oil; all have extensive undeveloped hydroelectric resources: in
short, if the economies of the various countries are developed in
coordination, the conditions exist for steadily growing trade and
economic interdependence.

Against this background it is easy to understand why the region's network of economic treaties—often covering not only trade
but also the coordination of economic plans—has been rapidly
expanding in the past two years. On the political side this general
movement has had its counterpart in treaties of friendship and
mutual assistance now bringing the whole region together, whereas
before the war such treaties and ententes were invariably diplo-
matic weapons of one group against another. Simultaneously,
traditional national hatreds—for example, between the Hungar-
ians and Rumanians or between the Yugoslavs and the Bulgarians
—have been combated by the authorities, whereas once they were
deliberately stimulated. Moreover, there has been a great deal of
talk about federation, and the expansion of Yugoslavia to take
in Albania and Bulgaria as federal republics (along with Serbia,
Croatia, Slovenia, Bosnia-Herzegovina, Macedonia, and Monte-
negro) may come in the near future. Wider schemes are perhaps
not likely to be realized for some time, but their eventual possibility is not to be discounted.

To summarize: the fundamental characteristics of the postwar
revolution in eastern Europe are (1) the distribution of land to
the peasants with a consequent destruction of the power of the
old landlord class; (2) nationalization of large-scale enterprise in
the fields of industry, finance, transport, and communication;
(3) the adoption of planning as a permanent principle of economic organization; and (4) the replacement of policies leading
to political and economic antagonisms by policies of mutual conciliation and collaboration. To what extent should the societies
which are emerging from this revolution be considered socialist?

Mixed Societies in Transition to Socialism

From a purely quantitative point of view the new eastern European societies are clearly not socialist, since the extent of public ownership of the means of production is relatively small.[2] This does not mean, however, that the countries are predominantly capitalist; on the contrary, the proportion of employees in the capitalist sector (that is, those hired by private employers) is and will remain much smaller than that in the public sector. The majority of the workers, including most of those engaged in agriculture, are what we have defined as simple commodity producers. It follows that, if we were to confine our attention to the quantitative aspect of the matter, we should have to classify these societies under the heading of simple commodity production.

To adopt this procedure, however, would lead to paradoxical results. Simple commodity production as such has nothing to do with economic planning, and yet, as we have seen, the countries of eastern Europe have all committed themselves to planned economies. The explanation is that the simple commodity producers, though numerically preponderant, are not in control of the situation and can influence the course of events only through the force of inertia. (The importance of this force, in the case of so large a segment of the population, must not be underestimated, but it can in no case be regarded as a creative or guiding force.) It is the socialists who are in power, and the initiative is in their hands. They have already put into operation the socialist principle of planning, and they are in a position to shape the future to their own ideas, even though the process may be slow and sometimes painful. Given these circumstances, the societies of eastern Europe can be accurately characterized only by taking account

[2] Figures for Poland are given below (p. 77). As far as the other countries are concerned, the extent of public ownership is likely to be greater only in Czechoslovakia.

both of their present structure and also of the long-range objectives of the groups which control them. When this is done, it will be seen that they are mixed societies (including elements of capitalism, socialism, and simple commodity production) which are in transition to socialism.

We have already analyzed one mixed society: the Soviet Union during the period of NEP. Evidently, the present-day societies of eastern Europe resemble NEP Russia in many important respects. Nevertheless, one must not jump to the conclusion that eastern Europe will travel exactly the same path to socialism as the Soviet Union. The similarities are unquestionably more fundamental than the differences, but even a brief consideration of the latter will show that they are by no means unimportant.

The first of these differences is that the Soviet Union was not ready to put a comprehensive economic plan into operation until a full decade after the revolutionary regime came to power; in fact, the very essence of NEP was reliance on the forces of the market to overcome the destruction of war and civil strife. On the other hand, the new regimes in eastern Europe are already planning on a national scale and with the specific purpose of guiding and hastening recovery from the effects of Nazi occupation and war. The reasons for this difference are to be found primarily in the results of Soviet experience. As Professor Carr has wisely said, "the economic impact of the Soviet Union on the rest of the world may be summed up in the single word 'planning.'" [3] After the First World War economic planning was no more than an untried idea; no one was sure how to go about it or even whether it would work. The success of the Soviet Five-year plans changed all that. From the early 1930's both the methods and the tremendous potentialities of economic planning were widely known. All socialists, regardless of party affiliation, put economic planning in the forefront of their programs. [4] It was

[3] E. H. Carr, *The Soviet Impact on the Western World* (1947), p. 20.

[4] For the case of the British Labor Party see p. 37.

therefore only natural that they should proceed to plan as soon as they could get hold of the essential levers of economic control, a preliminary condition which in eastern Europe was satisfied through the nationalization of large-scale industry and finance.

The immediate adoption of economic planning will, of course, affect the entire future development of the eastern European societies. There will be no sharp break between reconstruction and long-range development, as there was in the Soviet Union at the time of the abandonment of NEP and the launching of the First Five-year Plan. For example, the present Polish plan states that "in the final stages of the Plan it will be possible . . . to lay foundations for the further development of the Polish economy in accordance with the Long Term Plan." Moreover, the experience gained and the personnel trained during the reconstruction phase should make it possible to embark upon more ambitious projects in the future while avoiding the kind of waste and confusion which inevitably accompanied the first pioneering efforts of the Soviet Union.

A second vital difference between the Soviet Union and the eastern European countries lies in the fact that the former had to make its way in a completely hostile capitalist environment, while the latter have the great advantage of a powerful socialist neighbor and ally. Hence, while the Soviet Union could count on no outside economic support and had to build up its own military strength as rapidly as possible, the new regimes in eastern Europe are in a much more favorable position in both these respects. Indeed, in view of the fact that they are not richly endowed with natural resources and that they are extremely vulnerable to attack from the west, it is doubtful whether any of them would be able to survive without Soviet support. Such an event as the drought of 1947, for example, would have put them at the mercy of capitalist countries if they had not been able to rely on Soviet aid. As it is, these countries are in a position to dispense with assistance from the capitalist world, however much they might be able to profit from such assistance if it were available on acceptable terms.

The benefits arising from military alliance with the Soviet Union are no less important. From the very beginning the possibility of raising living standards in the Soviet Union has been severely restricted by the necessity of building up military strength. Many of the harshest features of the Soviet regime can be directly traced to the same cause. The eastern European countries, on the other hand, recognize that their security depends on alliance with the Soviet Union rather than on their own military strength. Moreover, they have been able to equip what forces they do need largely with Russian armaments and hence have been spared the necessity of heavy investment in war industries. The Polish Minister of Industry and Commerce, Hilary Minc, undoubtedly expressed what is true of all the eastern European countries when he said, in a speech on June 2, 1946: "Were our barely revived economy now to take up the burden of equipping a large and modern army, all economic progress would necessarily be halted, living standards could not be raised, and consumers' goods could not be produced." [5] And yet Minc was defining a dilemma which the Soviet Union had not been able to avoid at a comparable stage of development. The fact that the new regimes in eastern Europe have been able to avoid it means that their future progress should be smoother and more rapid than was the case in Russia.

Finally, a third difference, closely related to the second, concerns the problem of agriculture. As we have seen in Chapter 2, collectivization of agriculture was a matter of life and death for the Soviet Union. It had to be pushed through rapidly in order to ensure economic self-sufficiency and national defense. This necessity was the fundamental reason for the Second Revolution, with all its attendant suffering and hardship. The eastern European countries face no such emergency. This does not mean that

[5] *Poland of Today* (monthly bulletin of the Polish Research and Information Service, New York), August, 1946, p. 10.

they are likely to remain satisfied with the type of small-scale, inefficient agriculture which characterizes the region at the present time. But it does mean that they should be able to develop larger scale cooperative farming gradually and in such a way as to convince the peasants of its inherent superiority from the point of view of their own interests. Peasant mentality is conservative, but it is not immutable. If industry can be built up to the point where agricultural machinery and consumers' goods are available, and if the state can demonstrate in a practical way how the one can be used to acquire the other, there should be no insuperable obstacle in the way of a "revolution by consent" in the countryside. The great significance of this possibility for the future of the eastern European countries needs no special emphasis.

Our analysis of the differences between NEP Russia and the present-day eastern European countries points to the conclusion that in the latter the transition to socialism should be smoother and less painful. The reasons for these differences can in every case be traced back to the circumstance that the Soviet Union came first and that, as a consequence, its experience and its support can be drawn upon by those who enter the path to socialism at a later stage. This is, of course, not surprising. History teaches that in the field of social change, no less than in the opening up of new territory to human settlement, it is the pioneer who has the hardest time.

The New Poland

Poland is by a considerable margin the largest and most populous country in eastern Europe; and though its industry is less developed than that of Czechoslovakia, there is no doubt that in the long run its economic potential is greater. For both these reasons the experience of Poland is likely to exercise a strong influence among its immediate neighbors and also among the more industrialized countries of western Europe.

Poland has undergone a drastic change not only in its institutions but also in its territorial and demographic base. The prewar territory of Poland was 150,000 square miles. Of this total, 70,000 were lost to the Soviet Union in the east. On the other hand, 40,000 square miles have been gained from Germany in the north and west. Hence Poland today, with a territory of 120,000 square miles, is 20 per cent smaller than before the war. The decline of population has been even greater. After allowance has been made for wartime deaths (probably about six million), the return of displaced persons from abroad, the net loss in the east (this loss does not equal the total population of the ceded territory because of the number who elect to retain Polish citizenship and migrate to Poland proper), and the net gain in the west (similarly, this gain is less than the total population of the gained territory because of the number of expelled Germans), it is estimated that the population of the new Poland will be approximately 24 million. Since the population of prewar Poland was 35 million, this means that the total decline will be about one-third.

At a first glance these figures might suggest that Poland has been seriously weakened and that the chances of building a strong and stable society are smaller than they would have been before the war. Actually, this impression is misleading. Prewar Poland suffered from chronic overpopulation; the territory subsequently lost to the Soviet Union was industrially undeveloped and agriculturally backward; moreover, this territory was largely inhabited by Ukrainians and Byelorussians, disaffected peoples who were a source of weakness rather than of strength to the Polish state; the territory acquired from Germany, especially in Silesia and Pomerania, is rich in both industrial and agricultural resources; and finally, the new Poland has a much longer coastline and three good harbors whereas before she had only one. There can thus be no doubt that the new Poland is richer in economic resources than its predecessor and that the population density is more favorable to economic progress than it was before the war.

The government of Poland is a coalition of five parties. Its

history is complicated, and only those features which are necessary to an understanding of its political complexion can be noted
here. After the Germans had overrun Poland in the autumn of
1939, a government in exile was set up in London. The London
Government represented the prewar Polish social system, which
was antisocialist and anti-Soviet to the core. For this reason, the
possibility of a genuine *rapprochement* between the London
Government and the Soviet Union was always remote; and when
it began to appear that the Red Army would be responsible for
liberating Poland, the possibility disappeared altogether.

During the winter of 1943–1944 the Soviet authorities encouraged friendly Poles on Russian territory to establish a body
known as the Union of Polish Patriots. In the summer of 1944
the Red Army advanced to the gates of Warsaw, and the Union
of Polish Patriots transformed itself into a Committee of National
Liberation with headquarters at Lublin. The Lublin Committee
assumed responsibility for civil administration in the liberated
portion of Poland, thus becoming a *de facto* government. This
situation was formally recognized on the last day of 1944 by the
organization of the first Provisional Government of Poland with
representatives of the following three parties: the Polish Workers'
Party (Communist), the Polish Socialist Party (the prewar Social
Democratic party minus its extreme right wing, which continued
to support the London Government), and the Peasant Party (a
splinter from the prewar Polish Peasant Party, which constituted
the backbone of the London Government). Both the origin and
the composition of the Provisional Government guaranteed that
it would adopt a fundamentally socialist domestic policy and a
pro-Soviet foreign policy.

Subsequent events have brought extensive changes in the personnel and legal status of the Polish Government, but nothing
has happened to alter its essential character. In June, 1945, following the terms of the agreement on Poland concluded by the Big
Three at Yalta, the Provisional Government was broadened to
include three members of the Polish Peasant Party and one mem-

ber of the newly formed Democratic Party, a small party which draws most of its support from middle-class intellectual circles. All available evidence suggests that the Polish Peasant Party, under the leadership of Stanislaw Mikolajczyk, who had been Premier of the London Government, entered the government merely as a tactical move in a campaign to reverse the trend of postwar Polish politics and eventually to set up an antisocialist, western-oriented regime. Mikolajczyk's popular support among the peasants and the urban middle classes was unquestionably strong, but in every other respect his position was hopelessly inferior to that of the Socialist-Communist coalition, which dominated the government and controlled the entire state apparatus. Moreover, Mikolajczyk's foreign supporters were far away and could offer him little concrete assistance, while the Soviet Union, which had backed the Socialist-Communist alliance from the beginning, had troops in Poland guarding communications with the Soviet zone of Germany and was in a position to lend economic aid of a kind which was crucial to the recovery of the country. Under the circumstances the outcome of the struggle was a foregone conclusion. During 1946 Mikolajczyk's supporters split into two factions; and when elections were at length held in January, 1947—elections, incidentally, which were reasonably honest by prewar eastern European standards—the Polish Peasant Party was overwhelmingly defeated and effectually eliminated as an important factor in Polish political life.

The government which was formed as a result of the elections remains in power up to the time of writing. It is a coalition under a Socialist Prime Minister, containing representatives of the Socialist Party (seven ministers), the Workers' Party (five ministers), the Peasant Party (six ministers), the Democratic Party (three ministers), and the Christian Labor Party (two ministers). (The Christian Labor Party is a Catholic Party which has its main strength in the western provinces.) The bare figures, however, understate the predominant position of the Communist-Socialist alliance. These two parties hold the crucial portfolios and can count on the solid support of the Peasant Party, which, indeed, is essentially their creation. The other parties can doubtless secure consideration for the groups they represent in the execution of policy, but they have no power to determine its content.

The political reality, then, is that Poland has been under a two-party socialist government ever since the first days of the liberation. The two parties are of roughly equal strength, each having a membership of approximately three-quarters of a million. Their alliance is embodied in a formal agreement pledging the two parties to work together but recognizing their organizational independence. This arrangement has, on the whole, worked smoothly, but it is probable that sooner or later the two parties will merge into a single working-class party. In any case, the only thing that would be likely to wreck the Communist-Socialist alliance would be an attempt on the part of a segment of the Socialists to adopt a "western" orientation. If such an attempt were made, it might cause a split in the Socialist Party. Such a split, in turn, could easily lead to what would be in effect a Communist government. But the indications are that the responsible Socialist leaders are aware of these dangers and mean to steer clear of them. If this view is correct, something like the present setup will probably last at least through the period of reconstruction covered by the Three-year Plan.

Three fundamental economic reforms have been put into effect in postwar Poland: land reform, nationalization of large-scale business, and economic planning on a national scale. We shall describe these reforms in turn, leaving a separate section for the subject of economic planning.

Land reform was initiated shortly after the Lublin Committee had established itself on Polish territory; and though the process is not yet finished, it is now possible to give a reasonably accurate account of its general character and scope. The basic principles of the Polish land reform are few and simple. All property of Germans and of certain categories of collaborators is confiscated outright. Other landowners are allowed to retain a specified maximum of land (50 hectares in the old parts and 100 hectares in the so-called Recovered Territories [6]). Everything beyond this maximum is taken over by the state without compensation and distributed, together with the land formerly belonging to Germans and collaborators, to the landless and to those whose holdings are considered insufficient to provide a livelihood.

Quantitatively, the reform has affected a larger area, both relatively and absolutely, in the Recovered Territories than in the regions which were part of prewar Poland. In the latter there are about 11.5 million hectares of arable land; of this total about 2 million hectares (17 per cent) are affected by the reform. (In judging this figure, it must be kept in mind that the part of prewar Poland which was particularly characterized by large estates was the region subsequently ceded to the Soviet Union.) In the Recovered Territories, on the other hand, of a total arable surface of nearly 5 million hectares, more than 4 million (80 per cent) are affected. The difference is striking and is of course accounted for primarily by the expulsion of Germans from the Recovered Territories. Nevertheless, from the point of view of the structure of Polish society it is the figures for the whole country which are most significant; by the time the reform is completed between 35 and 40 per cent of all arable land within the new boundaries of Poland will have been redistributed.

When account is taken of the fact that this redistribution of land is being accompanied by an extensive migration from the overcrowded regions of central and southern Poland, it will be seen that this is indeed a far-reaching agrarian reform which should go a long way toward solving that most intractable of prewar Poland's problems, the problem of rural overpopulation with its attendant evils of poverty, ignorance, and wasted manpower. Not only will the average amount of arable land per farm be larger (7.8 hectares planned for 1949 compared with 5.5 hectares in 1938), but also the number of farms with less than

[6] One hectare equals approximately 2.5 acres.

the average will be drastically reduced. This does not mean, however, that Poland's agrarian problem can be solved by land reform alone. There is still a need for alternative employments for the rural population as well as for a considerable increase in agricultural productivity. Both of these objectives require industrialization, and the need for industrialization has been one of the underlying motives for the nationalization measures to which we now turn our attention.

The property system of Poland was thoroughly scrambled as a result of German economic penetration, the virtual annihilation of the Jews, and the ravages of war. The government was obliged to take charge of so many establishments that, in the words of an official publication, "the question to be decided was not as to which undertakings should be taken over by the State, but rather which undertakings under State administration should be returned to private owners." [7] Given the predominantly socialist complexion of the Polish government, it was only to be expected that this question would be settled in favor of extensive nationalization, the scope and terms of which were fixed by a law of Jan. 3, 1946. All former German property was taken over by the state, including, of course, all such property in the Recovered Territories. Certain industries were nationalized *in toto:* mining, oil, public utilities, transportation and communications, certain branches of metallurgy, armaments, basic food processing, large- and medium-scale textile manufacturing, and printing. In addition, all establishments capable of employing more than 50 workers per shift, regardless of the nature of the industry, were nationalized. Finally, the government was granted permission to nationalize certain other types of undertakings, including banks and storage facilities. The Nationalization Law recognizes the principle of compensation to Polish nationals and to nationals of friendly states. In actual fact, however, about three-quarters of

[7] Preface to "The Nationalization of Industry in Poland: Speech by the Minister of Industry, Hilary Minc, at the Ninth Session of the National Council of the Homeland," Warsaw, 1946.

the value of assets taken over by the state either belonged to Germans or collaborators or was "ownerless." Hence the problem of compensation is not likely to create any serious financial difficulties.

The Nationalization Law contains provision for transferring properties taken over by the state to municipalities and cooperatives; and Minister of Industry Minc, in introducing the bill, emphasized the government's intention to proceed in this direction:

> In this economic pattern [of democratic Poland], the development of Cooperative Societies occupies an essential position. It is not our intention to confine their activities to distribution of goods, to the part of an intermediary between the producer and the consumer. We are of the opinion that Cooperative Societies should also take an important place in the production in various branches of industry. Next to the big undertakings administered by the State the cooperative form of economy should be predominant. This applies in the first place to the food industry, *i.e.,* the processing and improving of agricultural produce.[8]

Statements of this sort—and they have been frequent in the speeches and writings of Polish leaders—have given rise in some quarters to the impression that the new Polish economy consists of three roughly coordinate sectors: nationalized, private, and cooperative. This impression is misleading. It is expected that in 1949, the last year of the Three-year Plan, less than 2 per cent of total Polish manpower will be employed in the cooperative sector (see Table 9). Cooperatives will no doubt play an important role in the new Poland, but at the present stage of development it is hardly justifiable to put them on a par with either nationalized or private business.

No single set of figures, of course, can give a completely ade-

[8] *Ibid.,* p. 29.

quate picture of the structure of a particular society. Nevertheless, no statistics are more relevant in this connection than the
distribution of manpower among various employments. For this

Table 9. *Planned Distribution of Polish Manpower for 1949* *

	Thousands		Per cent	
Grand total...................		13,244.8		100.0
Nationalized sector............		3,043.8		23.0
Industry †..................	1,243.0		9.4	
Government service ‡.........	618.6		4.7	
Transport and communications	548.5		4.1	
Construction................	326.0		2.5	
Forestry....................	105.5		0.8	
Public utilities..............	97.0		0.7	
State farms.................	76.0		0.6	
National defense.............	18.2		0.1	
Banks......................	11.0		0.1	
Cooperative sector............		250.0		1.9
Private-business sector.........		8,595.0		64.9
Agriculture.................	6,665.0		50.3	
Handicraft..................	1,100.0		8.3	
Trade and free professions......	530.0		4.0	
Industry....................	300.0		2.3	
Housewives and students §.......		1,356.0		10.2

* A rearrangement of figures given in the *Polish National Economic Plan*
(Warsaw, 1946), pp. 89–92. The total figure is the estimated population between eighteen and fifty-nine years of age inclusive.

† Including state monopolies.

‡ Including health, social insurance, education, and public information.

§ The category "Housewives and students" is not explained. The author
assumes that it includes only housewives who have no other employment.

reason, we close this section with Table 9, which reproduces, in
somewhat rearranged form, data from the Three-year Plan covering 1949, its last year. In spite of the fact that the nationalized
sector includes government as well as business, less than a quarter
of all manpower will be in the direct employment of the state,

while less than a fifth of total business employment will be in state enterprises. On the other hand, by far the greater part of private employment will be in agriculture, handicrafts, and professions. Inasmuch as most private traders are also self-employed, it is apparent that private employers (capitalism) will play a very small part in the new Poland.[9] What the figures reflect above all, however, is the relatively backward state of the Polish economy, even when the resources of the Recovered Territories, which are expected to be fully integrated by 1949, are taken into account. In the final section of this chapter, we shall touch upon the general nature of the changes which are likely to be brought about when Poland leaves the period of postwar rehabilitation and enters the path of positive construction.

Planning in Poland

Poland officially adopted a system of planned economy on Sept. 21, 1946, when the provisional legislature accepted the Polish National Economic Plan, drawn up by the Central Board of Planning in conjunction with the various economic ministries. In form the Plan covers a period of four years from Jan. 1, 1946, to Dec. 31, 1949. Actually, however, the figures for 1946 are not (and in the nature of the case could not be) targets to be aimed at; rather they appear to be estimates of production, distribution of manpower, and so forth, which are designed to provide a base from which the projected changes of the later years of the Plan can be measured. The practice of referring to the Plan as the Three-year Plan is thus entirely logical. During the summer of 1947 a revised version of the Plan was adopted by the Diet, which had been elected on Jan. 19, 1947. The revised Plan has not been published in English, but according to available information its

[9] It will be noted that the relative size of the public and private sectors is practically the same in Poland as in Britain (see pp. 45–47). The decisive difference between the two countries lies in the composition and strength of the private sector.

basic assumptions do not differ from those of the original. Certain important quantitative changes were introduced, however, and these will be noted below.[10]

The essential nature of the Three-year Plan is somewhat obscured by the method used in making comparisons with prewar years. For example, when one reads that the output of production goods per head is expected to reach 250 (1938 = 100) in the last year of the Plan, one immediately receives the impression of massive investment activity in the industries concerned. And, knowing something of the damaged and disorganized state of the Polish economy at the time of the Plan's adoption, one is likely to conclude that the whole project must be based more on sanguine hopes than on real possibilities. This, however, is in the nature of an optical illusion deriving from the fact that the 1938 figures refer to prewar territory and population, while the 1949 figures refer to present territory and estimated 1949 population. As we have already seen, Polish population has declined by about one-third, and furthermore the Recovered Territories are industrially much richer than the region ceded to the Soviet Union. The Plan, far from contemplating grandiose schemes for building up the production goods industries, merely expresses the hope that by 1949 "decrease of productive capital should be completely stopped." [11] There are excellent reasons for stating the comparisons with prewar years in the way the Plan does. Not only are prewar data for those parts of Poland within its present boundaries difficult (and often impossible) to calculate, but the comparison of the new Poland with the old Poland, the postwar *nation* with the prewar *nation,* is what most interests the Polish public. Nevertheless, in analyzing the Plan one must always remember that a careless use of the data given in the Plan can be extremely misleading.

[10] I am indebted to the Polish Research and Information Service, of New York, for supplying me with information about the revised Plan. The responsibility for interpretations is entirely my own.

[11] *Polish National Economic Plan,* p. 9.

The essence of the Three-year Plan is an attempt to solve two fundamental problems: first, to repair and put back into operation the facilities for producing and distributing goods which already exist within the present boundaries of the country; and second, to unite the old and the new territories into an integrated, smoothly functioning economy. Furthermore, certain tasks are imposed on the Plan by the structural changes in Polish society which have taken place since the war. In particular the agrarian reforms must be assimilated, and the composition of the output of consumers' goods must be altered to correspond with the new class structure of Polish society. Finally—and this applies mainly to the last year of the Plan—a bridge must be laid between the Three-year Plan of *reconstruction* and the projected Long-Term Plan of *development,* which will be inaugurated in 1950. If all these problems can be successfully solved, what is stated to be the "chief aim" of the Plan, "the raising of the standard of living of the working masses above the pre-war level," [12] will be automatically achieved.

The Three-year Plan consists of three parts: first, a Resolution of the National Council setting forth the general objectives of the Plan; second, 10 pages devoted to "General Guiding Principles"; and third, 60 statistical tables grouped under the following headings: "Agriculture," "Industry," "Transport and Communications," "Production and Consumption in Basic Investment Industries," "Foreign Trade," "Employment," "Education, Health, and Social Welfare," "Consumption," "National Income," and "Indices of Economic and Social Development." The over-all national character of the Plan can be inferred from even this brief description. But within this comprehensive pattern the treatment of the various fields is by no means uniform. Thus, for example, "the industrial tables contain principally only the State industries, and in some cases the co-operative industries. The character of private industry and handicraft does not allow plan-

[12] *Ibid.,* p. 7.

ning of production to the extent possible in State or co-operative industry." [13] On the other hand, as far as nationalized industry is concerned, the figures are considered to be definite operative targets which are to control the policies of the various responsible authorities. Many of the agricultural tables have a still different significance: "Owing to the instability of the economic situation and of agricultural production, and the lack of basic statistical data, a considerable number of estimates used in the agricultural tables are given only for orientation." [14] And if the reader asks "for whose orientation?", the answer is certainly "not for the orientation of the farmers themselves." For, as Minc frankly admitted in his speech introducing the Plan, "as far as agriculture is concerned, the plan contains no directive to guide it as such, its [the Plan's] influence confines itself to providing the necessary equipment, the necessary aids." [15] Thus the agricultural tables must be for the orientation of those nationalized industries which are responsible for supplying the necessary equipment and aids to agriculture.

If we now take into account the facts that private industry is largely omitted from the Plan and that agriculture is dealt with for the most part indirectly, it will be seen that the Plan is essentially a plan for the nationalized sector, its basic premise being that by controlling the development of the nationalized sector the state can in fact control the development of the whole economy. In introducing the Nationalization Bill, Minc had clearly stated this philosophy of planning:

> . . . a realistic plan can only be created and carried out when means of realising it are at the disposal of the state. It is possible to guide a state organism, like a ship, in a definite direction if one holds the rudder. The rudder in this case is the essential branches of national economy such as produc-

[13] *Ibid.*, p. 32.
[14] *Ibid.*
[15] *Poland of Today*, November, 1946, p. 5.

tion of coal, iron, steel, electrical power, artificial fertilizers, textiles, agricultural implements and machine tools, transport networks and telecommunications, and lastly the banking system. Without holding the rudder, there is no plan. . . . That is why the state is taking over.[16]

And Minc described the relation of private industry to the Plan as follows:

So far private industry has existed either by drawing from old resources, or from other accidental, not to say illegal, sources. Now that these possibilities are coming to an end, it is clear that the development of private industry will not be possible without access to raw materials and auxiliary products held by the state. The state will offer such assistance on condition that private industry will join the state's economic plan.[17]

It is too early to say how well this system will work, but in any case there is no ambiguity about the Polish conception of economic planning. The Plan itself exists as a carefully worked-out document, and its underlying principles have been clearly stated. This is in sharp contrast to the treatment of planning in Great Britain, where, as we saw in the previous chapter, there is much discussion of planning but no plan, and where in practice planning is little more than a collective name for a wide range of governmental economic policies. The difference can doubtless be accounted for by the fact that the Polish Government feels that it has the necessary means to plan, while the British Government feels in this respect less sure of itself.

Industrial production as a whole has increased very satisfactorily since the inauguration of the Three-year Plan. A monthly index of production of 20 basic commodities (1937 = 100) averaged 91 for 1946 and remained in the neighborhood of 100 during

[16] *The Nationalization of Industry in Poland,* p. 17.
[17] *Ibid.,* p. 28.

the last half of the year. During the first eight months of 1947, it rose more or less steadily and stood at 124 for August.[18] The record of plan fulfillment in individual industries, however, is

Table 10. Polish Plan Fulfillment, First Half of 1947 *

Industry and unit	Planned production	Actual production	Percentage excess or deficit †
Electric power, billion kilowatt-hours...	1.7	1.7	
Hard coal, million tons...............	27.1	27.2	
Brown coal, million tons.............	1.9	2.4	+32
Smelting, million tons................	3.0	3.1	+3
Machine tools, thousand pieces........	1.7	1.2	−29
Agricultural machinery, thousand pieces.	149.7	154.1	+3
Wiring and forged parts, thousand tons	67.4	76.4	+13
Electrotechnical, thousand tons........	14.4	14.0	−3
Chemicals, million tons...............	1.9	2.3	+21
Crude oil, thousand tons..............	60.9	60.9	
Natural gas, million cubic yards.......	85.5	106.4	+24
Cotton yarn, thousand tons...........	32.1	26.6	−17
Cotton fabrics, million yards..........	137.6	124.7	−9
Woolen fabrics, million yards..........	15.3	15.5	+2
Garments, million pieces..............	18.7	21.0	+12
Leather, billion zlotys................	1.7	1.3	−24
Paper, thousand tons.................	361.3	337.1	−7

* Data furnished by Polish Research and Information Service.
† Approximate.

somewhat uneven, as may be seen in Table 10. Of 17 important industries listed, 3 fulfilled their quotas exactly; 4 came within 5 per cent; 5 missed by between 5 and 20 per cent; and the remaining 5 missed by more than 20 per cent. The 10 deviations of more than 5 per cent are divided equally between surpluses and deficits,

[18] *Statistical News of the Central Statistical Office* (in Polish and English), Nov. 5, 1947, p. 322.

a fact which suggests that they arise more from inexperience in planning than from any underlying bias in the plan as a whole. In some cases, moreover, it is clear that deficits can be traced to causes over which the Polish authorities had no control. For example, the large deficit in machine-tool production (29 per cent) is explained largely by a shortage of ball bearings, which have to be imported, and which have not yet been obtainable in required quantities. Polish spokesmen have never made any attempt to hide the imperfections of the original Plan, and it would seem that by their own standards they have no reason to be disappointed by the record of achievement during the first months of its operation.

Comparable data for agriculture are not available at the time of writing, but there is little doubt that results in agriculture have been less favorable than in industry. The main reason for this, of course, was the severe drought of 1947, which affected all Europe west of the Soviet Union. Another contributing factor is a continuing shortage of draught power on Polish farms. The number of horses was drastically reduced by occupation and war, and it has been impossible to import tractors on the scale originally planned. From a long-term point of view, indeed, this is likely to be the most serious obstacle to full agricultural recovery.

Changes in the Plan adopted by the Diet on July 2, 1947, were intended partly to rectify errors and partly to meet changed conditions. It is probably safe to classify most of the alterations of individual industry targets as rectifications, while the shift in livestock breeding from cattle, pigs, and sheep to horses evidently reflects the difficulty of importing tractors. The most general changes—those affecting the disposition of the national income and the total of investment—are probably motivated by considerations of both these types. The Diet version of the Plan raises per capita national income in each year by an average of about 6 per cent. Per capita consumption, however, is increased by almost twice as much, and this, of course, implies a decline in the percentage of national income going to investment. At the same time, total investment is cut by an even larger percentage figure.

How can we explain these changes? It would be logical to suppose that there must be at least two factors involved. First, productivity and consumption are closely related, and it is quite likely that the original Plan did not take adequate account of this fact. Second, the original Plan was based on the assumption that from 15 to 20 per cent of total investment, or approximately 400 million dollars for the three-year period, would come from abroad, and under present circumstances most of this sum would have to come from the United States. Since the United States has so far been unwilling to lend to pro-Soviet countries, the Poles have undoubtedly had to reduce their expectations regarding foreign capital and to cut total investment accordingly.

The Outlook for Socialism in Poland

Poland is now passing through a very trying period of reconstruction, as indeed was inevitable after the devastation of Nazi occupation and war. Nevertheless, the prospects of the most urgently immediate problems' being successfully solved seem favorable. The socialist-dominated government is firmly in the saddle and has shown energy and determination in the face of great difficulties. The disappointment of hopes for continued large-scale foreign aid—it must not be forgotten that the contribution of UNNRA to Polish recovery in the first year and a half after liberation was of inestimable value—is a hard, but probably not a fatal, blow. The reconstruction of the economy, and especially of agriculture, by the end of the Three-year Plan will be less thorough than had been originally contemplated. But the general objectives of the Plan as revised in 1947 can probably be achieved. If so, the most difficult phase will have been passed, and Poland should be in a position to go forward with genuine confidence.[19]

[19] After this chapter had been written, it was announced from Moscow on Jan. 27, 1948, that a series of agreements had been signed between Poland and the Soviet Union. These provide for (1) 200,000 tons of grain from the

What of the more distant future, of the period of the projected Long-Term Plan scheduled to be inaugurated in 1950? The Polish Government has given assurances that there will be no new acts nationalizing property which is now private. If this pledge is kept, will it mean the permanent retention of the present mixed social system and an end to all hopes (or fears) that Poland is on the way to becoming a thoroughly socialist country?

One must, of course, refrain from concrete predictions about events which lie so far in the future, for in the rapidly changing world of today even 5 or 10 years is a long time. But one can safely say that in principle there is no incompatibility between the promise of the Polish Government not to nationalize property which is now private and an intention, presumably shared by the two dominant government parties, to work for a socialist Poland. For the new Poland has everything necessary for extensive industrial growth; and with industry largely nationalized, industrial growth will mean the growth of the nationalized sector of the economy. The Three-year Plan, even though it is only a plan of reconstruction, already contemplates the relative growth of industry: not only is the entire natural increase of population expected to be absorbed in the cities, but also a net migration of 300,000 workers from rural to urban employments is anticipated. There is no doubt that this process can be pushed much further in subsequent plans, and it goes without saying that it will be large-scale nationalized industry, not petty production, which will do the growing. In this way the socialist element in Polish society

---

Soviet Union to Poland during the next three months; (2) an exchange of goods averaging 200 million dollars a year for the next five years; and (3) Soviet loans for Polish industrialization averaging 50 million dollars a year for the next nine years. These agreements, aside from enabling Poland to overcome an immediate food crisis, should go far toward compensating her for the absence of aid from the United States. This is an excellent illustration of the point made on pp. 66–69 that the assistance of an already established socialist country can be of enormous importance to a country just entering the path to socialism.

can, and presumably will, become steadily larger without any fresh acts of nationalization.

The perspective for agriculture—aside from the essentially negative probability that it will decline relatively to industry—is much less clear. But to suppose that the Polish peasant will cling indefinitely to the present system of individual small holdings is to make the untenable assumption that he is by nature incapable of appreciating the advantages of modern methods of mechanized farming even when they finally become available to him. We do not need to assume that Polish agriculture is likely to develop along the lines of the Soviet collective farm, for after all the kolkhoz was the Soviet answer to a specifically Soviet problem. But it seems possible that there may evolve in Poland a system of cooperative farming which will be as compatible with socialist society as the collective farm has already proved to be under Soviet conditions.

Part Two

The Development of Socialism

CHAPTER 5

The Origins of Present-day Socialism

THERE ARE many misconceptions about the origin and nature
of socialism. Two of the most widespread are particularly obstruc-
tive to a clear understanding of the subject as a whole. One of
these is that socialism is as old as recorded history, that every age
has its socialists, and that ours is therefore in this respect not at
all peculiar. The other—which evidently derives from the fact that
socialism has had its first trial in the Soviet Union, an eastern
European and Asian country—is that socialism is in some sense
alien to the traditions of the western world of which the United
States is a part.

It is one of the main purposes of this chapter to show that
socialism is on the contrary both a modern and a western phenomenon. It is as modern as industrial capitalism and as western
as the idea that all men are created equal. In fact, capitalism and
the doctrine of human equality can be described without exaggeration as the true parents of socialism. Unless this is understood,
it is impossible to grasp the historical meaning of socialism and
the role which it is playing in the world today.

"Socialism" in Ancient and Medieval Times

Much has been written about ancient and medieval socialism,
but on closer examination this literature turns out to be concerned with something quite different from the subject matter
of this book. Let us review briefly some of the most frequently
cited examples of ancient and medieval socialism.

Some writers have claimed to find evidences of socialism in
the Old Testament—in the Mosaic law and in the utterances of

the prophets. These claims can be vindicated, however, only by identifying socialism with injunctions to succor the poor and condemnations of the abuse of wealth. In reality, the social system which the Old Testament presupposes and to a large degree illuminates is one of pastoralism based on unrestricted private ownership of animal herds.

The Essenes have been more plausibly cited as an example of socialism among the ancient Jews, for there seems to be no doubt that the group did hold its worldly goods in common. But here we have to do with the practice of a religious sect and not at all with a program for society as a whole. The mere fact that the Essenes practiced celibacy proves that they were attempting to set themselves apart from the rest of the world rather than to make it over according to their own ideas. The contrast with modern socialism could hardly be sharper.

The supposedly socialist tendencies of primitive Christianity have been a common theme of modern writers. And yet one will search the New Testament in vain for any conscious concern with the nature of the social order. Christ taught his followers that they should seek the Kingdom of God, not a reform of the system of society under which they lived. They could do so only by shunning the temptations of wealth and practicing the virtues of generosity and love of others. Socialists may believe that only under socialism will it be possible for the ideals of the primitive Christians to be realized, but to make this a ground for identifying socialism with primitive Christianity is merely a case of confused thinking.

Of all the alleged examples of ancient socialism, none is so widely known or so extensively discussed as Plato's *Republic*. Yet the truth is that the *Republic* has nothing in common with modern socialism. Since many readers, having been often told differently, may be inclined to doubt this, it may be well to quote the view of an eminent authority. According to Professor Ernest Barker,

There is . . . no common ownership in the Platonic system; there is only common consumption, and that only
among the class of the guardians. The members of the farming class own, cultivate, and consume in severalty—subject
only to two conditions, first that they pay a quota of their
produce to the guardians, for *their* common use, and sec-
ondly that the amount of land which each may own is
restricted.[1]

It is, of course, true that some of the arguments which Plato
advances to support the proposal of communal living for his
guardians can be used to justify socialism, but it would be a
simple *non sequitur* to conclude from this that Plato had any
conception of a socialist order of society.

Generally speaking, Roman history seems to have yielded fewer
examples of alleged socialist tendencies than Jewish or Greek
culture. Nevertheless, not a few writers have found evidence of
a practical struggle for socialism in the numerous civil wars and
slave uprisings which punctuated the stormy career of the Roman
state. One has only to examine the facts with critical attention,
however, to perceive that nothing even resembling socialism was
involved in these internal Roman disturbances. Most often the
question at issue was the simple one of which group should
enjoy the fruits of power. The movement led by the Gracchi, in
contrast, was certainly concerned with the Roman social system,
but what it aimed at was not socialism but a return to an earlier
system of individual peasant farming. Finally, the slave uprisings
—such as that led by the famous Spartacus in the first century
B.C.—represented an elemental reaction to savage exploitation.
Their objectives were liberty and revenge; there is no evidence
that any thought of changing the social order ever entered the
heads of the leaders, still less of the rank and file.

Turning now to the Middle Ages, we see that the most frequently cited examples of supposed socialism are found in mon-

[1] Ernest Barker (ed.), *The Politics of Aristotle* (1946), p. 56.

astic movements or in heretical religious sects. As to the former, the very principle of monasticism is antithetical to socialism. The monastery, whatever its constitution, is a place apart from the world, while socialism is a program for the reconstruction of the world. To characterize the religious sects satisfactorily is more difficult, especially in view of the fact that we know about them mostly from their persecutors, who were, at least ostensibly, concerned entirely with questions of religious doctrine. Still, there is enough evidence to suggest that, if we leave out of account millenarian visions of a golden age, the medieval sects were much more concerned with abuses of power and wealth, especially in the Church, than with the structure of society. By excluding millenarian visions, we do not mean to suggest that there is nothing in common between the psychology of millenarianism and the psychology of socialism; indeed it is obvious that both arise from strong negative reactions to a present environment and positive hopes for a better future. But that is as far as the similarity goes, and to confuse millenarianism with socialism on this basis is to miss the crucial point that at one stage of history the oppressed react to a harsh environment by hoping for a miracle, while at another they react by proposing to build a better world.

A somewhat different problem is presented by the violent social upheavals which were particularly characteristic of the fourteenth and early fifteen centuries: for example, the rising in western Flanders during the 1320's, the *Jacquerie* in France in 1357, the peasant insurrection in England in 1381, and—somewhat later—the famous Peasant War in Germany, which broke out in 1525. These disturbances invariably had a religious overtone, but both in origin and in aim they were almost wholly secular. Fundamentally they bear a strong resemblance to the slave rebellions of the ancient world, which have already been characterized above. It has often been noted, however, that these medieval social struggles had a marked flavor of communism about them, and this has sometimes led to their being classified as definitely socialist movements. But this seems to be going too far; Petegorsky is probably nearer to the truth when he says that the "communism" of these medieval movements "is generally a vague and mystical affair, and, at best, a general demand for a common and equal division of the social product rather than for a system of common production. In no instance does it derive from a reasoned examination of social and historical forces." [2]

It should be noted that in none of the foregoing examples of alleged socialism in ancient and medieval times is there any analysis of the problems of production. This fact in itself is enough to prove that they are far removed from socialism in the modern sense of the term, for the essential feature of modern socialism is a system of production based on common ownership. Clearly, if the problems of production are altogether ignored, it is impossible to attain to such a conception. Ancient and medieval thinkers tended to take for granted the existing system of production and sought improvements within this framework. Class divisions, the coexistence of rich and poor—these things seemed natural and unavoidable. On the other hand, the rich had obligations to take care of the poor and not to abuse their power. It was generally against the violation of these obligations, and not against the social system as such, that ancient and medieval radical thought was directed.

Why this should have been so is an important historical question which has not received the attention it deserves. To go into it in any detail would be clearly beyond the scope of the present book. Yet it is important that we should not entirely ignore the subject, for it casts a revealing, if indirect, light on the actual origins of socialism in modern times.

No doubt a full explanation would have to take account of many contributory factors, but the underlying cause, which is basic to all the others, must be sought in the extremely low level of human productivity which characterized ancient and medieval times. Civilization itself, which necessarily presupposes at least a

[2] D. W. Petegorsky, *Left-wing Democracy in the English Civil War* (1940), pp. 150–151.

small class of people freed from the problems of securing a bare living, rested on a very narrow margin. With the existing low levels of productivity it was literally impossible for more than a small proportion of the population to become educated and to enjoy the fruits of culture. The vast majority was doomed to a life of backbreaking toil. Under these circumstances people could see no way out of the dilemma—except through a miracle. And a problem that has no earthly solution is not an earthly problem. Socialism—which, if it is anything, is an earthly solution to an earthly problem—could hardly take root in such a world.

The Forerunners of Socialism

The ideal of common ownership for the whole of society rather than simply for a small ruling class or a religiously motivated sect was first clearly set forth in Thomas More's *Utopia,* published (in Latin) in 1516. More himself was strongly influenced by Plato, and there are passages in *Utopia* which indicate that he thought he was copying the property system of the *Republic.* The fact is, however, that in this respect the two have little in common. The "communism" of Plato is simply a device for isolating his ruling caste from the contamination of the world of economic affairs. In Utopia, on the other hand, common ownership is the basis of the community's entire system of production and distribution. It is this fact that has given to More's great work an honored position in the literature of socialism.

Nevertheless, it would be a mistake to attribute a large influence to Thomas More in the development of socialism. The chief purpose of *Utopia* was probably—there is no way of being certain, and the experts are far from agreed—to serve as a medium for a searching criticism of conditions in England at a time when enclosures were uprooting peasants from the land and casting them adrift to beg or steal and too often to die on the gallows. And the chief influence of the book is indicated by the fate of its title, which has come to mean any ideal imaginary society which achieves perfection by conveniently disregarding the hard facts of the real world. Socialists have created their share of Utopias, but they are by no means the only ones; and all, whatever their vision of the perfect state may be, trace their ancestry back to Thomas More. More's conception of a society based on common ownership of the means of production, coming as it did at the very dawn of the modern era, was a flash of genius and a harbinger of things to come, but it can hardly be said to have exercised a direct influence on the course of social thought.

Modern socialism has its real beginnings in the period of the English Civil War (1642–1652), one of the decisive events in the shaping of our own world. The shock of the crisis produced an outburst of social and political thinking which, both in quantity and in quality, would be hard to match in any age or country. The ideas of two centuries were anticipated in less than two decades.

It must not be supposed that socialism was an important issue in the Civil War. It was, in fact, confined to a numerically insignificant group, called the Diggers, on the extreme left wing of the democratic movement. But Gerrard Winstanley, the chief spokesman and theorist of the Diggers, was a man of genius, whose clarity of thought and breadth of vision place him in the top rank of socialist thinkers. Furthermore, Winstanley mirrors in his own development the transition from medieval religious mysticism to modern rational socialism.

Winstanley's first two tracts, published early in 1648, are typical of much of the mystical millenarian religious literature of the period. But before the end of the same year he had produced the first of a series of short works, which, despite a continued use of religious language, enunciated a brilliantly clear and rational system of social thought. Winstanley argued that throughout the course of history, war and civil strife had their origin in that division of society which had as its basis the private ownership of the land. Private property not only divided society into rich and poor, it dehumanized the rich and debased the poor. Governments were established and maintained to protect the interests of the property owners, and organized religion was called into existence to encourage submission on the part of the poor by attributing divine approval to the social order. This analysis of history and society, which anticipates the doctrines of modern socialism at many points, could lead to but one conclusion—that a righteous social order which would recognize the principles of human equality and dignity could be built only on the basis of common ownership of the land. "The Earth," said Winstanley, "was made by Almighty God to be a Common Treasury of Livelihood to the whole of mankind in all its branches, without respect of persons." [3]

But Winstanley's analysis led him even farther in the direction of modern socialism. Since the existing social order was conceived and maintained in the interests of the rich, it followed that they and their representatives in church and state could not be expected to be sympathetic to its abolition. Since, on the other hand, it was the highest interest of the poor to effect such a change, they themselves would have to bring it about.

These conclusions were necessary logical deductions from his theory, and Winstanley did not hesitate to draw them. It was only when he came to the methods to be followed in achieving the new order that he faltered, and this was due to a lack of relevant experience rather than to any intellectual fault. Winstanley urged the poor to start immediately to work on uncultivated common land (whence the name "Diggers"); and he expected the movement, once begun, to lead peacefully, but by an otherwise unspecified path, to the new society. The method was, of course, unrealistic; and Winstanley's one attempt to put it into practice soon convinced him of the fact. In his last and most important work, *The Law of Freedom* (1652), Winstanley virtually confessed his inability to solve the central political problem of socialism; in dedicating the book to Cromwell, he wrote, "I have set the

[3] Quoted in *ibid.*, p. 201.

candle at your door; for you have power in your hand to act for Common Freedom, if you will; I have no power." [4] But his own theory should have warned him—and perhaps it did—that his plea would go unanswered.

Though Winstanley's works enjoyed some success in their day, their profoundly original character was not appreciated by his contemporaries; and his name was soon buried along with those of hundreds of other seventeenth-century religious and political pamphleteers. He was too far ahead of his time, and when history had caught up with him he was already forgotten. It was not until the end of the nineteenth century that Eduard Bernstein, a German socialist, rediscovered Winstanley, and it is possible even today for a British historian to write a long volume on socialist thought without even mentioning his name.[5] Yet for an understanding of the nature of socialism, Winstanley is a crucial figure. He stands at one of the decisive watersheds of modern history; his own writings reflect the age that was passing as well as the age that was to come; he sensed the tremendous potentialities of the new science and technique which capitalism was bringing with it; and he spoke out on behalf of a landless proletariat which was still young and feeble but which was to grow into a mighty social force in the centuries ahead.

During the eighteenth century numerous writers, especially in France, approached (some actually achieved) a socialist standpoint; but they were more or less isolated individuals, and none attracted a significant following. Moreover, in point of theoretical range and depth no socialist writer of this period was the equal of Winstanley. In a brief survey, therefore, we are justified in passing over men like Meslier, Mably, Morelly, and Boissel, even though they figure prominently in the standard histories of socialism. From our present point of view, the next decisive period in the development of socialism after the English Revolution was the French Revolution.

[4] *Ibid.,* p. 213.

[5] Alexander Gray, *The Socialist Tradition: Moses to Lenin* (1946).

The French Revolution was, of course, in no sense a socialist revolution; on the contrary, it was the purest of middle-class revolutions. But just because of this, the French Revolution cleared away the last ideological and psychological barriers to the development of a genuine socialist movement. It did this by firmly implanting the idea of human equality in the consciousness—and also in the conscience—of western Europe.

The leaders of the French Revolution meant by equality no more than the abrogation of special privileges based on birth or social status, in other words, equality before the law. But the idea could not be contained within such narrow limits; once formal equality had been attained, it was only to be expected that the lower classes would raise the question of the real inequality of living conditions, an inequality which now seemed to lack all justification. The next step, and it was but a short one, was to bring into question the property system, which was the root of inequality of living conditions. It was the spread of this mode of thinking in the half century after the outbreak of the French Revolution that laid the psychological foundations for a genuine mass socialist movement.

This new development was clearly foreshadowed in the writings and activities of Babeuf, the one important socialist figure of the French Revolution. Babeuf was a passionate believer in equality, which he gradually came to interpret in the most literal and strict sense. When it became apparent to him in 1795–1796 that the Revolution had not only stopped far short of his developing ideal but was actually losing ground to reaction, he and a small group of associates decided that the time had come for drastic action. This is the background of the famous "Conspiracy of the Equals" which boldly proclaimed thoroughgoing communism as its aim and revolution as its method. A few excerpts from the "Manifesto of the Equals" will indicate the extent to which Babeuf and his comrades were products of the French Revolution and at the same time prophets of a coming socialism:

Equality! First promise of nature! First need of man and principal bond of all legitimate association! . . . Equality has been nothing but a fine-sounding and sterile fiction of the law. Today when we demand it more loudly than ever, we are told: "Silence, wretches! Real equality is a chimera; content yourselves with conditional equality; you are all equal before the law. Swine, what more do you want?" What more do we want? . . . We claim the right henceforth to live and die as equals just as we were born as equals, and we want real equality or death. The French Revolution is only the harbinger of a still greater and more solemn revolution which will be the last. . . . We demand something more sublime and more equitable [than the agrarian law]: the common good or community of goods. No more individual property in the land. The land belongs to no one; its fruits belong to all. . . .[6]

It is not only in linking the doctrine of equality and the demand for collective ownership that Babeuf and the Equals are important for the development of socialism. They understood much more clearly than any of their predecessors that their aims could be realized only through the acquisition of political power, and the essence of the Conspiracy was an elaborate and carefully conceived plan of insurrection, which involved winning the support of both the civilian population and the army. Conditions were not ripe; the Conspiracy failed; Babeuf and his comrade Darthé were tried and executed. But the example which they set lived on as an inspiration, and even to a certain extent as a model, for future generations of socialists.

The Formative Period of Socialism

The first half of the nineteenth century was the formative period of modern socialism. Before 1800 socialism consisted of

[6] Paul Louis, *Histoire du socialisme en France* (1946), pp. 34–35.

a few relatively isolated thinkers and two small, short-lived movements, the Diggers and the Equals, both the product of special
revolutionary conditions. After 1800 the individual thinkers gave
way to schools of thought, and the movements, gradually taking
on a more stable character, came to reflect the normal conditions
of life of an ever-expanding sector of the population. That these
conditions of life were peculiar to capitalism is proved by the fact
that until the very end of the period under review the development of socialism was practically confined to England and France,
the two major nations in which capitalism, owing in large part
to the revolutions of the seventeenth and eighteenth centuries,
was already predominant and rapidly expanding.

The most prominent and influential of the early nineteenth-
century socialists were St. Simon, Fourier, and Owen—the first
two French, and the third an Englishman. Though these three
men differed widely in their backgrounds, in their temperaments,
and even in their interests, they were alike in certain important
respects. They were all sensitive humanitarians and keen observers of their environment. At the same time they were children
of the Enlightenment, distrustful of received authority and con-
fident in the power of reason to solve the problems of human
society. The contradiction between their ideals and what they saw
around them led them, each in his own way, to draw up a searching indictment of the existing social order and to formulate the
principles of a better society. Moreover, since there was no movement working for fundamental change to which they could attach
themselves, they could see no other course than to attempt by
their own reasoning and eloquence to persuade those who already
possessed power and wealth to support their plans for reform.

It was this choice of method, which was natural enough under
the circumstances, that has led to the classification of St. Simon,
Fourier, and Owen as Utopian socialists. Moreover, there can be
no doubt that the same factor was decisive in determining both
the character of their activities and the nature of their influence
on others. They were, so to speak, attempting to sell a new form

of society in much the same way that a manufacturer attempts to sell a new machine. In the one case, as in the other, it is necessary to set out the specifications of the product in detail, to describe its merits in the most attractive terms, to advertise it far and wide, and if possible to provide models for the inspection and approval of prospective customers. Performing these various functions took up much of the time and energy of the Utopian socialists and prevented them from giving consideration to alternative approaches to the problems of social reconstruction. It was thus entirely characteristic of them that they shunned politics—not incidentally but as a matter of principle. And when their hopes were shattered and their ambitions frustrated, as they were bound to be, it was natural that they should become embittered if not disillusioned. Finally, it was inevitable that the followings which they attracted, at first including many able men inspired by the enthusiasm and vision of the masters, should gradually dwindle away and eventually degenerate into narrow sects cut off from all contact with the main stream of history.

If one concentrates on this aspect of the great Utopian socialists —and it is probably the aspect that they themselves would have stressed—one can only conclude that they were tragic failures. But the viewpoint is altogether too one-sided; it entirely overlooks their extremely important positive contributions to the development of socialism. If the Utopians were unrealistic in their approach to the future, the same cannot be said of their treatment of the past and present. In their criticism of the existing social order, in their analysis of history, in their insights into individual and social psychology, the Utopians vastly enriched the socialist heritage and provided much of the raw material which Marx and Engels were later to fashion into the world view of the present-day socialist movement. Nor was this the only positive contribution of the Utopians. They were the first to make socialism into a genuine public issue, to stir up impassioned debate not only among their adherents but with and among their opponents, to spread the new ideas from their birthplace in

France and England to Germany, Switzerland, and Belgium in the east and to America in the west. As far as the western European and American public was concerned, socialism came into the world through the agency of St. Simon, Fourier, and Owen.

We have called the first half of the nineteenth century the formative period of socialism. The achievements of the Utopians would be enough to justify the designation, but there is another and equally important justification. It was in England during the 1830's and '40's that socialism first acquired the character of a working-class political movement, which it has ever since retained. The Chartist movement was the first example in history of large-scale independent political action on the part of the working class.

The demand for the People's Charter followed logically after the passage of the Reform Bill of 1832. The Reform Bill gave the vote and a share of political power to the middle classes. The working class, now very numerous and increasingly active in its own interest, helped to force the reform down the throats of the unwilling Tories, but any hopes that it would benefit the workers themselves were quickly shattered by the drastic Poor Law Reform Bill of 1834. During most of the next two decades—right up to the new era which opened with the suppression of the revolutions of 1848—the British working class concentrated on winning its own reform, the People's Charter.

Anyone reading the Charter today who is unfamiliar with the period in which it made its appearance will almost certainly conclude that there is nothing socialistic about the document [7] and that the movement which demanded its enactment must have been devoted to quite ordinary and very unrevolutionary democratic objectives. To reason in this way, however, is a serious mistake. It is necessary to remember that in the 1830's noth-

[7] The six points of the Charter were universal suffrage, abolition of all property qualification, annual parliaments, equal constituencies, salaries for members of Parliament, and the secret ballot.

ing approaching universal suffrage existed anywhere outside the United States, and even in the United States it was not general. English political thinkers of the time were unanimous in holding the opinion that universal suffrage would be immediately followed by an attack on private property; indeed, "democrat" and "communist" were virtually synonymous terms. Today, it is true, the Charter would be looked upon as a purely political reform; but in the 1830's it was looked upon as the political means to a radical reconstruction of society.

The concentration of the Chartists on the question of political rights, which in their eyes was identical with the question of political power, was responsible for their failure to elaborate a program of economic and social reforms. To most of them it seemed futile to propose measures which they had no power to carry out; conversely, once the workers had political power they would not long be in doubt as to how to use it in their own interests. Many, perhaps most, of the Chartists took it for granted that this would involve the adoption of a socialist form of society. This comes out most clearly in their numerous and often heated controversies with the Owenites, who were very active at the same time and who for a few years had a considerable working-class following.

The Chartists for the most part did not quarrel with the ultimate aims of Owen, but they regarded his rejection of politics as stupid and irresponsible. The proposals of the Owenites, wrote Henry Hetherington, a leading Chartist,

> are essentially practical and beneficial, if the people had a free stage and no favour. When the people have equal rights and their consequent equal laws, the superiority of Mr. Owen's principles will admit of demonstration, but not till then. To attempt to establish, even partially, on independent grounds, any of Mr. Owen's philanthropic views in the present state of the country and before the working classes

are politically emancipated is only putting the cart before the horse and will end in an abortion.[8]

This criticism of Owenism was eminently justified, and it shows that one must not judge the whole character of the Chartist movement by the particular demands of the Charter. Implicitly, if not explicitly, Chartism was a socialist movement. Moreover, it showed for the first time that the working class is capable of concerted action aimed at building a better world. By this demonstration, Chartism in effect dealt the *coup de grâce* to Utopian socialism; henceforth socialism was either a working-class movement or it was a farce or a swindle.

The foregoing sketch may give the impression that Chartism was strong in the field of practical action and weak in the field of theory. To leave the matter there, however, would be misleading. It is true that many of the Chartists were primarily men of action, but their ranks were by no means devoid of able thinkers. Probably the most remarkable of these was James Bronterre O'Brien, an Irishman and a journalist of exceptional talents, who drew much of his inspiration from the French Revolution and the heroic example of Babeuf. Bronterre O'Brien had a very clear conception of the class structure of existing society. He knew that it was useless to expect the ruling class to act against its own interests, and he understood that a fundamental change could be brought about only by those who were the special victims of the existing order, the propertyless working class. He regarded the state as an instrument of oppression in the hands of the ruling class, and he taught the workers the necessity of acquiring political power as a prerequisite to effective reform.

In later life O'Brien became a rather commonplace currency crank, and this has unfortunately tended to obscure the fact that in his prime during the 1830's he was one of the most vigorous

[8] Quoted in Theodore Rothstein, *From Chartism to Labourism* (1929), pp. 119–120.

and original thinkers yet produced by the British working-class movement.

Socialism's Coming of Age

If socialism may be said to have been conceived in the early sixteenth century and born in the English Civil War, it no less clearly came of age in the 1840's. The great achievement of Karl Marx and Friedrich Engels was combining the rich but scattered materials to be found all around them into a new socialist synthesis which is both a coherent system of social science and a purposeful movement of social reconstruction.

It is perhaps a commonplace, but nevertheless an important one, to insist that Marx and Engels could play this role in the development of socialism because they arrived on the stage of history at precisely the right moment. Marx was born in 1818, Engels in 1820. They were thus growing to full maturity in the early forties at a time when a continent-wide movement of revolt against the *status quo* was coming to a head; when capitalism, already firmly established in England and France, had demonstrated the enormous potential productivity of human labor; when the working class in the more advanced industrial areas was beginning to prove that it was capable of taking the initiative and fighting for its own interests; and when socialism, thanks to the efforts of the Utopians, was the subject of widespread and passionate public debate. Clearly, great changes were occurring and even greater seemed to be in the offing. Socialists, if they were to take full advantage of their new opportunities, could no longer be satisfied with a critique of the existing order and a vision of a better world. They would have to find out why things were as they were, how they were changing, and in what direction they were tending; for only through such understanding could they lay the basis for rational and effective action. This was a challenge posed by the character of the times.

Marx and Engels were well prepared by background and training to recognize and accept the challenge. Both came from western Germany, an area which had felt the impact of the French Revolution, which was economically relatively advanced, and which was responsive to pressures from both east and west. Marx's father was a baptized Jew, a lawyer by occupation, who brought his son up in the liberal tradition of the eighteenth-century Enlightenment. Engels's father was a prosperous industrialist who owned textile factories both in Barmen (now a part of the city of Wuppertal) and in Lancashire.

Marx received a university education and took a doctorate in philosophy; Engels, rebelling against the commercial training his father designed for him, began at an early age to write essays and literary criticism. Both fell in with the so-called Young Hegelian movement which was at that time the *avant garde* of German intellectual life. Each was led by his personal experiences (and within the space of a couple of years) to adopt a socialist position. In Engels's case the decisive factor was his experiences in England, where he was sent for business reasons by his father, at a time when the Chartist movement was in full swing. This contact had the effect of giving definite form and direction to a radicalism which had hitherto been largely emotional and philosophical. In Marx's case the decisive factor was contact with Prussian reaction, first when he found that a university career was closed to him, and again when he was forced out of his first job as editor of the newly founded *Rheinische Zeitung*. Shortly before leaving this job Marx became entangled in a controversy with a rival paper over the question of the socialist and communist doctrines which were then (1842) beginning to penetrate Germany from their native France. He complained that his adversary was too ready to dismiss the new theories: "I do not know communism," he wrote, "but a social philosophy that has as its aim the defence of the oppressed cannot be condemned so lightly. One must acquaint oneself thoroughly with this trend of thought ere he dare dismiss it." In the process of acquainting himself he was completely won over.

In 1843 Marx moved to Paris, and the following year he and Engels, renewing what had been until then a casual friendship, discovered that they had arrived by independent paths at substantially the same intellectual and political position. This was the beginning of a collaboration which was to be one of the closest and most fruitful in history.

It was during the next four years, while the revolutionary storm blew up all over the continent, that Marx and Engels hammered out the basic framework of their new socialist synthesis. Their method of procedure was something quite new in the history of socialism. Instead of rushing out to convert the world to their new-found faith, they settled down to a searching study of history, political economy, and existing socialist doctrines; they wrote two long books [9] to settle accounts with their own intellectual past; they painstakingly discussed and criticized the ideas of their contemporaries, both orally and in print; [10] they threw themselves into the arduous task of organizing an international revolutionary association, which they hoped would be able to play a guiding role in the social upheavals lying ahead.

Most earlier socialists had been men who arrived at their conclusions through their own experiences and their own independent thinking; they were, in other words, self-educated in questions of social theory. It is well known that the autodidact, while often a brilliant and original thinker, is almost always a narrowly limited thinker who exaggerates his own importance and lacks a sense of perspective and proportion. Marx and Engels belonged to a very different type. They were certainly among the most learned men of the nineteenth century; but they were also perpetual students, always taking up new subjects, always tapping afresh the accumulated stock of human knowledge. With them, socialism was neither a finished dogma nor a collection of brilliant insights; it was a carefully thought-out system of ideas which stood

[9] *The Holy Family* and *The German Ideology.*

[10] The best known example is Marx's polemic against Proudhon, *The Poverty of Philosophy* (1847).

squarely in the mainstream of intellectual development and which had to be continually tested in practice and improved in the light of experience. In approach and method Marx and Engels found socialism a Utopia and left it a science.

A comprehensive outline of the new socialism was given to the world in the form of the *Communist Manifesto,* written by Marx and Engels for the Communist League in late 1847 and early 1848, and issued a few days before the outbreak of the February Revolution in Paris. The publication of the *Manifesto* marks a true turning point in the history of socialism. All earlier brands of socialism have long since disappeared; the Marxian brand, which can be traced back in a direct line to the *Manifesto,* is today, exactly a century later, a world-wide movement, larger and more powerful than ever before.

It is hard to summarize the *Manifesto* because its thirty-odd pages are already a very compact and lucid summary of a vast body of material. And yet it is essential to indicate the nature of its central theme if we are to understand the difference between the socialism of Marx and Engels and that of their predecessors.

The *Manifesto* opens with the famous statement: "The history of all hitherto existing society is the history of class struggles." In one sense this was an old idea; one can, for example, find something very similar in content if not in form in Winstanley 200 years earlier, and it is very clearly expressed in the writings of Bronterre O'Brien. Nevertheless, it soon becomes apparent that Marx and Engels mean very much more than these earlier writers; and it is hardly an exaggeration to say that this additional content, with all that it implies, is what is most essential to Marxism. Winstanley and O'Brien could see only one class struggle in history, the struggle between the rich and the poor, between the propertied and the propertyless. Since the first establishment of private property, history had been all of a piece, a constant repetition of the same acts of exploitation, punctuated by occasional rebellions and followed in each case by repression. Since this was so, one did not need to study history; one needed only to sample it to

learn all that it could teach. To this view Marx and Engels opposed the conception of history as a series of qualitatively different
class struggles, each taking place within the framework of a specific form of society and each in turn giving rise to a new form
of society. Each form of society was related to that which went
before and that which came after, and yet each had its own particular structure and hence its own laws and tendencies. It followed that a thorough study of history was the only way to understand the present, while an understanding of the present was a
prerequisite to effective action for the future. It followed, too,
that the bases of socialism must be on the one hand a theory of
history and on the other a theory of the existing social order.
It was the central purpose of the *Manifesto* to sketch these theories
in a few bold and sweeping strokes.

The first Section, entitled "Bourgeoisie and Proletarians," [11] is
the core of the *Manifesto*. It is a wonderfully lucid account of the
transition from feudalism to capitalism, of the development of
capitalism to its mid-nineteenth-century form in the industrially
advanced countries of western Europe, and of the forces and tendencies which were working to produce a future socialist society.
The language is sometimes charged with emotional overtones,
but in both form and content the exposition is strictly objective
and scientific. The essence of the argument is that capitalism,
having come into the world by breaking the bonds of feudal
society and having established the *bourgeoisie* as the ruling class,
had developed the productivity of human labor to previously
unimagined heights. (There are, incidentally, probably no passages in all literature which paint the achievements of capitalism

[11] The following quotation, a footnote supplied by Engels to later editions
of the *Manifesto*, explains how these terms are used throughout Marxian
literature and hence also from time to time in the present work: "By
bourgeoisie is meant the class of modern capitalists, owners of the means of
social production and employers of wage-labour; by proletariat, the class
of modern wage-labourers who, having no means of production of their own,
are reduced to selling their labour power in order to live."

in more glowing terms than those devoted to the subject in the *Manifesto*.)

But capitalism, for all its accomplishments, had not done away with exploitation and class struggle; it had simply substituted new forms which, like those they replaced, had their own inherent logic. The proletariat was the special and indispensable creation of capitalism: as capitalism expanded so also must the proletariat. Moreover, the proletariat's conditions of life were such as to force it to organize to fight for its own interests. Eventually, when capitalism had developed to a certain stage, it revealed a more and more glaring contradiction between the enormous powers of production which it had set loose and the narrow consuming base provided by the exploited and impoverished proletariat. The consequence of this contradiction was a series of increasingly disastrous commercial crises, each overcome only by means which intensified its successor. There is no escape within the framework of capitalism: "Society can no longer live under this bourgeoisie, in other words, its existence is no longer compatible with society." Finally, the last paragraph of Section I contains the following summary and conclusion:

> The essential condition for the existence and sway of the bourgeois class is the formation and augmentation of capital; the condition for capital is wage-labour. Wage-labour rests exclusively on competition between the labourers. The advance of industry, whose involuntary promoter is the bourgeoisie, replaces the isolation of the labourers, due to competition, by their revolutionary combination due to association. The development of modern industry, therefore, cuts from under its feet the very foundation on which the bourgeoisie produces and appropriates products. What the bourgeoisie therefore produces, above all, are its own grave-diggers. Its fall and the victory of the proletariat are equally inevitable.

It is not necessary, from our present standpoint, to summarize the rest of the *Manifesto;* but to understand its significance for the development of socialism one further passage is crucial:

> The theoretical conclusions of the Communists are in no way based on ideas or principles that have been invented, or discovered, by this or that would-be universal reformer. They merely express, in general terms, actual relations springing from an existing class struggle, from a historical movement going on under our very eyes.

The implication of this view is that the role of socialists is not to sell socialism as a more just and humane form of society—though socialists obviously believe that it is both—but to demonstrate that it is the next step forward in the historical development of the human race and to teach the working class how to hasten and ease the transition. Before the *Manifesto* the socialist was a preacher of revolution; after the *Manifesto* he became a scientist of revolution. In this transformation is summed up the most fundamental of Marx's and Engels's contributions to the development of socialism.

CHAPTER 6

Marxism: Philosophy, History, Politics

THE LAST CHAPTER sketched the development of socialism from its beginnings in early modern times through the publication of the *Communist Manifesto* in 1848. It was shown that in the *Manifesto* Marx and Engels drew the outlines of a new socialist synthesis, which, on its theoretical side, was essentially a science of society and history. After playing a brief role in the revolutionary events of 1848, Marx and Engels settled down in England and devoted most of the remainder of their lives—Marx died in 1883, Engels in 1895—to developing this new science, which, in recognition of the fact that Marx was undoubtedly the more original and powerful thinker of the two, has come to be known as Marxism. In this and the following chapters, we shall attempt to give a condensed account of the fundamentals of Marxism, taking into consideration such additions and extensions by followers of Marx and Engels as have stood the tests of time and experience.

Philosophy

The philosophical ideas of Marx and Engels were derived from two main sources: Hegelian dialectics and eighteenth-century French materialism. For this reason Marxian philosophy is usually referred to as "dialectical materialism." Let us examine the two components of this perhaps forbidding label.

Materialism, in its Marxian usage, is not a doctrine of the nature of "matter," however defined; it is rather a doctrine of the nature of the relationship between man and his environment and, as such, is opposed to all forms of idealism. Marxism holds that the world of nature exists independently of any one's perception or thinking, that life and hence also consciousness are natural phenomena which arise under certain favorable conditions and which would disappear if those conditions no longer existed. Human beings, the most developed and complex organisms known to us, receive knowledge of the world through their sense organs and adapt themselves to the world by making use of their capacity to think. The only meaningful way of testing the validity of knowledge and thought is through experiment and activity; to the extent that we can make things, and force them to serve our own purposes, we know that our knowledge is accurate and our thinking correct. Two conclusions of cardinal practical importance follow from the doctrine of materialism so conceived. One is that a belief in the supernatural, including much of the content of all religions, arises from the attempt of people to furnish themselves with explanations of what they do not understand. The other conclusion is that understanding of, and hence control over, nature can be indefinitely extended by the methods of science, that is to say, by generalization from observation and experiment.

The term "dialectical" as applied to Marxian philosophy has a broad and relatively simple meaning, though this fact has been obscured by much that has been written by friend and foe alike. There are two ways of regarding an object or an idea (more generally, a system of objects or ideas). One is to abstract it from its spatial and temporal context and to examine it in isolation; the other is to leave it in its context and to seek to understand it as an element in a spatial pattern and a temporal process. The basis of Marxian dialectics is a conviction that reality can be adequately comprehended only by combining *both* these methods. The examination of things in isolation is an essential part of the process of scientific investigation, but if it is allowed to become a dominant habit of thought it leads to a distorted picture of the world. As Engels explained:

The analysis of Nature into its individual parts, the grouping of the different natural processes and natural objects in definite classes, the study of the internal anatomy of organic bodies in their manifold forms—these were the fundamental conditions of the gigantic strides in our knowledge of Nature which have been made during the last four hundred years. But this method of investigation has also left us as a legacy the habit of observing natural objects and natural processes in their isolation, detached from the whole vast interconnection of things; and therefore not in their motion, but in their repose; not as essentially changing, but as fixed constants; not in their life, but in their death. And when as was the case with Bacon and Locke, this way of looking at things was transferred from natural science to philosophy, it produced the specific limitations of last century, the metaphysical mode of thought.[1]

The method of dialectics rejects this "metaphysical mode of thought" without rejecting the scientific procedures on which it is based. The examination of things in isolation is admittedly necessary, but not as an end in itself. A picture cannot be understood by even the most painstaking analysis of details if the interrelation of the details is ignored. In the real world, the whole is always more than the simple sum of its parts. The essence of the dialectical method is always to study both the parts and the way they combine to make up the whole. To quote Engels again, the dialectical method "grasps things and their images, ideas, essentially in their interconnection, in their sequence, their movement, their birth and death." [2]

The metaphysician, according to Marxism, is the dupe of his own method. In order to understand the world, he chops it up, classifies it, draws dividing lines, accentuates contrasts. From these elements he then creates a mental picture of the world, which he

[1] *Anti-Dühring* (International Publishers Co. edition), pp. 27–28.
[2] *Ibid.*, p. 29.

perversely assumes to be accurate and reliable. The dialectician understands the necessity of the method but refuses to be dominated by it.

> The recognition [Engels wrote] that these antagonisms and distinctions are in fact to be found in nature, but only with relative validity, and that on the other hand their imagined rigidity and absoluteness have been introduced into nature only by our minds—this recognition is the kernel of the dialectical conception of nature.[3]

Important practical conclusions follow from the Marxian conception of dialectics, just as they do from the Marxian conception of materialism. From the standpoint of social science the chief of these practical conclusions is that society—which, according to the materialist view, is as much a part of nature as the sun and the stars—cannot be torn apart and farmed out for study to a series of independent sciences. Society must be seen as a whole and in its historical development. To be sure, many distinctions can and must be made—for example, between economics and politics, or between the medieval and modern periods—but they have only a provisional and relative validity, and they do not define independent, much less mutually exclusive, fields of study. It follows that the science of society must be as unified and integrated as the subject matter which it investigates. Thus the fact that Marxism attempts to deal with all aspects of society and history, and is not split up into a number of carefully delimited disciplines in the manner of traditional academic social science, is a necessary consequence of the most fundamental Marxian views on the nature of reality and knowledge.

As a rule, discussions of dialectical materialism make much of certain Hegelian formulas which Marx and Engels occasionally used for their own purposes. Most famous of these are the thesis-antithesis-synthesis triad, the "transformation of quantity into

[3] *Ibid.*, p. 19.

quality," and "the negation of the negation." These are, however, minor aspects of Marxian philosophy and must be omitted
from a brief review of fundamentals. We need only remark, by
way of explanation, that each of these formulas is an extremely
condensed, and hence more or less unsatisfactory, description of
one *form* which change has frequently been observed to assume.
As such they do not *prove* anything; they merely indicate patterns
of common occurrence which may help to bring order and meaning into what otherwise would be a formless mass of data. Any
one wishing to pursue the matter further should consult Chapters
12 and 13 of Engels's *Anti-Dühring,* where, under the titles
"Quantity and Quality" and "Negation of the Negation," these
subjects are discussed in considerable detail.

History

The Marxian analysis of history has been given a variety of
names, of which historical materialism is perhaps the most general and the most appropriate. It must be remembered that in
this context, as well as in the context of Marxian philosophy, the
term "materialism" does not refer to a particular doctrine of the
nature of matter but signifies the rejection of all supernatural or
idealist interpretations of history. Historical materialism can perhaps best be characterized as the application of the principles of
dialectical materialism to the development of society. As such, it
constitutes the foundation and general framework of the entire
structure of Marxian social science.

The first principle of historical materialism is that the way
people think is determined by the way they live. This principle
has often been wrongly interpreted to mean that intellectual
activity plays only a passive role in the historical process. What
it does mean is something quite different—that intellectual activity influences the course of history primarily through its impact
on the way people live. But intellectual activity does not take
place in a vacuum; it grows out of past and present experience.

Hence, though intellectual activity is a vital link in the chain of historical causation, it cannot be said to be an independent variable, as the various idealist and psychological schools of historical interpretation assume.

The role attributed to intellectual activity in historical materialism has probably been the source of more misunderstandings and misrepresentations than any other aspect of the doctrine. For this reason it should be worth while to illustrate the Marxian position by means of a specific example.

At present much is being said and written about the tremendous historical importance of atomic energy, the release of which can certainly be described as the culmination of a long series of intellectual achievements. Historical materialism neither denies nor minimizes the significance of atomic energy; what it does is to attempt to put the problem in an intelligible historical framework. First, historical materialism asserts that the discovery of atomic energy could happen only in a country where not only scientific knowledge but also industrial technique had reached a high degree of development; in other words, the discovery of atomic energy is itself the outcome of a long and complex economic evolution. And second, historical materialism does not expect, as many present-day commentators apparently do, that the discovery of atomic energy *by itself* will or can exercise a profound historical influence. The impact of atomic energy will be felt through its application to the techniques of warfare and industry. In this way, and only in this way, will atomic energy affect conditions of life, alter the composition of society, and hence influence fundamentally the way people think.

So far we have spoken very generally about "conditions of life" and "people" as though every one lived under the same conditions and thought and acted in the same way. This is, of course, not the case, and historical materialism has much more to say on the subject. There are two closely related problems here: first, the structure of society at any given time, and second, the changes which occur in the course of time.

It is obviously impossible to analyze society without adopting some system of classifying people into groups. Many modern historians assume that nationality is the most important criterion of division; others assign a similar role to religion. Historical materialism does not deny the relevance of these criteria to many problems, but it asserts that more fundamental than either is the division of society into social classes.

How are we to define social classes? Historical materialism answers this question in terms of its basic principles. If conditions of life determine people's thinking and behavior, social classes must be composed of those whose conditions of life are similar. As Marx wrote, "In so far as millions of families live under economic conditions of existence that divide their mode of life, their interests, and their culture from those of the other classes, and put them in hostile contrast to the latter, they form a class." [4] Since the way people live is in the final analysis dominated by the way they get their living, it follows that the *differentia specifica* of a social class is the economic status of its members. Thus the chief classes of a slave society are masters and slaves; of feudal society, lords and serfs; of capitalist society, capitalists and wage earners. In any given society, in other words, it is the character of the economic system which determines the structure of classes, their interests, their ideologies, and their relations with one another. And, according to historical materialism, it is these factors which determine how the society functions and how it develops in the course of time.

These, then, are the leading ideas of historical materialism: that the foundation of any society is its economic system; that to every economic system there corresponds a definite structure of social classes, each with its own outlook and interests; and that history is essentially the record of the strivings and conflicts of classes. It must be stressed that these ideas outline a method of

[4] *The Eighteenth Brumaire of Louis Bonaparte* (International Publishers Co. edition), p. 109.

investigation and are not intended, as many critics of Marxism seem to assume, to constitute a sovereign formula which will automatically reveal historical truth. In particular, there is no implication of the existence in history of the kind of precise and invariant relationships which are found in the natural sciences. For example, one is not entitled to assume that a given economic system will give rise to a uniquely determined historical process. Japan in the period before the Meiji Restoration (1868) and western Europe in the Middle Ages were both feudal societies, and yet the history of pre-Restoration Japan was very different from the history of medieval Europe. The differences can be explained in terms of differences in geography, previous history, and surrounding societies. Marxism does not in the least deny the importance of these factors; on the contrary, we have already seen that the first principle of dialectics is that nothing can be understood apart from its spatial and temporal context. But historical materialism does insist that the only key which can unlock the secrets of pre-Restoration Japan and Europe in the Middle Ages is a thorough understanding of the feudal system.

This example indicates how the method of historical materialism should be applied to the study of particular problems. If the historian wants to understand what happened in a given region during a given period, he must first investigate the prevailing economic system and the social structure which corresponds to it; he must uncover the elements in this system which make for instability and change; he must study the interests, ideologies, and potentialities of the decisive social classes, taking account of traditions and behavior patterns inherited from past ages; and finally he must give proper weight to influences and pressures emanating from societies outside the immediate field of study. By skillfully fitting all these factors together—and it should not be forgotten that scientific procedure can never dispense with the skill of the investigator—he should be able to arrive at an explanation of historical phenomena which is both consistent and comprehensive.

The Marxist may be asked: how do you know that your explanation is the true one? It was pointed out above that in the Marxian view, the truth or falsity of knowledge and ideas can be tested only in practice; and this holds in the field of history as well as anywhere else. At first glance it might seem that we have here a hopeless contradiction: history, it could be argued, is what has happened in the past, and bygones are forever bygones; *no* explanation can be put to any sort of practical test.

For Marxists, however, the contradiction does not exist. In their view history is not only what happened yesterday but also what is happening today and what will happen tomorrow. It follows that the methods of historical materialism are as applicable to the present as they are to the past, and that they should allow us, within limits which are more or less narrow according to the extent and accuracy of our observations, to diagnose the future. That is to say, the methods of historical materialism should allow us to diagnose the future *if they yield true interpretations of historical phenomena*. But the soundness of our diagnosis can be tested in practice: we can observe whether events conform to our expectations, and we can act upon our diagnosis and find out how reliable it is for our own purposes. Marxists hold that ever since the *Communist Manifesto* events have amply confirmed the diagnosis which it contains; and they believe that the history of the socialist movement in the last hundred years provides innumerable proofs of the reliability of historical materialism as a guide to action. They conclude, therefore, that historical materialism does in fact yield true explanations of historical phenomena.

The reader will have noticed that the application of historical materialism is no simple task. A knowledge of the structure and functioning of various different social systems is needed, and such knowledge can be acquired only through painstaking theoretical and empirical research. It is no exaggeration to say that when Marx and Engels began their labors not a single social system had been subjected to the kind of study which historical materialism presupposes if it is to be applied with full effectiveness. This does not mean, of course, that the new principles of historical interpretation were useless; on the contrary, they immediately.threw a flood of light on both past and present, as the *Communist Manifesto* itself proves; and they provided a powerful stimulus to important new research in dozens of different fields. But it does mean that the full potentialities of historical materialism could not yet be realized; the various social systems which have appeared in history still needed to be studied from their economic foundations up.

It was obviously up to Marx and Engels to lead the way in tackling this vast—in principle, endless—task. Moreover, for men who were as interested in changing the world as in understanding it, there was only one possible starting point, the dominant social system of their own day. This explains why, following the defeat of the revolutions of 1848, Marx settled down in London and, with indispensable financial and intellectual support from Engels, devoted most of the rest of his life to an exhaustive study of capitalism. The chief product of this study was *Capital,* the first volume of which was published in 1867.

It is well known that *Capital* is concerned almost exclusively with the economics of capitalist society, and we shall deal with this aspect of Marxism in the next chapter. The point to be emphasized here is that *Capital* is not at all a general treatise on economics in the manner of the classical and neoclassical schools. Rather, *Capital* has a well-defined place as a part of a much more comprehensive science of history and society. In other words, *Capital* is the first fruit of an intensive application of the method of historical materialism. Much has been added since Marx's day, both to the understanding of capitalism and to the understanding of other historically important forms of society; but even today the filling in of the outline of the comprehensive social science implied in the doctrine of historical materialism is still far from complete.

Politics

Our next task is to explain the Marxian approach to the problems of political power and the state. For this purpose we need not enter into the controversial question of the origins of the state; it is enough to recognize that something very like a state, in the modern sense of the word, has been a common feature of all known literate societies and that literate societies have dominated the history of the last three or four thousand years.

The first problem requiring clarification is the role of force in social life. All states are based on the actual or potential use of force. What are the implications of this for the understanding of history and politics?

Engels gave the Marxian answer to this question in his polemic against Dühring, who argued, as many before him had done, that the

> formation of *political* relationships is, *historically, the fundamental fact,* and the *economic* conditions dependent on this are only an *effect* or a particular case, and are consequently always facts of the second order. . . . The *primitive* phenomenon must be sought in direct political force and not in any indirect economic power.[5]

The fallacy in Dühring's reasoning is apparent. Force by itself is powerless to create. The instruments of force, the methods of its application, and the purposes to which it is put are all dependent on technical and economic conditions. Take, for example, the case of slavery, which Dühring cited as a pure manifestation of force. Engels had no difficulty in showing that slavery presupposes a certain level of economic development; the slave must be able to produce not only his own keep but also a surplus for his master. Before this level had been reached, prisoners of war were either eaten or simply killed. Thus the introduction of slavery reflects

[5] *Anti-Dühring,* p. 180. Italics in original.

a definite economic advance, even for the slaves themselves. In more recent times slavery in the United States was based primarily on the needs of the English cotton industry; in non-cotton-growing regions it died out of its own accord, and eventually it proved to be too wasteful and uneconomic to survive in a struggle with an economic system of superior productivity.

Or take the case of European feudalism, a social system in which originally a virtual monopoly of force was enjoyed by the nobility. The feudal lords had every interest in using force to maintain the system, and yet their failure to do so was complete. Why? Because they were powerless to prevent the growth of trade and industry, which brought into existence the new class of burghers. In the fourteenth century the introduction of gun-powder into western Europe revolutionized the technique of war-fare. From this time on, control over the superior instruments of force gradually came into the hands of the burghers, who enjoyed an enormous advantage in the manufacture of the new weapons. Throughout this whole development, the economic fac-tor was of decisive importance; force was merely the servant of economic power. And, according to Engels, this has been the general rule in every historical epoch.

It will be noted that the treatment of force in Marxism is similar to the treatment of intellectual activity, which was dis-cussed in the previous section. There is no disposition in Marxian thought to deny the importance of either, but the view that they can be in any sense regarded as primary or independent variables is rejected. Force operates entirely within a given economic and social context; even more, what constitutes effective force at any time is determined by economic conditions.

Let us now turn to the closely related question of the state. According to the Marxian view, the state is a public organization which possesses a legal monopoly of the use of force. Such an organization is evidently necessary to the very existence of any society which is divided into classes with conflicting interests. If individuals or groups were free to use force in furtherance of their private interests, the result could only be something like the Hobbesian "war of each against all." The question then arises as to who will succeed in establishing a supreme coercive organ and making good a claim to the legal monopoly of force. Our discussion of force has prepared us for the Marxian answer. According to Engels:

> The state is the result of the desire to keep down class conflicts. But having arisen amid these conflicts, it is as a rule the state of the most powerful economic class that by force of its economic supremacy becomes also the ruling political class and thus acquires new means of subduing and exploiting the oppressed masses. The antique state was, therefore, the state of the slaveowners for the purpose of holding the slaves in check. The feudal state was the organ of the nobility for the oppression of the serfs and dependent farmers. The modern representative state is the tool of the capitalist exploiters of wage labor. At certain periods it occurs exceptionally that the struggling classes balance each other so nearly that the public power gains a certain degree of independence by posing as the mediator between them.[6]

The primary function of the state is thus to safeguard the existing economic and social order in the interest of the class or classes which dominate it and benefit from it. In other words, the first duty of the state is to protect the existing property system.

This, then, is the core of the Marxian theory of the state. But it is by no means the whole of the theory, as some hostile critics have been too ready to assume. Once the state has come into existence as the guarantor of a given social order, it does not simply stand aside and let nature take its course. (This, incidentally, was the role cut out for the state by nineteenth-century liberalism, and it came close to being realized in English practice

[6] *The Origin of the Family, Private Property, and the State* (Kerr edition), pp. 208–209.

during the middle decades of the century. But history records no other comparable episode.) On the contrary, the state normally plays an active part in the functioning of the system.

The state may foster the normal developmental tendencies of the system. In this case, there is no conflict; economic and social development are both accelerated. This is a characteristic situation in the early stages of development of a new social order. For example, what is usually called the period of mercantilism (roughly the seventeenth and eighteenth centuries) is chiefly notable for the close connection which existed between the growth of capitalism and the policies of the more advanced European states. The state may, on the other hand, attempt to interfere with the normal developmental tendencies of the system, blocking them here, turning them into new channels there, and softening their impact in another place. In this case there is a conflict; the state is trying to buck a system which it is at the same time pledged to uphold. This is a characteristic situation in the dying days of an old social order. Imperial Rome attempted for a long time to stem the decay of ancient society by increasingly rigid state interference—without success. And in our day we see a comparable effort to curb the self-destructive tendencies of the capitalist system—so far also without success. As Engels said—and he was here using "force" as synonymous with "state power"—force may "work against economic development; in this case, as a rule, with but few exceptions, force succumbs to it." [7]

We shall have occasion in the next chapter to analyze various ways in which the state plays a role in the development of capitalism; for the present we are concerned only with establishing the fact that Marxian theory in no way excludes the possibility of such a role. In the Marxian view the state is at the same time a power above society and an integral part of society. If it is said that such a dual role often leads to contradictions and difficulties, the Marxist will agree; but he will insist that these contradictions

[7] *Anti-Dühring*, p. 208.

and difficulties arise from the nature of the case and not from faulty reasoning on his part.

We come now to the question of the part played by the state in transitions from one social order to another, in other words to the problem of *State and Revolution*. [8] The Marxian view is that a ruling class will fight to the last to maintain the social system from which it benefits. Since the state is the instrument of the ruling class, it follows that a state, once firmly established, must always be expected to be a conservative and, if necessary, a counterrevolutionary force. On the other hand, the meaning of a successful revolution is the coming to power of a new ruling class, which needs a state as much as its predecessor did; and the state of this new ruling class performs a revolutionary function, often for long periods, in liquidating the remnants of the old order and in laying the foundations of the new. Thus there is no simple generalization which will cover the relation of the state to revolution; all that can be said with assurance is that *the same state* (that is, the same administrative and coercive apparatus) will not play both a revolutionary and a counterrevolutionary role. Though it may sound paradoxical, it is nevertheless true that a revolution involves both the destruction of a state and the creation of a state.

According to Marxian theory a revolution is a period in which two or more classes contend for the immediate possession of political power and for the ultimate right to organize society in accordance with their own interests and ideas. That both sides use force in such a struggle goes without saying; as Marx put it, force is the midwife of every old society pregnant with the new. But force must not be confused with violence. So far are the two from being identical that the completely successful use of force implies the absence of violence, because those against whom force is used recognize the futility of resistance.

As a matter of historical experience, of course, revolutions have

[8] The title of one of Lenin's most famous works.

usually been accompanied by violence, but Marxists have always held that circumstances can arise in which a peaceful revolution is possible. Thus Marx himself, speaking in 1872, conceded the possibility of a peaceful transition to socialism in England and the United States. Three years after Marx's death, Engels wrote of England as a country in which a peaceful socialist revolution was possible. Lenin granted that these views were correct when they were put forward but thought that by 1917, when he wrote *State and Revolution,* such possibilities no longer existed.

The triumph of socialism in Russia changed the situation once again, and by 1924 Stalin was able to envisage the possibility (which still seemed "extremely hypothetical") of a peaceful transition to socialism in certain capitalist countries which might become subject to what he called a "socialist encirclement." Since the Second World War such a socialist encirclement has actually materialized as far as the countries of eastern Europe are concerned; and, as we have seen in our discussion of this region, Stalin's view has proved to be well founded. It is not surprising that eastern European Marxists are now stressing the possibility and desirability of a peaceful transition to socialism in their own countries.[9] In doing so, they are not breaking with traditional Marxian theory.

We may close this discussion with a few words about the long-run relation between socialism and the state. The Marxian position, which was first formulated in answer to the anarchists' demand for immediate abolition of the state, is that the working class will need *its* state to anchor the new socialist society and protect it until it is fully developed, just as the bourgeois state was needed in the early stages of capitalist society. But here the parallel with earlier experience ends, because the long-run goal of socialism is not to substitute one form of class rule for another but to abolish all classes and to establish a society in which the

[9] See, for example, the speeches by Georgi Dimitrov, Communist Premier of Bulgaria, and Wladyslaw Gomulka, Communist Vice-Premier of Poland, translated and published in *Political Affairs,* August, 1946, and April, 1947.

instruments of labor are owned in common and production is organized on the basis of a free and equal association of the producers. From such a society the exploitation, the tensions, and the gross inequalities which inevitably characterize class societies will be absent.

> People [as Lenin wrote] will gradually *become accustomed* to the observance of the elementary rules of social life that have been known for centuries and repeated for thousands of years in all school books; they will become accustomed to observing them without force, without compulsion, without subordination, without the *special apparatus* for compulsion which is known as the state.[10]

Under these circumstances the state, in the sense of the coercive and punitive organs of government, will have less and less to do. In the much-quoted phrase of Engels, it will gradually "wither away."

Lack of space prevents our discussing in detail the heated controversy which has long raged around this theory. We shall here merely point out certain common misconceptions which have tended to stand in the way of any attempt to understand what the theory actually implies.

First, the withering away of the state does not imply the disappearance either of authority or of administration. Engels, in refuting the theories of the anarchists, ridiculed the idea that a factory or a railway or a ship, to say nothing of a complex society, could be run without some persons' being in authority over others. If the anarchists, he wrote,

> had been content to say that the social organization of the future would permit authority only within the limits in which the relations of production made it inevitable, then it would have been possible to come to an understanding with

[10] *State and Revolution,* Chap. V, Sec. 2. Italics in original.

them; but they are blind to all facts which make authority necessary, and they fight passionately against the word.[11] [And as to administration,] public functions will lose their political character and be transformed into simple administrative functions of watching over social interests.[12]

One can, of course, reject this perspective, but one cannot legitimately say that it neglects the obvious need for organization and direction in a planned economy. The question is whether people will come to accept this need as a matter of course and do their share willingly, or whether they will have to be kept in line by the use or threat of force.

Second, arguments from the experience of the Soviet Union are irrelevant to the theory of the withering away of the state. As long as the world is divided into socialist and capitalist sectors, and as long as each sector consists of sovereign nations, it is obvious that all countries will maintain armies and navies, not to mention all the auxiliary coercive and punitive organs that go with them. Under these circumstances it is absurd even to talk in terms of the withering away of the state. The doctrine was formulated with an international (or perhaps it would be better to say supranational) socialist society in mind. It is not relevant in any other context.

Finally, it should be pointed out that much of the criticism of the theory of the withering away of the state derives, implicitly or explicitly, from the supposed axiom that "you can't change human nature." If "human nature" means only that which is natural to human beings, then this is, of course, a meaningless truism. But if it means that certain human behavior patterns—such as those implied in the exploitation of man by man—are permanent and unchangeable, then it is a statement about facts and is subject to proof or disproof. In the Marxian view, as this chapter has attempted to show, all human history refutes the

[11] Quoted in *ibid.*, Chap. IV, Sec. 2.
[12] *Ibid.*

theory of unchangeable behavior patterns and underlines the indefinite variability of society and consequently also of the individuals composing it. To any one holding this view of "human nature" the withering away of the state in a future socialist society will seem like a reasonable, even if still unprovable, hypothesis.

Summary

Before we proceed to a discussion of capitalism, it may prove useful to present a brief summary of the Marxian theories of philosophy, history, and politics. The Marxian theory of capitalism is not independent of the theories which we have been examining; it is rather the consequence of their application to a specific form of social organization.

Dialectical materialism, as Marxian philosophy is usually called, is a general view of the nature of the world and of the place of human beings in the world. Human life is regarded as a product of natural evolution. Thought is a reflection of the actual conditions of life and enables human beings not only to adapt themselves to their environment but to mold their environment to their own purposes. Ideas are true and trustworthy in so far as they accurately represent reality. Reality is a complex, interrelated whole and not merely a collection of more or less independent parts which can be abstracted from their context and understood in isolation. The essence of the dialectical approach, in the words of Engels, is a recognition that "antagonisms and distinctions are in fact to be found in nature, but only with relative validity, and that on the other hand their imagined rigidity and absoluteness have been introduced into nature only by our minds."

Historical materialism is the application of dialectical materialism to the development of society. The way people live and think is determined by the way they get their living, in other words by the economic system under which they live and their place in that economic system. Thus to every economic system there corresponds a certain structure of social classes, each with its own outlook and interests. History is essentially the record of the strivings and conflicts of classes. The study of a particular historical problem requires an investigation of the prevailing economic system or systems, the class structures to which they give rise, the interests and ideologies of the decisive classes, and the manner in which conflicts are fought out or resolved. The truth or falsity of historical materialism can be tested by applying it to the present and the future. To the extent that events conform to our expectations, and if our diagnosis provides a reliable guide to action, we know—in the only way we can ever know—that our methods yield true explanations of historical phenomena.

The Marxian theory of politics deals basically with the use of force in the historical process. Force is subordinate to economic power, but its use is indispensable to the stability and functioning of all class societies. The state is an organization having a legal monopoly of the use of force. Any given state is established and maintained by an economically dominant class to preserve the system which assures its dominance. The state, however, not only protects the system but also operates within it. Either the state fosters the inherent tendencies of the system, or it attempts to arrest or divert the tendencies of the system. In the first case development is accelerated; in the second case the state normally fails and eventually goes under. A revolution is a period in which the state of an existing ruling class is destroyed and replaced by the state of a new ruling class. In the early stages of socialism, the working class will need a state, just as earlier ruling classes have needed a state. But as socialism develops, all classes will disappear and with them the need for the use of organized force in social life. As this stage is approached, the socialist state will gradually "wither away."

In the next chapter we shall see how these general ideas can be applied to the study and understanding of capitalism, the social system which dominates the history of the last three or four centuries.

CHAPTER 7

Marxism: Political Economy

IT WAS POINTED OUT in the last chapter that the application of the method of historical materialism requires a thorough study, from the economic foundations up, of the various historically important forms of society. It was also pointed out that Marx and Engels quite naturally turned their attention first to capitalism, as the form of society under which they lived. In this chapter we shall examine the essentials of the Marxian theory of capitalism.

The Nature of Capitalism

It is generally agreed that capitalism is the system which came to dominance in western Europe between the sixteenth and nineteenth centuries. What is the distinguishing characteristic of this system? Many writers have answered, "production for the market" or "the purchase and sale of commodities for profit"—and have gone on to conclude—quite rightly on the basis of either of these definitions—that capitalism is in no sense peculiar to the modern period. Thus Michael Rostovtzeff, well-known historian of the ancient world, has a great deal to say about capitalism in Greco-Roman times; while, to take another example, Henri Pirenne, the great Belgian medievalist, found ample evidence of the existence of capitalism in the later Middle Ages.[1] If one accepts the standpoint of these writers, the modern period is

[1] On Rostovtzeff see Meyer Reinhold, "Historian of the Classic World: A Critique of Rostovtzeff," *Science and Society*, Fall, 1946, and the sources there cited. A summary of Pirenne's views is presented in his *Economic and Social History of Medieval Europe*.

135

distinguished from its predecessors not by the birth and development of capitalism but by its spread to additional sectors of the economy and to new geographical regions.

It should be apparent from the discussion in the last chapter, however, that Marxism necessarily rejects any definition of a social system which puts primary emphasis on the method of distributing goods. According to the Marxian view the basis of all social life is production, and the distinguishing characteristic of a social system must accordingly be sought in the sphere of production proper. Once this standpoint is adopted, it becomes apparent that the differences between the ancient and medieval social systems, or between either of these and the modern system, are differences of kind and not merely of degree.

In both the ancient and the medieval periods production was overwhelmingly agricultural; in the former it was carried on either by individual peasant farmers or by the system of plantation slavery, while in the latter the dominant unit was the feudal manor. In both, industry was of secondary importance and was for the most part centered in artisan workshops. In the modern period, on the other hand, industry has increasingly outstripped agriculture, and the decisive productive unit has become the large-scale factory operated by free wage labor. Clearly, we have to do with three different systems of production, and the Marxist maintains that the existence of trading for profit in all three of them is an important but essentially subordinate fact.

Marxism, then, defines capitalism as a system of society in which production is predominantly carried on in private enterprises operated by free wage labor. In such a system there must be at least two classes: the capitalists, who pay wages, and the workers, who receive wages. In practice there are always other classes as well—for example, landlords, self-employed peasants or artisans—but the decisive classes in capitalist society are capitalists and workers, and it is their relations with each other that constitute the central theme of the Marxian theory of capitalism.

The relations between capitalists and workers are not so simple as the master-and-slave or lord-and-serf relations of earlier forms of society. It is true that inside the workshop the capitalist is the boss and the worker does what he is ordered to do. But before the worker enters the workshop, he is hired on terms which are determined independently of his own will or of the will of the capitalist who hires him. If we ask who does fix the terms of employment, the answer is no one; the terms are fixed by the impersonal forces of the market. The analysis of capitalism must therefore start with the market or, to use the traditional terminology of economics, with the general problem of value.

Before we proceed to an examination of Marxian value theory, we should be clear that it applies to simple commodity production [2] as well as to capitalism and that this fact tends to obscure the crucial differences between the two forms of society. Marx explained these differences by means of two ingenious formulas.

In simple commodity production the producer sells his product in order to be in a position to purchase other products which satisfy his own needs. He comes to market with a commodity (C), turns it into money (M), and then reconverts the money into another commodity (C). The characteristic market transaction of simple commodity production can thus be represented as $C–M–C$. The capitalist, however, is in a different position. He comes to market with money (M), buys labor power and materials (C), and then (after a process of production has been performed) returns to market with a product which he reconverts into money (M). The characteristic market transaction of capitalism is thus $M–C–M$.

According to Marx, the difference between $C–M–C$ and $M–C–M$ is of fundamental importance. In $C–M–C$ the two C's are equal in terms of exchange value but, since they are different commodities, they are unequal in terms of use value. For the producer himself the second C has a greater use value than the first C, and it is this fact which provides the operation with its rationale. In $M–C–M$, on the other hand, the two M's are quali-

[2] See n. 2, p. 18.

tatively homogeneous, and if the second M is not larger than the first, the transaction as a whole is pointless. Marx indicated this by rewriting the formula as $M–C–M'$, where M' is larger than M. Thus, the purpose of production under simple commodity production is the qualitative transformation of use value, while under capitalism the purpose of production is the quantitative expansion of exchange value.

From this analysis, Marx drew certain important conclusions about the specific characteristics of capitalism:

> The circulation of money as capital is . . . an end in itself, for the expansion of value takes place only within this constantly renewed movement [$M–C–M'$]. The circulation of capital has therefore no limits. Thus the conscious representative of this movement, the possessor of money, becomes a capitalist. His person, or rather his pocket, is the point from which the money starts and to which it returns. The expansion of value . . . becomes his subjective aim, and it is only in so far as the appropriation of ever more and more wealth in the abstract becomes the sole motive of his operations that he functions as a capitalist. . . . Use values must therefore never be looked on as the real aim of the capitalist; neither must the profit on any single transaction. The restless neverending process of profit-making alone is what he aims at.[3]

The central purpose of Marxian economics is to track down the consequences of this "never-ending process," which is thus set in motion by the capitalist. To this we shall return after taking up the problem of value.

Value and Surplus Value

Marx started from the classical theory, according to which the value of a commodity is proportionate to the quantity of labor

[3] *Capital,* Vol. I, pp. 169–170. All quotations from *Capital* are from the Kerr edition.

required to produce it. He knew, just as the classical economists had known, that this is not true under all circumstances, but he regarded it as a first approximation well suited to bringing out the main characteristics of a commodity-producing economy.

We can perhaps best appreciate the implications of the "law of value" if we consider a famous illustration from Adam Smith's *Wealth of Nations*.[4]

> If among a nation of hunters [Smith reasoned], it usually costs twice the labour to kill a beaver which it does to kill a deer, one beaver should naturally exchange for or be worth two deer. It is natural that what is usually the produce of two days' or two hours' labour, should be worth double of what is usually the produce of one day's or one hour's labour.

It is not hard to show that Smith was right, if we assume that his hunters would "naturally" behave like buyers and sellers on a competitive market. For if beavers and deer were exchanging, say, on a one-to-one basis (still assuming that to kill a beaver costs twice the labor necessary for killing a deer), no one would bother to hunt beavers, since by catching a deer and exchanging it for a beaver it would be possible to get a beaver in half the time it would take to catch one directly. Obviously the one-to-one price could not last long; the supply of beavers would soon dry up. It can be shown, by a process of elimination, that no price except two deer for one beaver would be stable. Adam Smith's proposition, which is nothing but the law of value in a simplified form, is thus shown to be correct.

In order to arrive at this conclusion, we had to assume that hunters can move freely from beaver-hunting to deer-hunting and vice versa. The same assumption in generalized form is implied in Marx's theory of value. Any deviation of market prices from values will lead to the transfer of labor from some industries into others as the production of some commodities expands and the

[4] Book I, Chap. 6.

production of others contracts. All this is part of the mechanism of the law of value; if this mechanism failed to operate, values as determined by labor-time ratios would have no practical economic significance. We can conclude that the law of value in reality covers the entire process by which exchange ratios, quantities produced, and the distribution of the labor force are simultaneously determined in a commodity-producing society. No one is directly concerned with these problems, and yet everyone's action contributes to solving them. Speaking of capitalism, Marx made the point in the following terms:

> Since individual capitalists meet one another only as owners of commodities, and every one seeks to sell his commodity as dearly as possible (being apparently guided in the regulation of his production by his own arbitrary will), the internal law enforces itself only through their competition, their mutual pressure on one another, by means of which the various deviations are evened out. Only as an internal law, and from the point of view of the individual agents as a blind law, does the law of value exert its influence and maintain the social equilibrium of production in the midst of accidental fluctuations.[5]

The law of value, in other words, is the integrating principle of a commodity-producing society. It explains why what at first sight appears to be nothing but a collection of individuals is in fact a coherent social system; it welds the private labor of innumerable separate producers into an effective aggregate social labor force.

It is against this background that we must interpret Marx's famous doctrine of commodity fetishism. On the surface, value appears to be merely a quantitative relation between inanimate objects; but, as our discussion of the law of value shows, it really

[5] *Capital,* Vol. III, p. 1026. The translation of this passage from the original German has been corrected in several places.

hides a complex set of relations among the members of society. This appearance of relations among people in the guise of relations among things has peculiar consequences. It veils the real nature of commodity production and causes people either not to understand the social system they live under at all or to assume that it is a manifestation of natural forces over which man himself has no control. It thus comes about that commodity production is a state of society "in which the process of production has the mastery over man instead of being controlled by him." [6] Marx spoke in this connection of "commodity fetishism" to indicate that the citizen of a commodity-producing society has much the same superstitious attitude toward social forces as the primitive savage has toward natural forces. In the Marxian view this attitude can be overcome only when society takes direct charge of the means of production and plans their use for the benefit of all its members; it can be overcome, that is to say, only under socialism. In the meantime, it can be understood only by means of the labor theory of value and the critical analysis of commodity production which this theory makes possible.

It was pointed out above that the distinguishing characteristic of capitalism is the prevalence of wage labor; in other words, labor power itself is typically a commodity, which is bought and sold on the market just like all other commodities. The question therefore arises as to what constitutes the value of labor power and how it is determined.

The capitalist does not buy actual labor but rather a certain specified amount of the laborer's time or the laborer for a specified amount of time, which comes to the same thing. What is called labor power in Marxian economics is therefore in reality the laborer, a fact which is obvious enough in a slave society but which under capitalism is hidden by legal limitations on the duration and finality of the labor contract. It follows that the value of labor power is the value of the laborer. If we now apply

[6] *Ibid.,* Vol. I, p. 93.

the labor theory of value to the value of the laborer, we see that the quantity of labor required to produce the laborer is but another way of saying the quantity of labor required to produce the laborer's means of subsistence. Thus, finally, we conclude that the value of the special commodity, labor power, can be reduced to the value of a certain number of ordinary commodities.

This leads naturally to the theory of surplus value. In discussing the formula $M–C–M$ it was noted that the operation of purchase and sale which it represents is meaningless unless the final M is larger than the original M, or, to put it otherwise, unless not only the original value is returned but a surplus as well. But this in itself is not enough to explain the emergence of such a surplus. Now that we have analyzed the value of the commodity labor power, however, we are in a position to understand the source of surplus value.

We assume that the capitalist buys labor power at its value, that is to say, pays to the worker a wage equal to the value of the worker's means of subsistence. Let us say, for the sake of illustration, that this value is the product of six hours' labor. After production has proceeded for six hours the worker has produced enough value to cover his wages. If the process were to break off at this point, the capitalist would just come out even. But the capitalist has bought the worker for a day, and there is no reason why a working day should be limited to six hours. Let us assume that it is ten hours. Then in the last four hours the worker continues to add value over and above his wages, and it is this which constitutes the surplus value in which the capitalist is interested.

It is apparent from this example that the working day can be divided into two parts: first, that which produces a value equivalent to the worker's wage (Marx called this necessary labor); and second, that which produces surplus value (Marx called this surplus labor). The ratio of surplus labor to necessary labor, or of surplus value to wages, Marx called the rate of surplus value. Other things being equal, a lengthening of the working day, a lowering of the real wage, or an increase in the productivity of labor will raise the rate of surplus value; while a shortening of the working day, a rise in the real wage, or a decline in the productivity of labor will reduce the rate of surplus value. More than a quarter of the first volume of *Capital* is devoted to analyzing the variation of these determinants of the rate of surplus value in the history of English capitalism.

Let us now take the value of a finished commodity and break it down into its component parts. First, it contains the value of the materials which went into its production, including a certain amount of wear and tear on machinery and equipment; second, it contains the value of labor power; and third, it contains surplus value. Marx called the first component constant capital (c), the second variable capital (v), and the third surplus value (s). Thus the total value of a commodity is represented by the formula $c + v + s$. This formula is not necessarily limited in its application to a given commodity; it can also be applied to the output during a certain period of time of one or more enterprises. Moreover, if we apply it to all enterprises, we have a convenient method of arranging and analyzing what present-day economists call the national income. In Marxian economics the formula is used for all these purposes, with the context making clear which is meant.

Before we leave the problem of value it is necessary to note certain frequently used ratios which are derived from the $c + v + s$ formula. One, the rate of surplus value, or s/v, has already been mentioned. Another is the ratio of surplus value to total capital, $s/(c + v)$, which is the traditional formula for the rate of profit. Finally, there is the ratio of constant to total capital, $c/(c + v)$, which in Marxian economics is called the organic composition of capital. For the sake of convenience, let us adopt a symbol for each of these ratios: let s' stand for the rate of surplus value, p for the rate of profit, and q for the organic composition of capital. By simple algebra it can be shown that

$$p = s'(1 - q)$$

which means that the rate of profit changes in the same direction as the rate of surplus value but in the direction opposite to the organic composition of capital. As we shall see, these relations figure in the Marxian analysis of the process of capitalist development.

Accumulation and Crises

We return now to the investigation of the accumulation process set in motion by the capitalist. But let us first look a little more closely at the roots of this process, especially since on this point Marxian economics, while quite in the classical tradition, differs very widely from modern orthodox economics.

It is usually held by non-Marxian economists that all economic behavior is motivated by a desire to maximize consumption satisfactions. Accumulation is therefore looked upon as abstinence from consumption, and it is assumed that a definite reward in the form of profits (or interest) is required to induce people to accumulate. Further, it is assumed that a higher rate of return will call forth more accumulation and a lower rate less accumulation. On the basis of these assumptions elaborate theories have been built.

Marx swept all this aside as irrelevant. According to him the capitalist "shares with the miser the passion for wealth as wealth. But that which in the miser is a mere idiosyncrasy, is, in the capitalist, the effect of the social mechanism of which he is but one of the wheels." [7] The position of the capitalist in society, unlike that of the miser, is dependent upon the quantity of his wealth. If the capitalist loses his wealth, he ceases to count; if he increases it, he moves up in the social scale. As Marx put it, "to accumulate is to conquer the world of social wealth, to increase the mass of human beings exploited by him, and thus to extend both the direct and the indirect sway of the capitalist." [8] More-

[7] *Ibid.*, p. 649.
[8] *Ibid.*

over, there is an additional reason for accumulation inherent in the capitalist system which is of hardly less importance:

> . . . the development of capitalist production makes it constantly necessary to keep increasing the amount of capital laid out in a given industrial undertaking, and competition makes the immanent laws of capitalist production to be felt by each individual capitalist as external coercive laws. It compels him to keep constantly extending his capital, in order to preserve it, but extend it he cannot except by means of progressive accumulation.[9]

Thus we see that the Marxian analysis relates accumulation to the basic structural characteristics of the capitalist system. The road to power and position lies through accumulation, and the capitalist who refuses to enter the race risks losing everything.

We are now ready to trace the consequences of accumulation.

Capital consists of two parts, constant capital and variable capital. In the general case, accumulation means an addition to both parts. In other words, accumulation means an increased demand for materials and machinery on the one hand and for labor power on the other. But here we meet a puzzle: given the fact that accumulation raises the demand for labor power, what is to prevent wages from rising steadily above the value of labor power until the very existence of surplus value, and with it of the capitalist system, is threatened? The classical economists had already run into this problem, and they found a solution in the Malthusian theory of population. When wages rise and the standard of living goes up, they argued, workers will have larger families, the supply of labor will increase, and eventually wages will come down again. Marx, however, rejected the classical population theory out of hand and worked out a solution of his own to the problem, which was not only original but also immune from the attacks which eventually brought the Malthusian dogma into general discredit.

Briefly, Marx's solution was that the accumulation process

[9] *Ibid.*

begets a pool of unemployed workers—what he called the "reserve army of labor" or "relative surplus population"—whose competition on the labor market keeps the rise of wages in check. To quote the key passage:

> The industrial reserve army, during the periods of stagnation and average prosperity, weighs down the active labour army; during the periods of overproduction and paroxysm, it holds its pretensions in check. *Relative surplus population is therefore the pivot upon which the law of demand and supply of labour works.* It confines the field of action of this law within the limits absolutely convenient to the activity of exploitation and to the domination of capital.[10]

From what sources are the ranks of the industrial reserve army recruited? According to Marx there are two chief sources. The first is what economists today would call technological unemployment. As wages rise under the impact of accumulation, capitalists react by introducing laborsaving machinery. The laborers who are thrown out of work join the ranks of the industrial reserve army and compete for the remaining jobs. But if this is not enough to keep wages in check, another mechanism comes into play. Capitalists temporarily reduce the rate of accumulation or even stop accumulating altogether. The result is a crisis followed by a depression; the ranks of the reserve army are quickly filled up and wages fall until conditions are once again favorable for a resumption of accumulation.

Thus we see that unemployment and depression occupy a key position in the Marxian analysis of capitalism. The classical economists had largely ignored these phenomena or had attempted to explain them away as accidents. Most modern economists regard them as defects in the capitalist system which can be removed by a proper policy on the part of the state. Marxists, on the other hand, regard them as an essential part of the mechanism of the

[10] *Ibid.*, p. 701. Italics added.

system without which its continued existence would be impossible. This interpretation of unemployment and depression is one of the most significant and distinctive features of Marxian economics.

Our picture of the accumulation process so far includes a continuous substitution of machinery for labor and recurring depressions when wages nevertheless get out of hand and threaten the margin of surplus value. These are, so to speak, normal accompaniments of accumulation, and there is no particular reason to assume that they would grow more or less severe as the capitalist system develops. In addition, however, the accumulation process generates other difficulties—what Marxists often call "contradictions"—which grow in intensity as the system develops. The theory of these long-run tendencies is the most complicated and controversial part of Marxian economics, and the reader will therefore understand that the following summary is necessarily oversimplified and incomplete.

First, there is what Marx called the falling tendency of the rate of profit. It will be recalled that the formula for the rate of profit is $p = s'(1 - q)$, where s' is the rate of surplus value and q the organic composition of capital. Now there can be no question that in the course of capitalist development there is a strong tendency for the organic composition of capital to rise, that is to say, for workers on the average to be equipped with better and more expensive machinery and to process greater quantities of material; and it appears at once from the formula that this in itself is sufficient to create a tendency for the rate of profit to fall. There are, of course, offsetting factors—particularly the tendency for s' to rise as the productivity of labor increases—but Marx believed that in the long run the rising organic composition of capital must assert itself and bring about a declining trend in the rate of profit.

What will be the consequence of such a trend? To answer this question it is necessary to understand that the rate of profit is, so to speak, the barometer by which each individual capitalist tries to regulate his course. A steady rate of profit indicates no

change in the economic weather; the higher the level, the fairer
the weather, and conversely the lower the level, the fouler the
weather. A rise in the rate of profit means clearing; a fall in the
rate of profit is a storm warning. Hence a long-run falling tendency of the rate of profit signifies that under capitalism there is
a more or less steady deterioration in the economic climate. The
vitality of the system is gradually sapped, its susceptibility to the
disease of depression is magnified, its recuperative powers undermined.

> It is here demonstrated [Marx wrote in commenting on
> what he called the fright of the English economists over the
> decline of the rate of profit] in a purely economic way, that
> is from a bourgeois point of view, within the confines of capi-
> talist understanding, from the standpoint of capitalist pro-
> duction itself, that it has a barrier, that it is relative, that it is
> not an absolute but only a historical mode of production cor-
> responding to a definite and limited epoch in the develop-
> ment of the material conditions of production.[11]

The second difficulty which grows more serious as capitalism
gets older can be called with almost equal appropriateness a tendency to underconsumption or a tendency to overproduction. It is
apparent that in a smoothly working economic system the growth
of production and the growth of consumption would move forward in step. This does not mean that there is an exact technically
determined relationship which must be maintained between production and consumption. It means only that production and
consumption are closely interdependent and that it is impossible
for them to conform to a pattern of development which is determined by considerations of an entirely different order. And yet,
according to the Marxian analysis, it is precisely this impossibility
which is demanded by capitalism. As a capitalist country becomes
wealthier, it tends to devote an ever larger share of its produc-

[11] *Ibid.*, Vol. III, p. 304.

tion to the purposes of accumulation, that is, to building up its capacity to produce still more in the future. At the same time, the system has a strong bias toward repressing the growth of consumption: first, because the workers' consumption is held in check by the millstone of unemployment; and second, because the capitalists deliberately keep their own consumption down in order to have more for accumulation. Lenin speaks in this connection of the contradiction "between the limitless striving for expansion of production, which is the very essence of capitalism, and the restricted consumption of the masses." [12] It is a contradiction which in the nature of the case grows more severe and intractable as the capitalist system develops and becomes more wealthy; it operates, along with the falling tendency of the rate of profit, to produce a state of chronic depression, which can be relieved only by "outside" developments such as the opening up of a continent to capitalist exploitation, the introduction of a new industry requiring massive capital investments, or war, with its unlimited demand for armaments and its vast destruction of existing wealth. [13]

[12] Lenin, *Sämtliche Werke*, Vol. III, p. 21. This volume of Lenin's *Works* has not yet been translated into English.

[13] There is an obvious similarity between the Marxian theory sketched in this paragraph and the analysis of the late Lord Keynes. Professor Harris, commenting on this aspect of Keynes's thought, has pointed out that by 1936 Keynes "had emphasized over-saving, excessive rates of interest, limited demand for capital, low marginal efficiency of capital, and had noted the more favorable demand conditions in the nineteenth century: population increase, wars, new inventions, opening up of new lands, were especially important." S. E. Harris, *The New Economics* (1947), p. 406. One school of Keynesians has developed these ideas into an elaborate theory of capitalist stagnation. Perhaps the most important work of this school is A. H. Hansen, *Full Recovery or Stagnation?* (1938). It would, however, take us far beyond the scope of this book to compare the Marxian and Keynesian analyses of capitalism: we must be content to point out that the similarities are less fundamental than the differences, and that in many respects the Marxian and Keynesian conclusions are diametrically opposed to each other.

It must be remembered, however, that there is not an indefinite number of unopened continents and that new industries requiring investments on the scale of the basic industries, like steel and railroads, which are built up in the earlier phases of capitalism, grow increasingly rare as industrialization proceeds. Hence the burden of keeping capitalism going falls more and more heavily on militarism and war. For quite independent reasons, which we shall discuss in the next section, capitalism also generates the purposes and the motives for ever greater and more destructive warlike enterprises.

Before we turn to the subject of imperialism, there is one more long-run tendency of capitalism to be taken into account. This is what Marx called the centralization of capital and what is usually described today as the development of monopoly and the concentration of economic power. The underlying cause of this trend, as practically all economists agree, is the steady increase in the optimum scale of production which accompanies technological advance. There are also other contributory causes; one of the most important is the development of the corporate form of business organization (together with all the financial machinery that goes with it) which greatly facilitates the assemblage and management of huge aggregations of capital. Marx was perhaps the first to understand the full significance of these phenomena; today they are widely recognized as among the most important accompaniments of capitalist development.

Some of the chief consequences of this trend will be analyzed in the next section. Here we need only note that monopoly tends to accentuate rather than to ameliorate those contradictions of the system which have already been passed in review and that it brings with it certain peculiar problems and difficulties on its own account. One of the most striking of the problems specifically related to the growth of monopoly is the mushrooming up in the later stages of capitalist development of an inflated and wasteful apparatus for selling and distributing commodities.

Imperialism

So far we have confined our attention largely to the functioning of a single self-contained capitalist system. Historically, however, capitalism has developed more or less independently in a number of countries, and this fact of separation into various national sectors has always been one of the decisive factors determining the behavior not only of the individual parts but also of the system as a whole.

Up to about 1875 England was by far the most advanced capitalist country, so much so in fact that the products of English industry enjoyed an unchallenged dominance in the world market. Under these circumstances the English capitalists were free traders and not very much interested in bearing the cost of an empire which they could exploit economically in any case. Capitalists of other countries were largely on the defensive, more interested in gaining control of their own domestic markets than in challenging English supremacy abroad. As long as these conditions lasted, international economic relations were relatively tranquil, and there seemed to be good grounds for the optimistic liberalism which at that time was the dominant bourgeois ideology.

All this changed with dramatic suddenness in the last quarter of the nineteenth century. Three factors combined to produce an entirely new phase of capitalist development, to which Lenin gave the name imperialism. First, following the American Civil War and the Franco-Prussian War, two new industrial giants, the United States and Germany, appeared on the world scene to challenge England's economic supremacy. Second, huge monopolies and cartels, demanding special privileges and protection from the state, began to make their appearance. And third, all the advanced capitalist countries began to feel the need of assured outlets abroad for the accumulations of capitalists who were finding domestic investments less and less profitable. All these factors were of prime importance in shaping the subsequent course of events, and their effects can to a certain extent be separately traced. In a brief survey like this, however, it is more important to stress that they all worked in the same general direction and reinforced one another in a thousand ways.

Beginning in the 1870's, a great scramble set in for unclaimed territories, for protected markets, for exclusive sources of raw materials. Economic peace gave way to economic warfare on all fronts. At first the chief victims were the weaker and more backward peoples, who were unable to oppose effective resistance to the aggressive designs of the great powers. But as this relatively safe margin for expansion was used up, the powers came into increasingly severe conflict with one another. By the early years of the present century, it was already clear that the capitalist world was irrevocably embarked upon the course which led to the general slaughter of 1914–1918.

These developments in the international sphere could not but have profound repercussions on the internal structure and policies of the capitalist countries. Armies and navies were built up to hitherto undreamed of proportions; a spirit of aggressive nationalism was sedulously fostered by monopoly-dominated governments and organs of publicity; the power and functions of the state in economic and social matters were vastly expanded. And all this served the domestic as well as the foreign interests of the capitalists. Militarism is profitable, especially to the biggest monopolies in the heavy industries; moreover, as was pointed out in the last section, it becomes increasingly necessary as a method of offsetting the tendency to underconsumption. International conflict turns attention away from class conflict, which for the ruling class always has only dangers and no rewards. Finally, a strong state is essential, both to deal with the growing disorder of the capitalist economy and to counter the potentially revolutionary threat of a rising socialist movement.

Thus, in the period of imperialism all the national and international contradictions of capitalism plunge toward the one supreme contradiction—that war and preparation for war become the only purposes capable of sustaining the system: that death becomes the only possible means of life. It is this condition which marks imperialism as the final stage of capitalism. War on the modern scale is not a force which can be controlled. The experience of our generation fully demonstrates that war is a force which destroys those who let it loose and undermines the system which lives according to its dictates. And yet capitalism, unable to overcome its mounting contradictions in any other way, has no choice but to continue on the road to Armageddon. According to the Marxian view, the alternatives before mankind are not socialism or capitalism, but socialism now or socialism later—when even greater devastation and bloodshed have finally driven home the lesson that capitalism has completed its historic function of building up man's productive forces and lingers on only to destroy its own achievements.

CHAPTER 8

The Socialist Movement, 1848–1914

CHAPTER 5 SKETCHED the development of socialism from the first beginnings in early modern times up to 1848. That year was not only the year of publication of the *Communist Manifesto;* it was also a year of revolutions: the discontents and tensions which had been building up almost continuously since the end of the Napoleonic Wars finally came to a head. The revolutions of 1848 were no more socialist in essence than the Great Revolution of 1789, but the activity of socialists was much more prominent and their role less episodic than had been the case with the Babeuvist conspiracy of 1795–1796. The movement, still diverse, inchoate, largely lacking in organization, nevertheless showed evidences of vigor and idealism in 1848 which added up to a clear indication that socialism had at last become a force which would have to be reckoned with and which might soon be capable of exercising an independent influence on the course of events. In this and the following chapters, we resume the story of the development of socialism. The reader is asked to bear in mind that in the brief space available only the high lights can be touched upon.

The First International

The revolutions of 1848 ended in a general victory for reaction over the greater part of Europe. Many radicals, especially Germans, were exiled or emigrated to the freer air of Britain and America. The decade of the fifties witnessed an unprecedentedly rapid expansion of capitalism. For all these reasons the socialist movement suffered a relapse, and it was only in the early sixties that it began to show signs of recovery. Then several events occurred which signalized a resumption of the advance throughout central and western Europe.

In 1862 an International Exhibition was held in London to which the Bonapartist regime in France made the mistake of sending what it regarded as a safe and tame delegation of French workers. The Frenchmen, however, proceeded to get in touch with their opposite numbers in London, and vital contacts were established which led directly to the great meeting in St. Martin's Hall, London, on Sept. 28, 1864, at which the International Workingmen's Association, more generally known as the First International, was formed. The English representatives were for the most part trade unionists, and their participation seems to have had its origin in a desire to set up some sort of machinery capable of checking the importation of continental workers to be used as strikebreakers in England. The other representatives, except for the deputation that had come from Paris for the specific purpose of attending the meeting, were mostly exiles living in London who were interested in taking up again where they had been obliged to leave off in 1848–1849.

The St. Martin's Hall meeting approved the appointment of a provisional committee to decide on the form of the new association. This committee included twenty-seven Englishmen, nine Frenchmen, nine Germans, six Italians, two Swiss, and two Poles. The preponderance of Englishmen was undoubtedly due to the fact of the meeting's being held in London, and it gives an exaggerated impression of the role of the English in the future development of the First International. Nevertheless, the composition of the committee does indicate clearly the main geographical locus of the International's operations. Branches were formed in the United States during the later sixties, but by and large it is correct to say that the First International remained throughout its life a western and central European institution.

It is probable that the International Workingmen's Association would have had no more influence in history than several previous attempts to organize international radical movements had exercised if it had not been for the fact that Karl Marx was invited to sit on the platform at the St. Martin's Hall meeting and was appointed to the provisional committee. He quickly came to the fore in the meetings of the committee, and both the Inaugural Address, which established the general outlook of the association, and the Provisional Rules, which formed its initial constitution, were entirely his work. Moreover, throughout most of the life of the First International Marx, later aided by Engels, sat on the General Council (the Association's highest organ) and exercised a decisive influence in shaping its policies. The First International thus became the medium through which the Marxian outlook reached the European working-class movement, and it is this fact, rather than its immediate practical achievements, which give it its unique historical importance.

The Inaugural Address, an example of Marx's writing at its best, established the socialist character of the International from the outset. Drawing on British experience, he emphasized three themes. First, despite the enormous expansion of wealth and trade which had taken place since 1850, the condition of the working class had not been materially improved. From this it followed that "on the present false base, every fresh development of the productive powers of labour must tend to deepen social contrasts and point social antagonisms." Second, the British workers had finally, after a struggle of 30 years, succeeded in forcing the Government to enact the Ten Hours' Bill. This was the first notable victory in "the great contest between the blind rule of the supply and demand laws which form the political economy of the middle class, and social production controlled by social foresight, which forms the political economy of the working class." And third, the success of a number of cooperative factories, "raised by the unassisted efforts of a few bold 'hands,'" had given a practical demonstration

that production on a large scale, and in accord with the behests of modern science, may be carried on without the existence of a class of masters employing a class of hands; that to bear fruit, the means of labour need not be monopolised as a means of dominion over, and extortion against, the labouring man himself; and that, like slave labour, like serf labour, hired labour is but a transitory and inferior form, destined to disappear before associated labour plying its toil with a willing hand, ready mind, and a joyous heart.

The Inaugural Address closes on the same note as the *Communist Manifesto* 16 years before: "Proletarians of all countries, Unite!"

The First International was not an association of national working-class parties; no such parties existed at the time. It was rather an organizational and educational center which aimed to create national working-class movements. Number 7 of the Provisional Rules gives us an insight into the existing state of affairs and into the task which the International set for itself:

7. Since the success of the workingmen's movement in each country cannot be secured but by the power of union and combination, while on the other hand, the usefulness of the International Central Council must greatly depend on the circumstance whether it has to deal with a few national centres of workingmen's associations, or with a great number of small and disconnected workingmen's societies; the members of the International Association shall use their utmost efforts to combine the disconnected workingmen's societies of their respective countries into national bodies, represented by central national organs. It is self-understood, however, that the appliance of this rule will depend upon the peculiar laws of each country, and that, apart from all legal obstacles, no independent local society shall be precluded from directly corresponding with the London Central Council.

Some progress was made toward the goal of united national working-class movements through the setting up of Federal Councils for several countries and regions, but on the whole the First

International remained what Marx later described as "isolated sections, sparsely distributed over various countries and held together by a General Council on the periphery." It is even true that where, as in Germany during the later sixties, really strong indigenous political parties began to develop, their preoccupation with their own struggle for survival and influence weakened their interest in, and the strength of their ties to, the International. In this way the very success of the International as it was then constituted tended to undermine its authority and usefulness.

It is impossible to measure accurately the achievements of the First International. Certainly it played an important part in the struggle of the English workers for the franchise, a struggle which was finally crowned with success in 1867; it mobilized effective support for numerous workers' battles for higher wages and better conditions; it spread socialist ideas as far east as Russia and as far west as America; by its attitude during the Franco-Prussian War it helped teach workers of all nationalities to defend their independence and to resist aggression regardless of its origin; it made the cause of the Paris Commune its own and by so doing, as Marx predicted, enshrined the Commune's martyrs "in the great heart of the working class"; and, finally, by the frenetic reaction it called forth in chancelleries and editorial rooms, the International revealed the haunting fear of working-class solidarity, which never lies very far beneath the surface of capitalist society. All these things were important; but in the long run it was probably even more important that the International first effectively identified the class interests of workers, regardless of nationality, with the scientific socialism of Marx and Engels. The First International might die, but during its lifetime it prepared the ground and sowed the seed from which future Internationals would spring as long as capitalism continued to divide society into exploited and exploiting classes.

The inner life of the First International was at no time free of conflict. Though Marx never lost control of a majority in the General Council and in the annual Congresses, he was continuously challenged by rival groupings and factions: trade unionists with purely liberal tendencies in England, Proudhonists and Blanquists in France, Bakuninists in Switzerland and the Latin countries, to name only the most prominent. In fact, the decline and eventual death of the First International have often been laid at the door of these factional struggles. Undoubtedly they were a contributing factor, but their intensity did not change sufficiently during the lifetime of the organization to explain why it flourished during the later sixties and fell to pieces during the earlier seventies. To understand this change in trend we must look to deeper causes: first, to the increasing strength of international reaction following the Franco-Prussian War and the defeat of the Commune; and second, to the emergence of national working-class movements which were so engrossed in their own affairs that they had no time for the International and tended to look upon external ties as a liability instead of an asset. Hence, when the General Council of the International was transferred to New York as a result of the Hague Congress of 1872, this was more than a move in a factional struggle for control; at bottom it represented an admission on the part of Marx and Engels that the International Workingmen's Association had played out its historical role and had better be left to die quietly in the relatively peaceful atmosphere of the New World.

Between the First and Second Internationals

The death of the First International was in a sense a setback for the socialist movement, and yet this setback had nothing in common with the temporary collapse which followed the defeat of the revolutions of 1848. The fifties were years of general inactivity, while the decade and a half which followed the transfer of the General Council to New York was a period of highly significant developments in a number of the most important countries. As a rough but suggestive index of activity, we may cite the total vote of all socialist parties and groupings: in 1874 it amounted to approximately 350,000, and by 1889 the figure had almost tripled to a million. The foundation for a new and quite different International had been laid.

The outstanding development of this period was the building of viable national parties, and in this respect Germany, which had already made a good start during the lifetime of the First International, was far ahead of all other countries. The reasons for the precocity of the German socialist movement are not far to seek. After 1850 capitalism developed rapidly in Germany but within a framework of feudal particularism which was quite unsuited to it. The unification of Germany, as essential as it was inevitable, could come about in one of two ways: either the middle class and the working class could cooperate in overthrowing the multifarious feudal regimes and unify the country on the basis of a bourgeois republic, or one of the German states could seize the initiative and establish a unified Empire under its own domination. The failure of the revolutions of 1848 made the first alternative impossible; German liberalism never recovered from the defeat. Soon after, Bismarck led the way along the second path, and the decisive elements of the capitalist class were not slow to climb aboard the Prussian bandwagon. There was thus no solid basis for an alliance between bourgeois liberals and workers, of the kind that played such an important role in English history during the later nineteenth and early twentieth centuries. The German workers were obliged to conduct their own struggle, no less for elementary political rights than for economic betterment and social reform.

Credit for first giving independent form to this struggle goes to Ferdinand Lassalle who founded the General German Workers' Association in 1863. Lassalle had been associated with Marx and Engels in 1848–1849 and remained much under the influence of Marxian ideas. Marx and Engels, however, suspected Lassalle of being too willing to play Bismarck's game, and an open breach would undoubtedly have taken place but for Lassalle's death a little more than a year after the founding of the new Association.

Thereafter the relations between Marx, Engels, and the International on the one hand and the Lassallean party on the other were marked by mutual suspicion and sometimes open hostility.

In the meantime a second working-class movement had made its appearance in south Germany under the leadership of Wilhelm Liebknecht, another old associate of Marx and Engels, and August Bebel. This movement took on definite shape as the Social Democratic Workers' Party at a Congress held in the Thuringian town of Eisenach in 1869. After a few years of rivalry and jockeying for position, the Lassalleans and the Eisenachers merged their forces at a Congress held at Gotha in 1875.[1] The new party first called itself the Socialist Workers' Party, but the name was soon changed to the Social Democratic Party of Germany, and under this designation it developed into the largest and most influential socialist party in the world in the period before the First World War.

During the period under review France and England, which had led the way in the earlier development of socialism, lagged far behind Germany. In England the main reason for this backwardness was that the trade unions, which were composed for the most part of the better paid urban workers, who had won the franchise in 1867, found it to their advantage to collaborate with the Liberals rather than attempting to build up their own political party. A Marxian party, the Social Democratic Federation, was formed by H. M. Hyndman in 1881, but it was isolated from the main body of the workers and soon developed into a relatively ineffective sect. It was not until the rise of the so-called "new unionism" among unskilled and semiskilled workers in the late eighties and early nineties that socialism really began to make progress again in the ranks of the English working class, this time under the leadership of the non-Marxian Independent Labor Party.

In France the situation was complicated by the cruel and bloody

[1] Concerning Marx's reaction to the Gotha Program, see pp. 9–10.

suppression of the Commune, which wiped out or drove into exile the strongest leaders of the French working class and set the socialist movement back by at least a decade. A more or less orthodox Marxian party finally took shape in 1879–1880 under the leadership of Jules Guesde, a returned Communard exile, and Paul Lafargue, who in the course of his wanderings abroad had met Marx and married his daughter. But in France, as in England, the policy of alliance with bourgeois radicals had its supporters, and the new party split over this issue in 1882. For the next two decades the development of French socialism was marked by schisms and factional struggles, while the trade-union movement fell under the influence of syndicalists who rejected political action altogether. At the turn of the century there were no fewer than five socialist parties of varying strength and importance.

Under these circumstances it is not surprising that the socialist movements in the smaller countries of western and central Europe tended to be more strongly influenced by the example of Germany than by that of England or France. German Social Democracy was not only the largest and best organized socialist party, its prestige was greatly enhanced by the valiant and ultimately successful struggle which it opposed to Bismarck's antisocialist laws during the decade of the eighties; and it enjoyed the precious asset of close intellectual and moral guidance from the founders of scientific socialism right up to the death of Engels in 1895. By the end of the eighties most of the countries of central and western Europe had developed well-organized socialist parties which were under Marxist leadership and looked to Germany for inspiration and enlightenment. The stage was set for the founding of the new International.

Before we discuss the history of the Second International, however, it will be worth while to cast a glance at the development of socialism up to that time in the two great regions which have come to dominate the history of our epoch, the United States and Russia.

In the United States, to which Marxian doctrines had been

carried by refugees of '48 as well as by small but active sections of the First International, a socialist party on a national scale, called the Socialist Labor Party, was formed in 1877. This party, however, was largely confined to German-speaking workers, together with a few other foreign-language groups. Though it played a considerable role in the industrial struggles of the eighties and nineties, it never succeeded in winning a significant number of American workers away from their allegiance to one or the other of the two big capitalist parties. The naturalization of working-class socialism in America really dates from the formation of the Socialist Party in 1901.

The channels through which socialist ideas reached Russia were, of course, very different. To Czarist Russia western Europe represented freedom and progress, and thither went a steady stream of refugees and students. Those who were inclined to revolutionary views eagerly seized upon the writings of western radicals and attempted to adapt them to the special conditions of Russia. Hence the ideas of Marxism evoked a quick response among Russian intellectuals. Writing the Preface to the second edition of Volume I of *Das Kapital* early in 1873, Marx noted with obvious satisfaction that "an excellent Russian translation [of the first edition] appeared in the spring of 1872. The edition of 3,000 copies is already nearly exhausted." This was 14 years before the appearance of the first English edition. At about the same time the practical work of the International and the heroic example of the Paris Commune were creating a profound impression on the many Russians who had a chance to observe them at close range. Russia, however, was not yet ripe for a socialist movement, and it was only with the development of capitalist industry and the consequent growth of an urban working class in the late eighties and nineties that the necessary foundation was laid. Russia's entrance into the international socialist movement can be dated from the First Congress of the Russian Social Democratic Labor Party in 1898. The very name of the party is sufficient to indicate its Marxian and German inspiration.

The Second International

The Second International was formed at a Congress held in Paris in 1889 on the occasion of the celebration of the hundredth anniversary of the French Revolution. This Congress was attended by 221 Frenchmen and 170 delegates from 16 other countries of Europe and the United States. At its inception the Second International represented approximately the same general geographical region as its predecessor in the sixties and seventies. From the very outset, however, there was one great difference between the two organizations: the heart of the First International had been the General Council, without which it would have existed merely on paper; in contrast, the Second International was essentially a rather loose federation of already existing and functioning national parties, none of which was prepared to submit to the authority of an international body. The Second International did not even establish permanent administrative machinery until 1900. Prior to that it had existed only in and through the International Congresses of 1891 (Brussels), 1893 (Zurich), and 1896 (London); and even when the International Socialist Bureau was established at the Paris Congress of 1900 it was given little more than liaison and information-gathering functions.

The fact that the Second International had no executive authority over its constituent parties has been the subject of much comment on the part of historians of the socialist movement. Some have gone so far as to conclude that this organizational feature deprived the International of all but sentimental and propaganda value, and that its ultimate breakdown can be traced to this cause. Neither of these conclusions is justified. On numerous occasions the International demonstrated that its moral authority was considerable. For example, at the Amsterdam Congress of 1904 the chief subject of discussion was the situation in France, where two main socialist parties were at loggerheads over the question of participation in bourgeois ministries. The International voted against participation and urged the French parties to unify their ranks on this basis. This was agreed to by both French factions; and Jean Jaurès, who was already the most influential French leader and who had fought against the antiministerial resolution, accepted the decision of the International with good grace. The following year the French socialist movement united in a single party for the first time in 25 years. Such results could not have been achieved by an organization as impotent as historians of the Second International have often implied it to have been. We shall consider the causes of its breakdown later; here we need only say that they were much deeper than mere organizational defects.

The Second International lasted just a quarter of a century, from July 14, 1889, to the outbreak of war, in August, 1914. The Labor Parties of Australia and New Zealand—both of which, incidentally, antedated the British Labor Party—did not affiliate with the International, which otherwise included all socialist parties worthy of the name. The geographical composition of the International Congresses therefore gives us a good idea of the scope of the socialist movement. As we have already seen, the founding Congress was almost entirely confined to western and central Europe. The most important additions at later Congresses were from eastern Europe and the Balkans. With the adhesion of the Russians at the turn of the century, socialism became in the true sense an all-European movement. But very little progress was made overseas. To be sure, socialists from the United States were affiliated to the International from the outset, but they were really Europeans, who never played an important role in the political life of their adopted country. A small Argentine socialist party likewise sent representatives to the International. But for the rest, delegates from overseas were usually stray individuals representing nobody in particular.

An analysis of the make-up of two of the later Congresses will illustrate the actual situation with sufficient clarity. At Amsterdam in 1904 there were 476 delegates, of whom 460 came from 19

European countries; 11 of the remaining 16 came from the United States, 2 from Argentina, and 1 each from Australia, Canada, and Japan. At Copenhagen in 1910 there were 896 delegates, of whom 871 came from 21 European countries; 24 of the remaining 25 came from the United States and 1 from Argentina. In assessing the record of the Second International—what it did not accomplish as well as what it did—the fact that it was a European organization which never established contact with the masses of Asia, Africa, and South America must never be lost from view.

Table 11. Socialist Vote in Various European Countries, 1901–1914 *

(*In thousands*)

Country	Elections held during 1901–1906	Elections held during 1907–1910	Elections held during 1911–1914
Germany.........	3,011	3,259	4,250
France..........	878	1,106	1,389
Holland.........	66	82	162
Denmark.........	43	.....	107
Sweden..........	9	.....	173
Norway.........	25	92	125

* Compiled from S. F. Markham, *A History of Socialism* (1930), *passim.*

   In Europe itself the socialist movement grew very rapidly during the period of the Second International. A compilation of the socialist vote of the world (as we have seen, overwhelmingly a European world) made in 1904 showed that between 1889 and 1903 the figure had jumped from one million to more than six million, and there is no doubt that the advance continued unchecked, if not at an accelerated rate, during the next decade. Table 11, while not exhaustive, gives a generally correct impression of the growth of the socialist vote. Of course, one must not attach too much importance to mere number of votes; in fact, one of the cardinal weaknesses of the Second International was that it made just this mistake. But making all necessary allowances, there can be little doubt that the popularity and influence of the socialist parties did increase enormously during this period.

Ideologically the Second International was dominated by the German Social Democrats and, like the latter, was split into three tendencies, which can be fairly accurately described as Left, Center, and Right. In Germany the leaders of these three tendencies were, respectively, Rosa Luxemburg, Karl Kautsky, and Eduard Bernstein. Rosa Luxemburg and Kautsky both regarded themselves as orthodox followers of Marx and Engels, and on many questions they were in agreement, while Bernstein, only a few years after the death of Engels, proclaimed the necessity of revising Marxism in the light of events which had taken place since the publication of *Das Kapital*. (It is from this circumstance that Bernstein and his followers acquired the name "revisionists.") The differences between Left and Right were fairly clear-cut on most issues. The Left maintained that capitalism was headed for a period of crises and wars and that the only escape lay through a working-class revolution which would overthrow the capitalist state and open the way to a new socialist system of society. The Right, on the other hand, denied that catastrophes of the kind foreseen by the Left were inevitable and argued that capitalism was capable of indefinite expansion. From this analysis the Right drew the conclusion that the working class must aim at gradual reforms and that socialism would arrive more or less automatically as the end product of a long process of evolution.

Centrists like Kautsky could see clearly enough that the gradualism of the Right represented a break with Marxism rather than a revision of Marxism, and for this reason they felt obliged to combat the theories of Bernstein and his associates. Hence the views of the Center often seem to be very close to those of the Left, the only noticeable difference being a marked tendency on the part of the Center to slur over or ignore altogether the crucial issues of state and revolution. But what was most characteristic of the Center was that while it often talked the same language as the Left, in actual practice it sided more and more with the Right. This was the decisive fact not only in Germany but in the International as a whole, for throughout the greater part of the history of the International the Center and Right together constituted an overwhelming majority of most of the affiliated parties.

This is not to suggest, however, that all the parties were similar in their dominant ideas and policies. Indeed, the Left-Center-Right line-up existed among the different parties as well as within them. On the Left were the Russian Bolsheviks, under the leadership of Lenin.[2] In the Center were the German Social Democrats, under the ideological leadership of Kautsky and the political leadership of Bebel. And on the Right were the British Fabians and Laborites, whose political outlook was almost identical with that of Bernstein in spite of the fact that they arrived at it without ever having either accepted or "revised" Marxism. Generally speaking, the leadership of the other parties steered a middle course in the wake of the Germans.

If we are to understand the positive achievements as well as the ultimate failure of the Second International, it is necessary to recall the dominant characteristics of the quarter century in which it flourished. This period could be described as capitalism's Indian summer. The seventies and eighties—the interval between the two Internationals—were, on the whole, years of falling prices, low profits, abnormally high unemployment, and severe industrial strife. A turning point was reached, however, during the early nineties, and in the two decades preceding the catastrophe of 1914

[2] The name Bolshevik comes from the Russian word for "majority." It was applied to Lenin and his followers as a result of a party Congress held in London in 1903, at which they were in the majority. The Mensheviks, or minority group at the 1903 Congress, included both Right and Center elements. Formally, Bolsheviks and Mensheviks composed two wings of the same party until 1912, when a final split occurred; but in practice they functioned as two separate parties from 1903 on.

the leading capitalist countries enjoyed a relatively high degree of prosperity. This was undoubtedly one of the decisive factors in shaping the development of the International. A second factor, of no less importance, was the dependence of this prosperity in the advanced countries on imperialist expansion and the exploitation of colonial and semicolonial peoples.

Given the prosperity of the period, capitalism in the advanced countries could afford to make substantial concessions to the working class. The socialist parties and the trade unions, which in most countries were closely allied, were thus able to win significant improvements in living standards as well as important social reforms by working within the framework of capitalist society. It is not surprising that they tended to overlook the special and temporary character of the conditions which made these gains possible. The essence of revisionism, indeed, was an implicit assumption that these conditions, far from being exceptional, were normal in a fully developed capitalist society. And centrists like Kautsky, though rejecting this assumption in words, increasingly acted upon it in practice. Only the Left maintained a proper sense of perspective and insisted that the socialist movement should prepare for the storms that lay ahead.

Not, of course, that storm warnings were lacking. Increasing imperialist rivalries, mounting international tension, intensified preparations for war—these were obvious to everyone, including the Right and Center socialists; and the later Congresses of the International were increasingly preoccupied with the war danger. But by this time the leaders of the dominant parties were caught up in a hopeless contradiction. The very prosperity which they relied on, and which alone gave meaning to their policies of piecemeal reform, depended on the system of imperialist exploitation and expansion, and it was this system which was inexorably driving the world to war.

How benefit from a system and at the same time fight against it? There was no answer to the question. In the nature of the case there could be none. Hence the International passed antiwar resolutions but continued to act on what Kautsky once (1902) eloquently described as "that dream that now floats before our eyes, that wars and catastrophes are a thing of the past while before us stretches ahead the level road of peaceful, quiet progress." When the conflict finally broke upon the world in 1914, the International quickly dissolved into its component national sections and ideological tendencies. The parties of the western and central European belligerent nations accepted the logic of their past policies and supported their respective governments; the Russian Bolsheviks denounced the war and those socialists who supported it; within each national party the first signs of schism and regrouping began to appear almost immediately. An institution which had been built up on the assumption of peace and progress could not survive the hard reality of war and reaction.

CHAPTER 9

The Socialist Movement, 1914–1948

THE HISTORY of socialism during the First World War is extraordinarily complicated and confused; a brief summary must therefore be correspondingly oversimplified. The reader is asked to keep this in mind in reading the following section.

The First World War and the Founding of the Third International

The Right-Center-Left division of the socialist movement remained the basic framework within which wartime developments took place, but the composition and strength of the various tendencies diverged progressively from the situation which prevailed in the prewar period. Under war conditions the Right became identified with a win-the-war policy, the Center with a policy of pacifism, and the Left with a policy of revolution. At the outset the Right was dominant in the central and western belligerents, the Left was dominant in Russia, and the Center was dominant in the neutrals. The next four and a half years witnessed a decline in the strength of the Right, an increase in the strength of the Left, and a sharp struggle between the two extremes for the allegiance of the Center. This struggle culminated in 1919 with the founding of the Third International and a definitive split in the world socialist movement. Let us trace the development of these trends on a year-by-year basis.

1915. No decisive shifts took place during 1915. The International Socialist Bureau, the headquarters of which had been transferred from Brussels to The Hague soon after the war started, was unable to act because of the refusal of the dominant Right socialists in the belligerent countries to have anything to do with

enemy nationals. The first signs of organized protest against the
war came at a conference held in Zimmerwald, Switzerland, in
September. The Zimmerwald Conference was called by the Italian
and Swiss parties and included in addition representatives from
Germany, France, Russia, the Netherlands, Sweden, Norway,
Poland, Rumania, and Bulgaria. Though by no means all the
important Center parties and factions were represented, the
centrists had a clear majority and controlled the proceedings
throughout. The so-called Zimmerwald Left was dominated by
the Russian Bolsheviks, under the leadership of Lenin, who was
then in exile in Switzerland. By establishing an International
Socialist Commission to carry on its work, the Zimmerwald Conference planted the seeds of a new international, though the
majority of the Conference was in favor of reactivating the old
International and only Lenin and his followers openly demanded
a break. The Leninists were not satisfied with the results of the
Conference but regarded it as a hopeful sign for the future.

1916. Continued inactivity on the part of the International
Socialist Bureau, increasing dissatisfaction and war-weariness
among the masses, growing support for the antiwar and revolutionary tendencies within the various socialist parties—these were
the dominant trends during 1916. The Zimmerwald group held
a second, larger, and more representative conference at Kienthal,
Switzerland, in April. At Kienthal the Left was relatively stronger
than at Zimmerwald, but the Center still held a majority. Nevertheless, the resolutions of the Kienthal Conference were more
outspoken in condemning the war and its socialist supporters.
The inactivity of the Right and the growing pressure of the
masses was pushing the Center into the arms of the Left.

1917. In many respects 1917 was the decisive year of the war.
The first Russian Revolution in March stirred up the entire
socialist movement and gave a strong impetus to the antiwar and
revolutionary tendencies. A split which had long been building
up in Germany came to a head in April with the founding by
Center and Left of the Independent Social Democratic Party.

The so-called Minoritarians (centrists) in France very nearly cap-
tured control of their party in October. Lenin, who had previously been limited to a relatively inactive role in Switzerland,
returned to Russia and threw himself into the task of expanding
the organizational strength of the Left. Enthusiasm for the Russian Revolution and a desire for positive action to bring the
senseless bloodshed to an end were nearly universal in the socialist
movement.

The pressures were so great that even the die-hards of the Right
gave in and agreed to attend a conference in Stockholm called
jointly by a Dutch-Scandinavian committee and by the Petrograd
Soviet, which was then under centrist control. The Bolsheviks
and their allies of the Zimmerwald Left, foreseeing the possibility
of a revival of the International on substantially the old basis,
decided to have nothing to do with the Stockholm Conference.
It was indeed a dangerous proposal from their point of view.
Hitherto the Right had refused to budge from its prowar policy,
and the Center had been increasingly forced to cooperate with
the Left. Now it seemed as though the Right and the Center might
reunite their forces, leaving the Left in an isolated and exposed
position. But the Stockholm Conference never took place, largely
because of the refusal of the Entente governments to grant pass-
ports to their nationals. The Stockholm fiasco ended the last
chance to revive the International in anything like its prewar
form. In November came the second Russian Revolution, which
had an even sharper impact on the line-up of the socialist movement than its predecessor. From this time on the Center gradually
declined as an independent force as more and more elements
broke away and joined the Right or Left. In the meantime the
Zimmerwald organization remained the only active international
socialist body.

1918. The victory of the Bolshevik Revolution and the continuation of the war dominated the socialist movement during
most of 1918. Both factors tended to push the masses to the left.
Thus the French minority became the majority at the annual

convention of the French party, while in Germany the strength of the Independents and Sparticists (the left-wing group under the leadership of Rosa Luxemburg and Karl Liebknecht) increased rapidly. More and more socialists aspired to follow the example of the Russians and take power by revolutionary means. But the leaders of the Right and, as the war drew to a close, many who had taken an antiwar stand with the Center, recoiled before the reality of revolution in Russia and the threat of revolution at home. For this reason, the general swing to the left was accompanied by an increasing polarization of the movement. By January, 1919, only two months after the revolution broke out in Germany, the Right leaders had already entered into an alliance with the high command of the German army to suppress a Sparticist uprising. Among the victims of this alliance were Luxemburg and Liebknecht, the two most prominent and respected leaders of the German Left. The irreconcilability of the conflict between the two wings of international socialism was strikingly symbolized by the action of the Seventh Congress of the Bolsheviks (March, 1918) in changing the name of their party from Russian Social Democratic Labor Party to Russian Communist Party. The purpose clearly was to emphasize, officially and authoritatively, the break with the old International and to lay the groundwork for a new one.

It is against this background that we must interpret the events of February and March, 1919. First came a conference looking to the revival of the old International, held during February in Berne. It was attended by 102 delegates from 26 countries. The Right was in control and pushed through a resolution which guardedly condemned the Bolsheviks and the Russian Revolution. But the existence of a considerable Center group, under French and Austrian leadership, which still hoped for a reconstitution of the International on an all-inclusive basis, made it impossible for the Berne Conference to achieve concrete organizational results. Almost immediately afterwards, in early March, the Left's answer to the Berne Conference came in the form of the founding of the Third or Communist International (often referred to as the Comintern) at a hastily assembled conference of Left parties and groups in Moscow. The split in the socialist movement which had been building up since 1914 now received a definite institutional form. This split was fated to play a leading role in the history of socialism for a long time to come—just how long we are still not in a position to say.

The Communist International

During the years just before and after the end of the First World War the socialist movement reached the greatest degree of influence and popular support which it had yet enjoyed. The revolution in Russia had been won; revolutions were in progress or seemed on the verge of breaking out throughout eastern and central Europe; social unrest and discontent were mounting in western Europe. It was under these circumstances that the leaders of the Comintern worked out the form and policies which were officially adopted at the second World Congress in 1920.

They believed that the principal task of the Comintern was to provide the general staff for the impending world revolution, just as the Bolshevik Party had provided the general staff for the Russian Revolution. The structure of the Comintern, therefore, differed radically from that of its two predecessors: it was to be neither a coordinating body for a scattered group of local societies nor a loose federation of national parties; rather it was to be a single international Communist Party with tightly integrated national sections. Moreover, in order to perform the function of revolutionary leadership it needed the strictest kind of discipline and unquestioned obedience to the high command. It is important to remember that this conception of the International had its origin in what was believed to be a world revolutionary situation. Such a conception was much less appropriate for more normal times and had gradually to be relaxed as time went on. Nevertheless, the idea of the imminence of the revolution and of the consequent necessity for strict centralization and almost military discipline was too firmly planted in the Comintern at birth to be capable of anything like complete elimination. The persistence of this idea under changed conditions developed into a serious obstacle to the growth of the Comintern and helps to explain why it became less active and was eventually dissolved.

During its first year or so of existence the Comintern attracted the support of most of the militant socialists of Europe. In some cases (as in Italy) this took the form of affiliation by already existing socialist parties; in other cases (as in France and Germany) splits took place and new parties were formed by those who were prepared to accept the leadership of the new International. Students of the subject seem generally to agree that around 1920 a considerable majority of the continental socialist movement had actually joined or was strongly under the influence of the Comintern. When the revolutions in central and western Europe were defeated or failed to come off, however, the Comintern lost strength on the continent (it had never been strong in Britain). All the national movements outside Russia now split in two, and the Communists fell back into the minority position. This was the situation which continued to exist in Europe—or at least in those parts of Europe where socialism was not temporarily stamped out by fascism—right up to the outbreak of the Second World War.

It would be a mistake, however, to judge the interwar accomplishments of the Comintern solely on the basis of its record in Europe. It will be recalled that the Second International, with its main strength in the socialist movements of the advanced imperialist countries, had never succeeded in making contact with the oppressed masses of the colonial and backward regions of the world. It was quite otherwise with the Comintern, which had its main strength in the Soviet Union. For both ideological and tactical reasons the Bolsheviks fought from the beginning to establish socialism in those vast colonial regions of the Near East, Central Asia, and the Far East which they had inherited from the Czars;

and this attitude was carried over into the theory and practice of the Comintern. Hence it was under the guidance of the Comintern that socialism finally began to strike roots in continents other than Europe. Instead of the 25 or so countries which were represented at the later prewar Congresses of the Second International, as early as the Third (1921) Congress of the Comintern no fewer than 52 countries were represented.

Many of these new Communist parties, of course, remained small and relatively unimportant in the political life of their respective countries. We have already seen, however, in tracing the history of the socialist movement, that beginnings are not necessarily insignificant because they are small. Moreover, at least one Asian Communist party, the Chinese, raised itself to the position of one of the dominant factors in its own country even before the Second World War and in so doing worked out methods and tactics which may prove to be widely applicable to other areas. Future historians may well set down as the Comintern's greatest achievement the introduction of socialism to continents and regions which had been left untouched by the First and Second Internationals.

The most controversial aspect of the Comintern was always its relation to the Soviet Union and the Russian Communist Party. There can be no doubt that the Bolsheviks dominated the councils of the Comintern and that the Communist parties of the world, both before and after its dissolution, have regarded the defence of the Soviet Union as their first obligation. The enemies of the Comintern have, of course, used these facts as a basis for portraying the various Communist parties as mere agencies of the Soviet state quite on a par with the bought "fifth columns" of fascism. This explanation disregards both the theory of socialism and the specific historical conditions which surrounded the birth and development of the Comintern. The obligation to defend the Soviet Union follows quite logically from the fact that the Soviet Union is a socialist country. It is hardly surprising that those who accept the Marxian analysis of capitalism and socialism should feel that the success of socialism in its first stronghold is a matter of utmost importance and that its defeat would be a crushing blow to the whole socialist movement. The fact that during the lifetime of the Comintern this obligation extended only to the Soviet Union was simply due to the fact that in this period the Soviet Union was the only socialist country.

The dominance of the Bolsheviks in the councils of the Comintern rested on grounds which are no harder to understand and no more sinister. These grounds can be summed up in one word: success. The Bolsheviks had won their revolution and were engaged in building a socialist society in an area which covered one-sixth of the land surface of the globe. In stature and prestige the Bolshevik Party towered above the other Communist parties, most of which were small minorities struggling to stay alive against all kinds of obstacles and repressions. It is a safe rule that there can be no equality among unequals; the fact that the socialist movement is working for a greater degree of equality does not exempt it from the operation of this rule.

This is not to argue, of course, that either the preoccupation with the Soviet Union or the dominance of the Bolsheviks was a source of strength to the Comintern. On the contrary—and quite apart from the propaganda weapons which they put in the hands of its enemies—they were obvious sources of weakness. They produced a psychological fixation on everything Russian, which had nothing to do with socialism, and they gave rise to the stubborn conviction that the transition to socialism and the upbuilding of the new society must everywhere follow exactly the Soviet pattern. These were undoubtedly grave weaknesses. They drove many sincere socialists away from the Communist parties and prevented the latter from adapting themselves to the particular conditions of their own countries. They were weaknesses which go far to account for the ultimate dissolution of the Comintern; but at the same time they were weaknesses which could no more be avoided than the Second International could escape from the fact that its strength depended upon the very imperialist system which was heading for disaster. Finally, they are weaknesses which, taking the Communist movement as a whole and without regard to a possible revival of the International, will tend to disappear as other countries go socialist and Soviet Russia ceases to occupy the unique position which it held in the interwar period.

At every stage the development of the Comintern was conditioned by two factors, the international situation generally and the situation inside the Soviet Union. For the first few years hopes ran high for a victory of the revolution in central and western Europe, which would not only bring socialism to the whole continent but would also come to the rescue of the hard-pressed Soviet state. This was the period of the Comintern's greatest activity and influence, as evidenced by the fact that world Congresses were held every year from 1919 through 1922. By the latter date, however, it was clear that this hoped-for course of events would not materialize. In 1921, the Soviet Union turned to the NEP,[1] and the Communist parties elsewhere were obliged to begin to adjust themselves to a period of capitalist stabilization. Soon afterwards Lenin's death was followed by a struggle for control of the Bolshevik Party between Stalin and Trotsky, which was basically a struggle over whether the Soviet Union would try to build socialism in one country or continue to found its hopes on a world revolution. The Comintern was, of course, caught in these conflicting currents, and its capacity to formulate policies and act upon them was greatly impaired. This was reflected in the growing interval between world Congresses: the Fourth was held in 1922, the Fifth in 1924, and the Sixth not until 1928.

By 1928 Stalin had finally won out in the Soviet Union, but both the internal Russian situation and the international situation were almost immediately subjected to new strains, in the one case by the First Five-year Plan and the collectivization of agriculture, and in the other case by the Great Depression. The Comintern did not succeed in developing an effective policy to meet

[1] See p. 17.

these changed conditions; for seven years after 1928 no world Congress was called.

Events took a new turn with the rise of the Nazis to power in Germany. It soon became apparent that fascism represented a mortal threat both to the Soviet Union and to the socialist movement at large. Communists therefore adopted a policy of cooperating with all antifascists, and this policy was given official Comintern sanction at the Seventh World Congress, which was finally summoned in the summer of 1935. For the next few years, Communists everywhere took the lead in promoting national "popular fronts" and international collective security against the spread of fascism. The result was an upsurge of Communist strength in many countries (for example, in France) and an increase in the prestige and authority of the Comintern.

Unfortunately the western European capitalist countries refused to join the collective-security front against fascism and instead pursued a policy of turning Hitler against the Soviet Union. To counter this Anglo-French strategy the Soviet Union was obliged to abandon collective security and to buy time through a nonaggression pact with Hitler. The Comintern was now faced with an extraordinarily difficult problem. How could the officially friendly relations between socialist Russia and fascist Germany be reconciled with the obvious mortal enmity between fascism and the interests of the working class? The Comintern was unable to solve this problem, and as a consequence its influence suffered a severe blow.

In a very short time after Hitler's invasion of the Soviet Union, however, the world Communist movement more than made up for the losses suffered during the period of the Russian-German Pact. The act of invasion proved that the pact had never really been more than an armed truce, and the Soviet Union soon became the crucial factor in a world-wide antifascist coalition. But there was no longer any function for the Comintern to perform. Under wartime conditions the various national Communist parties were in fact on their own and could expect neither assistance nor guidance from an international center. Moreover, the dissolution of the Comintern would serve to allay suspicions and cement the alliance between the Soviet Union and the western capitalist countries. Hence in 1943, less than two years after the German invasion of Russia, the decision to dissolve was taken by the constituent parties.

Paradoxically, the Third International passed into history, following in the footsteps of its two predecessors, at a time when the Communist movement it represented was growing in numbers and strength more rapidly than ever before.

The Labor and Socialist International

Efforts to reconstruct the Second International did not cease with the abortive Berne Conference of February, 1919. A further conference was held at Lucerne in August, 1919; and finally at Geneva in July, 1920, a number of Right parties and groups decided to go ahead. Headquarters were now transferred to London, and Ramsay MacDonald, leader of the British Labor Party, was elected Secretary. The shift of the seat of the International to London symbolized the victory of reformism over Marxism, a victory which, despite the fact that many of the affiliated parties remained officially Marxist, turned out in practice to be definitive.

The International as it was reconstituted in 1920 was a mere rump of the prewar Second International. The Left had gone over to the Comintern, and the most important Center elements, including the French and the Austrians, who had together led the Center forces at Berne, had already withdrawn from the old organization. These Center parties, unwilling to accept either the old or the new International, proceeded to form one of their own which became known as the Second-and-a-half International and which devoted its energies to trying to get the three groups together again in one all-inclusive association.

Thus for a couple of years during the height of the postwar upheavals, the socialist movement was divided into three Internationals. This situation, however, was essentially temporary since the Second-and-a-half International could not, and probably never intended to, continue to lead an independent existence. After a meeting of representatives of all three Internationals, held in Berlin in 1922, failed to find any basis for agreement, the Second and Second-and-a-half reunited in a large Congress in Hamburg in May, 1923. This Congress voted to dissolve the two predecessor organizations and to form in their place a new Labor and Socialist International (often abbreviated as the LSI). From a legalistic standpoint the LSI was the successor of the old Second International and is frequently referred to by the same name.

Geographically the LSI continued to draw its main support from the same countries as the prewar International. We may take the situation which existed in the mid-twenties as representative of the composition and strength of the LSI under relatively favorable conditions. At the time of the Second (Marseilles) Congress, in 1925, 42 parties from 33 countries were affiliated. Of these only the following were non-European: United States, Argentina, British Guiana, Georgia, Palestine, and Turkey. The larger number of countries, as compared with the prewar Congresses of the Second International, was due mainly to the fact that the peace treaties had created additional states in central and eastern Europe. As to strength, a statistical compilation published on the occasion of the Third (Brussels) Congress, in 1928 showed a total membership of all affiliated parties amounting to 6.6 million, of which no less than 6.2 million, or 94 per cent, were from Britain, Germany, France, Belgium, Denmark, Sweden, Czechoslovakia, and Austria—in other words, from the old strongholds of the prewar International. In 1928 the only non-European party with a membership of over 20,000 was the Palestinian.

Ideologically and politically the LSI carried on in the tradition of the prewar Right. There was no longer an important left wing to fight for a revolutionary Marxist position; and the Center elements, led by the Austrians, were in a rather small minority. Moreover, the most famous of the prewar orthodox Marxist theorists—men like Kautsky and Rudolf Hilferding—who had fought a running battle against Bernstein and the British Fabians now modified their position to the point where it became practically indistinguishable from that of their former opponents. Writing in 1927, just two years before the greatest of all capitalist crises, Kautsky, who had once championed the view that capitalism was inevitably heading for a period of chronic depression, recanted in these words: "The expectation that crises would someday become so extensive and long-drawn-out as to render the continuation of capitalist production impossible and its replacement by a socialist order unavoidable finds no more support today." [2] In spite of the war and all that happened after it, including the suppression of democracy in many countries and the rise of fascism in Italy and Germany, most of the leaders of the LSI remained committed to the very end to a perspective of a long-drawn-out transition to socialism through purely legal and parliamentary methods. In their adherence to this point of view they were no less rigid than the leaders of the Comintern in insisting on the inevitability of the Russian pattern.

The foregoing discussion of the LSI may tend to give the impression that it occupied a position in the socialist movement comparable to that of either the prewar Second International or the Comintern. This was not the case. The LSI lacked the moral authority of the former and the centralized structure of the latter. Since the participating parties did not feel bound by its decisions, it could continue to exist only if it confined itself to generalities or to relatively minor problems like organizing relief and assistance for victims of political persecution. This is in fact what happened. As member organizations—leadership and rank and file alike—came to realize that nothing of importance would be decided or initiated by the LSI, they naturally tended to lose interest in its activities.

The impotence of the LSI is best illustrated by its role in the

[2] K. Kautsky, *Die materialistische Geschichtsauffassung* (2d ed.), Vol. II, p. 546.

struggle against fascism. While a considerable number of Social
Democratic parties—using the term "Social Democratic" in the
generic sense explained in Chapter 1—entered into popular fronts
with Communists and bourgeois democratic groups during the
mid-thirties, the LSI as such remained inactive. Its opposition to
fascism never went beyond the verbal level. This inactivity was
particularly glaring in the case of the Spanish Civil War, during
which the western powers followed the notorious policy of nonintervention, while Hitler and Mussolini beat down the Spanish
Republic with its popular front of Republicans, Socialists, and
Communists. Many Social Democrats, and not only from Spain
itself, called upon the LSI to get together with the Comintern
for the purpose of organizing practical support for the Spanish
Republic. It was precisely the kind of issue which urgently required effective international action, and there was hardly a socialist in the world who was not passionately committed to the Spanish Republican cause. Yet the LSI did nothing, and for reasons
which are not far to seek. The leadership of the British Labor
Party, which by this time was much the strongest party in the
LSI, had decided, despite heavy pressure from its own members,
to support the policy of nonintervention. Without Labor Party
participation, the LSI could accomplish nothing. Hence it was
faced with the alternative of keeping quiet or of openly proclaim-
ing its bankruptcy. Impotence was, so to speak, the price of
survival.

An observer who attended the meetings of the LSI Executive
from August, 1938, to the outbreak of the war has recorded his
impressions in the following terms:

> Because the presence of the International was a permanent
> reminder of the duty of international solidarity, it became
> intensely disliked in some Labour quarters. Delegates of some
> countries (including, curiously enough, the British delega-
> tion . . .) demanded insistently that the International should
> be divested of any political or moral function and reduced

to a mere clearing house for the exchange of information. Friedrich Adler, for sixteen years its General Secretary, answered this demand with his resignation a few weeks before the outbreak of the war. The crisis of humanity was preluded by a crisis of the Socialist International.[3]

Actually, it was more than a crisis of the Labor and Socialist International; it was the end.

The Second World War and After

Viewed in the longer perspective of history, there can be little doubt that the interwar period was one of solid gains for the world socialist movement. Three great achievements stand out. First, socialism became a reality for the first time in history, not in some out-of-the-way corner of the earth but in a country covering one-sixth of its land surface. Second, the socialist movement for the first time obtained a strong foothold among non-Europeans, and here again not in some insignificant backwater but in China, the world's most populous country. And third, a socialist party became the official opposition in Great Britain, metropolis of the world's greatest empire. It is important not to lose sight of these gains, as many have tended to do; they will in all probability count among the decisive events of our epoch as historians of the future will analyze it. But neither should these gains be allowed to obscure the reality or the magnitude of the losses suffered by the socialist movement before the advancing tide of reaction in the interwar period.

Beginning in Hungary as early as 1920, fascism (or near-fascism) spread over Europe west of the Soviet Union, by counterrevolution or by foreign conquest, until at the outbreak of war democratic institutions survived only in Switzerland, France, Belgium, the Netherlands, the Scandinavian countries, and Britain. In quantitative terms, of the 350 to 400 million people in Europe

[3] Julius Braunthal, *In Search of the Millennium* (1945), p. 298.

(excluding the U.S.S.R.), fascism had conquered more than two-thirds. And in every country that fell before the fascist advance, trade unions were smashed, socialist parties outlawed, leading Social Democrats and Communists murdered, imprisoned, or driven into exile. Nor was the damage confined to the fascist countries. The moral dry rot of defeatism was far advanced in the capitalist democracies and did not leave the labor movement untouched. Especially in France the Socialist Party was honeycombed with appeasers and capitulators. Clearly, by 1939 the fortunes of socialism had fallen very low in its historic homeland of western and central Europe.

But the worst was still to come. The Soviet-German Pact, concluded without warning or preparation, seriously weakened the Communist camp and added greatly to the bitterness of Communist-Social Democratic relations. The final blows came with the Nazi campaigns of 1940 and early 1941 which brought the whole region from the borders of the Soviet Union to the English Channel, with the exception of the small neutral states of Sweden and Switzerland, under Hitlerite domination. Those who predicted, some with relief and some with regret, that European socialism would never rise again seemed to have all the weight of the evidence on their side.

Then came the turn of the tide. Hitler attacked the Soviet Union on June 22, 1941. The outlines of the coalition that would finally crush the Rome-Berlin-Tokyo Axis could now be seen. The gloom of defeatism began to dissipate. Communists everywhere, released from the embarrassment and frustrations of the pact, threw themselves into the antifascist struggle once again as in the days of the popular front and the Spanish Civil War.

From this time on the story is a familiar one. The Soviet Union stood up to the Nazi onslaught and turned it back at Stalingrad; the viability and strength of socialism in action were demonstrated for all to see. As the Nazi armies were driven back, resistance movements, with socialists everywhere in the vanguard, grew by leaps and bounds throughout occupied Europe and Asia. The masses, believing now that they were fighting not only for survival but for a better world, turned steadily to the left. In the closing stages of the war the struggle against the foreign invader merged into a great movement of social reconstruction which, at least in Europe, could have no other aim than the establishment of a socialist order. The truth of this was eloquently attested by the programs of far-reaching reform, emphasizing economic planning and the nationalization of large-scale industry, which were adopted by the resistance movements and to which even the participating bourgeois groups felt constrained to agree.

The crucial moment for the resistance movements, and for the social revolutions which they hoped to bring about, was the liberation of their respective countries from Nazi occupation. At this moment there was no state in the proper sense of the word; there was only a disorganized administrative apparatus, which in every case was more or less compromised by having collaborated with the national enemy. There was likewise no indigenous armed force except that of the resistance movements themselves. At this moment, as Vice-Premier Gomulka of Poland has aptly said, "state power was lying in the street," [4] and the resistance movements were the only force ready and able to pick it up. Everything depended, then, upon the attitude of the Allied armies—the Red Army in the east and the Anglo-American armies in the west and south. If they permitted the resistance movements to take over, the basis would be laid for a gradual and relatively peaceful transition to socialism; if they held the resistance movements in check, there would be at least a possibility of a return to the *status quo ante*.

As was to be expected, the Red Army, representing a socialist country, acted differently from the Anglo-American armies, representing capitalist countries. The Russians encouraged resistance movements to take over while giving particular support to their

[4] Wladyslaw Gomulka, "People's Democracy: The Way to the Peaceful Development of Poland," *Political Affairs*, April, 1947, p. 330.

socialist elements. Since the resistance movements were already armed, this policy was relatively easy to carry out. The British and Americans, on the other hand, used their power to restore representatives of the old ruling class to positions of authority and helped them to disarm the resistance movements. Since the resistance movements were reluctant to surrender their arms, this policy could be carried out only at a cost of provoking severe political crises and, in the case of Greece, weeks of bloody fighting.

Everything that has happened since was in a very real sense determined by events at the time of liberation. In the east Communists and Social Democrats are in power and have generally entered into close working arrangements to solve the problems of economic reconstruction and social transformation. In the west Communists have everywhere been forced out of governments, and Social Democrats are generally following their interwar policy of cooperating with capitalist groups and parties. In the east the socialist aspirations of the resistance movements are being realized; in the west there is a strong tendency toward a return to the *status quo ante*.

There is no need to repeat here what has already been said in Part One about the present state of the world socialist movement. Before closing this survey, however, it may be appropriate to comment briefly on postwar developments in the field of international socialist organization, since much of the foregoing analysis has been integrated around the history of the Internationals.

By the end of 1947 seven international conferences of Social Democratic parties had been held since the outbreak of the Second World War (London, December, 1944; London, March, 1945; Clacton-on-Sea, May, 1946; Paris, August, 1946; Bournemouth, November, 1946; Zurich, June, 1947; and Antwerp, November–December, 1947). The initiative in every case was taken by the British Labor Party. At most of these conferences the question of reviving the old International has been raised, but every time the proposal has been made it has been either rejected or postponed for subsequent consideration. Thus while there is no formal Social Democratic International in existence, a sort of informal substitute under the guidance of the Labor Party is actually functioning.

This situation corresponds with the interests of the Labor Party, which, as a governing party, has no desire to bind itself by formal agreements and yet finds it useful to have a medium for communicating with and influencing the continental Social Democratic parties. But the importance of this "substitute International" is very limited, chiefly because of the deep division which exists between the eastern European parties (including the majority Socialist Party of Italy under the leadership of Pietro Nenni) and the western European parties. The eastern group believes in working with Communists, supports the Soviet Union, rejects cooperation with the German Social Democrats, and favors the eventual formation of an International to include all Social Democratic and Communist parties. The western group refuses to have anything to do with Communists, consistently attacks the Soviet Union, favors cooperation with the German Social Democrats, and flatly rejects the idea of an all-inclusive International. As long as profound differences of this kind exist, there is no possibility of the two groups' working together for the achievement of important practical objectives. It would seem rather that each is interested in meeting with the other for such purposes as getting information and urging its own point of view.

No international meetings of Communists were held from the time of the dissolution of the Comintern, in 1943, until 1947. The first signs of a revival of international activity came in February, 1947, with the calling in London, on the initiative of the British Communist Party, of a conference of British Empire Communist parties. The main purpose of this conference seems to have been the exchange of information and the establishment of contacts among Communist parties which obviously have many problems in common. There have, however, been no reports of the setting up of permanent machinery to facilitate continued cooperation among Empire parties.

In September, 1947, a more important and much more widely publicized conference was held in Poland of leading representatives of the Communist parties of nine European countries (the Soviet Union, Poland, Czechoslovakia, Rumania, Bulgaria, Yugoslavia, Hungary, Italy, and France). At this conference it was decided to establish a Communist Information Bureau (Cominform) with headquarters in Belgrade. The purpose of the Cominform will be "to exchange experience and in case of necessity to co-ordinate the activities of the Communist parties." The conference issued a statement analyzing the international situation and particularly emphasizing the danger arising from American imperialist expansion and the role of the right-wing Social Democrats of western Europe in supporting American aims.

The composition of the Cominform is sufficient to prove that it is designed to deal with European problems and hence to dispose of the theory that it represents a revival of the Comintern which, of course, was world-wide in scope. Two other striking features of the Cominform are worth noting. First, it consists only of Communist parties which either are government parties (as in the eastern European countries) or are clearly powerful and in a certain sense decisive factors in the political life of their countries (as in France and Italy). And second, the headquarters of the Cominform are not in Moscow but in Belgrade, which, in east-west terms, is about halfway between Moscow and Paris. These features of the Cominform reflect the great expansion in the scope and influence of the European Communist movement which has taken place during and since the war. Furthermore, they suggest that the new organization is intended to be something which the Comintern, with headquarters in Moscow, could never have been: a meeting place for parties which are mature and strong enough to work together as more or less equal partners in a common enterprise.

Both the British Empire Communist Conference and the Cominform seem to confirm the view that a revival of a world-wide Communist International is not likely in the near future. On the other hand, they also point to the possibility of further groupings of Communist parties on the basis of common problems. Thus, for example, a Pan-American Conference or an Asian Communist Conference would be a logical development of what seems to be present Communist thinking.

Throughout this and earlier chapters, we have been speaking of socialist Internationals only in the sense of specific, organized bodies. Antisocialists, however, frequently speak as though the Internationals, and especially the Communist International, continued to function regardless of the existence of conferences, congresses, secretariats, executives, and all the rest of the paraphernalia of formal associations. In the deepest sense, the antisocialists are perfectly justified. As long as socialists are true to their ideals, they *must* be internationalists, they *must* strive to cooperate and to coordinate their activities with their fellow socialists in other lands. In other words, as long as socialism continues to be a vital movement, a real International will be in existence no matter what organizational form or forms it may assume at any given time. This is what Marx himself meant in 1878, several years after the dissolution of the First International and a decade before the formation of the Second, when he wrote that

> far from dying out, the International has developed from one stage to another and higher one in which many of its original tendencies have already been fulfilled. During the course of this constant development it will experience many changes before the final chapter in its history can be written.[5]

Marx's words remain as applicable today as when they were written 70 years ago.

[5] Quoted in Franz Mehring, *Karl Marx,* p. 508.

Part Three

The Debate over Socialism

CHAPTER 10

Can Socialism Provide Incentives to Work and to Efficiency?

PRIVATE PROPERTY is much older than either capitalism or socialism and so also is hostility to private property, or at any rate—and this frequently comes to much the same in practice—hostility to large inequalities of private property. It is therefore natural that theories justifying and defending private property should be practically as old as the institution itself. When, in the modern epoch, capitalism rose in western Europe, the traditional theories of property were modified and adapted, without any sharp break in continuity, to serve the defence of capitalist property and to refute the socialist proposals which contemplated a fundamental alteration of the property system. If one is fully to understand the debate over socialism, which it is the purpose of this and the next two chapters to illuminate, one must always remember that it takes place in the context of a long and rich historical tradition.

The Theoretical Defences of Private Property

During the eighteenth and nineteenth centuries, three main lines of argument were developed to justify private property. The first (and also the earliest) is the theory that private property is based upon, and derives its sanction from, the labor of the owner. This theory, which received its classical formulation at the hands of John Locke in his *Two Treatises of Civil Government* (1690), was designed to answer criticisms of earlier theories which had attempted to ground private property in the Law of

Nature. According to Locke, in his *Second Treatise of Civil Government,* Chap. V,

> though the things of Nature are given in common, man (by being master of himself, and proprietor of his own person, and the actions of labour of it) had still in himself the great foundation of property; and that which made up the great part of what he applied to the support or comfort of his being . . . was perfectly his own and did not belong in common to others. Thus labour, in the beginning, gave a right to property.

(It is only fair to say that Locke was perfectly aware that this theory would not justify a large proportion of existing titles to property; he can therefore hardly be held responsible for the dogmatic form in which it was spread abroad, in print and from pulpit and platform, during the next two centuries.)

The great advantage of the Lockean theory was that it made of private property one of the natural rights of man which it was the duty of society to approve and of the state to protect. From this point of view it was not necessary to argue the merits of socialism, for socialism was by its very nature immoral and bound to be rejected by every right-thinking person. While strong vestiges of this way of thinking still survive, especially among editorial writers, hardly anyone attempts nowadays to base a rational argument on the conception of natural rights. Hence we need not concern ourselves further with the labor theory of property; even to demonstrate its internal weaknesses would be a work of supererogation.

The second justification of property referred to above is the utilitarian theory, first put forward in a logical and consistent fashion by David Hume (1711–1776) and subsequently popularized by Jeremy Bentham (1748–1832). According to this theory private property is a convention which men obey, and ought to obey, because it is in their interest to do so. In its most highly developed form—the form in which it exercised its greatest influence during the nineteenth century—the utilitarian theory rested its case primarily on the harmony of private and public interests which classical political economy was believed to have demonstrated. As long as capitalism worked reasonably well and produced a continuous expansion of trade and wealth, the utilitarian theory was both persuasive and popular. It appealed especially to those liberals and moderate conservatives who prided themselves on their rejection of dogma and who liked to think that their beliefs were always grounded in reason. It is probably no exaggeration to say that in the decades before the First World War, a period of capitalist expansion and prosperity, the utilitarian theory of property held the field without a serious rival.

Nevertheless it should be noted that utilitarian arguments have been used against private property as well as in its defence. From the very beginning socialists justified their proposals to abolish private property on the ground that such action would promote the well-being and happiness of the masses. And when, after the First World War, capitalism showed evident signs of retrogression and even collapse, when the peaceful world of the nineteenth-century liberals turned into the warring world of the twentieth-century imperialists, the utilitarian argument came increasingly to be used by the socialists against the defenders of private property. This is not to say that the utilitarian justification of private property was ever completely abandoned, but it does mean that the utilitarian justification was narrowed down and was relied on much less extensively than had hitherto been the case. Nowadays one seldom meets a sweeping defence of the capitalist system as a whole on utilitarian grounds; what is usually contended is that in the absence of private property there would be no adequate incentive to hard work, managerial efficiency, and technological progress. We shall consider these questions in some detail below; here it is sufficient to note that what is left of the utilitarian argument usually does not stand alone and is often overshadowed by other arguments believed to be more persuasive.

The third justification of private property to which we have referred came as a reaction to the natural-rights doctrine, which, as the French and American Revolutions showed, could be turned to purposes no conservative could approve. Edmund Burke, combating not only the French Revolution but also the English radicals who were inspired by it, put forward the historical, or prescriptive, theory of property. According to Burke prescription— a legal term which is roughly synonymous with traditional occupancy or possession—is the only safe title to anything; it embodies the experience of the ages and has the great advantage of stability, which comes with custom and habit. In the words of R. B. Schlatter, "for the abstract rights of man, he [Burke] substituted the traditional rights of Englishmen."[1] This theory is in one sense no more than a distillation of the conservative point of view, and as such it has its followers in every age, including our own. But the extent of its appeal to wider circles of the population is another matter. During the nineteenth century it enjoyed an extensive vogue and helped to inspire such important historical research as that of Sir Henry Maine (1822–1888) into the development of legal institutions. But before the century was over, the historical argument was, so to speak, torn out of the hands of the conservatives and turned against them; and it was the socialists, above all the Marxists, who accomplished this tour de force. For Marx showed that history not only creates and sanctifies; it also derogates and destroys. The historical justification of existing institutions, including private property, attained its greatest influence both on the continent and in England during the later nineteenth century. Thereafter it declined in importance and is today a relatively minor weapon in the antisocialist arsenal. Meanwhile, the socialists made increasingly good use of a similar line of argumentation to show that the system of private property is no longer in harmony with modern techniques of production

[1] In a forthcoming book, *The Theory of Property: An Historical Essay*. I am much indebted to Professor Schlatter for allowing me to read and draw upon his manuscript. His analysis of property theories and their interrelation is extremely valuable to the student of socialism.

and has become an obstacle to the further development of social wealth and consumption.

Thus, when capitalist society suffered its first shattering blow in the First World War, the theories of private property which had served to justify the existing social order for more than two hundred years were already losing their generality and force. The natural-rights theory was scarcely taken seriously any longer; the utilitarian theory had been practically whittled down to the proposition that without private property men would loaf and waste; and the historical theory was being more effectively used to attack than to defend the existing order. It was under these circumstances that bourgeois theorists began to cast about for new or previously neglected arguments to support capitalism and refute the case for socialism. Among those which were hit upon, two acquired such importance that it may fairly be said that, together with what is left of the utilitarian theory, they form the backbone of the antisocialist position today.

The first is a relatively new theory, traces of which can hardly be found before the beginning of the present century. It holds that a centrally controlled economy like that implied by socialism cannot utilize resources rationally and must therefore not only disappoint the hopes of its advocates but also drag society down from the levels attained by capitalism. This theory is somewhat too complicated to win widespread understanding and approval; but it has exercised a great fascination for certain types of intellectuals, and it may even be that its esoteric nature has been a source of strength rather than weakness. In any case, as influential a publicist as Walter Lippmann has declared that "an acquaintance with this school of socialist criticism is indispensable to all who would now discuss the problem of collectivism." [2]

The second theory, which is both older and vastly more popular today, holds that only a social order based upon private property is compatible with the maintenance of economic and political

[2] *The Good Society*, p. 94n.

freedom, that socialism is *The Road to Serfdom*.[3] This theory is probably almost as old as the idea of socialism itself; certainly it was strongly championed during the nineteenth century by such extreme advocates of *laissez faire* as Herbert Spencer and his followers. It began to come into its own only after the First World War, however, and its greatest successes have been scored since the end of the Second World War. So widespread is this theory today that one can scarcely open an American newspaper without finding it in some one of its many possible forms; and it is certainly no exaggeration to say that it is now an officially accepted doctrine of the United States Government.

This brief excursus into the history of property theory points to the conclusion that the three most influential arguments against socialism today are, first, the utilitarian theory in what might be called its waste-and-inefficiency version; second, the theory that socialism cannot utilize resources rationally; and third, the theory that socialism is incompatible with economic and political freedom. In the remainder of this chapter, we shall consider the first of these theories; the second and third will be dealt with in subsequent chapters.

Work under Capitalism and Socialism

The belief that people will work hard only under a system of private property is so widespread in the United States that it could almost be called an article of popular faith. The obverse of this belief, of course, is the conviction that a socialist system must necessarily stagnate or perhaps even collapse through failure to evoke from its population the necessary quantity and quality of labor. In order to judge this argument fairly it is necessary to examine the reasoning which lies behind it.

What motives are there for hard and conscientious work under capitalism? Let us concentrate for the moment on those

---

[3] The title of a much-discussed book, published in 1944, by Professor F. A. Hayek, of the London School of Economics.

who work under the direction of others, leaving the managerial function to the next section. Roughly, these motives may be described as being of two kinds: first, hope of higher earnings in a given job and of promotion to a better job; and second, fear of penalties, demotion, and ultimately dismissal. Hope of gain tends to call forth effort and initiative; fear of loss tends to check carelessness and maintain discipline.

There is no doubt—and certainly socialists never denied it— that under certain circumstances an appropriate combination of these motives can produce a well-disciplined and efficient labor force. Socialists maintain, however, that this fact by itself constitutes neither support for capitalism nor an argument against socialism. They claim that as capitalism matures it loses the capacity to make effective use of these motives; that socialism, notwithstanding a widespread belief to the contrary, can employ the same motives and can do so more scientifically than capitalism ever could; and finally, that some of the most important factors determining the quantity and quality of available labor lie altogether outside the realm of individual motivation and can operate positively only in a society from which private property and the class rule which goes with it have been eliminated. Let us examine these contentions in turn.

First, the argument that capitalism can make effective use of the motives of hope of gain and fear of loss usually proceeds on the explicit or implicit assumption that the labor force is unorganized and that each worker looks out only for himself regardless of what happens to his fellows. This assumption is never in complete accord with the facts, although in the early stages of capitalism it has generally been a fair approximation to the truth. One of the most characteristic phenomena of capitalist development, however, is the growth and spread of trade unionism. Now, whatever may be thought of trade unions in general (and socialists, of course, are among their strongest supporters), there can be no doubt that they fundamentally alter the terms on which the worker earns his livelihood. Unions deliberately blunt the edge of the motives on which the employer relies in a competitive labor market to get the most out of his labor force. Thus unions are generally hostile to incentive wage systems and accept them only under careful safeguards; they fight for a system of promotion by seniority; they place various limitations on the right of the employer to penalize and fire; and they insist that layoffs in time of depression shall follow the reverse order of seniority. This is not to argue, of course, that organized workers cease to hope for gain and to fear loss, but it does mean that these hopes and fears are now much less closely related to the quantity and quality of the work they perform. Moreover, in so far as such a relation continues to exist, it is not by any means of the simple sort which the theory we are examining assumes. To illustrate this point, compare the effect of heavy unemployment on a trade which is unorganized with its effect on a trade which is completely organized. In the unorganized trade each individual worker tends to exert himself to the utmost so that he can hold his job against those who are waiting to take his place and so that in the event of further layoffs he can avoid being one of the victims. In the organized trade, on the other hand, the workers as a group deliberately slow down and impose all sorts of make-work rules in order that whatever demand there is shall furnish a maximum of employment. Clearly, in the one case fear of loss makes for efficiency, in the other case for inefficiency.

It is impossible to make an accurate estimate of the impact of trade unions and the labor psychology which they represent on the traditional mechanisms of capitalism; and it is certainly true, as "pure and simple" unionists always point out, that their influence is by no means 100 per cent adverse to effort and efficiency. But one thing is certain, that capitalists themselves have no illusions about the importance of the problem, and in this case at any rate socialists can accept their opinion as authoritative. Where the two will differ is in their interpretation of the phenomenon, capitalists maintaining that trade unions are a disease of the system and socialists holding that trade unions are an inevitable and on the whole beneficial feature of the system.

Second, we come to the socialists' contention that socialism can make use of the traditional motives of hope of gain and fear of loss more effectively and scientifically than capitalism ever could. There are two reasons for this. In the first place workers do not object to the principle of rewarding efficiency and penalizing inefficiency as such; what they object to is that this principle should be used for the profit of a small class of capitalists rather than for the benefit of the workers themselves. Since under socialism production is planned in the interests of the community as a whole and since the community consists only of workers, this objection obviously loses its force. And in the second place, a socialist society can deliberately study and plan a system of rewards and penalties which will operate over the whole field of industry and hence contribute to the maximum degree not only to getting the best out of every worker but also to putting the right man in the right job.

In this connection, however, it must be remembered that the rewards and penalties need not (indeed cannot) be in every case identical with those upon which capitalism relics. To be sure, the level of money earnings is likely to be the most important element under both systems, but there is one extremely important capitalist penalty which socialism deliberately renounces, the fear of unemployment. A worker under socialism may be demoted, he may even be fired, but as long as a state of full employment is maintained—and a socialist system not only can maintain a state of full employment but has every interest in doing so [4]—he will always be able to get another job. This fact may, especially in the early stages of socialist development, seriously complicate the problem of maintaining labor discipline. It will not, however, make the problem insoluble. What it really means is that a socialist society will have to develop a code of labor law which ensures

[4] See the discussion of full employment in the Soviet Union, p. 34; also pp. 213–214.

the maintenance of labor discipline, in much the same way that capitalism has evolved a code of commercial law which ensures the maintenance of discipline in such matters as payment of debts, fulfillment of contracts, and the like. This suggestion will shock only those who believe that loss of income and possibly starvation imposed by private individuals are more rational penalties than a fine or a temporary restriction on freedom of movement imposed by duly constituted courts of law.

We now come to the third and probably the most important socialist contention in the field of labor efficiency, namely that a class society cannot evoke the enthusiastic and conscientious cooperation of the underprivileged classes. When the traditional mechanism of individual spurs and checks has been thrown out of gear by the growth of labor solidarity and trade unionism, there is no substitute for capitalism to fall back on. As Professor Tawney has well said, "it is useless to urge that he [the worker] should produce more wealth for the community, unless at the same time he is assured that it is the community which will benefit in proportion as more wealth is produced." [5] Moreover, he can be given no such assurance

> as long as he is directly the servant of a profit-making company, and only indirectly the servant of the community. . . .
> It can be offered only in so far as he stands in an immediate and direct relation to the public for whom industry is carried on, so that, when all costs have been met, any surplus will pass to it, and not to private individuals. It will be accepted only in so far as the workers in each industry are not merely servants executing orders, but themselves have a collective responsibility for the character of the service, and can use their organizations not merely to protect themselves against exploitation, but to make positive contributions to the administration and development of their industry.[6]

[5] *The Acquisitive Society*, pp. 136–137.
[6] *Ibid.*, pp. 137–138.

The case for socialism, in so far as it is based on grounds of labor efficiency, has never been stated more clearly or concisely.

Economic Leadership under Capitalism and Socialism

No one who is familiar with the history of the last two centuries can doubt that the greatest triumphs of the capitalist system have been won in the field of economic leadership. Marx and Engels could say a century ago, in the *Manifesto:*

> The bourgeoisie, during its rule of scarce one hundred years, has created more massive and more colossal productive forces than have all preceding generations together. Subjection of nature's forces to man, machinery, application of chemistry to industry and agriculture, steam-navigation, railways, electric telegraphs, clearing of whole continents for cultivation, canalisation of rivers, whole populations conjured out of the ground—what earlier century had even a presentiment that such productive forces slumbered in the lap of social labour?

And today we must say that the second century of bourgeois rule has produced at least as many remarkable achievements in the fields of technique and construction.

Defenders of capitalism maintain that these accomplishments are attributable to the driving force of the profit motive,[7] and in this they are largely correct. All things considered, the profit motive has proved to be one of the most powerful social forces

[7] It should be clearly understood that the term "profit motive," as it is generally used, does not mean simply the desire for material gain, though some writers confuse the two ideas when it suits their purpose to do so. The desire for material gain has existed in most, if not all, societies with which we are familiar. The profit motive, on the other hand, means the desire to maximize a specific category of income which does not exist in all forms of society and which acquires decisive importance only under capitalism. See the discussion of the nature of capitalism in Chap. 6.

in the history of the human race. If one could somehow imagine
that it had never been allowed to operate outside the narrow
limits of trade and moneylending, one would have to picture the
twentieth century as being no more advanced compared to, say,
the fifteenth century than the fifteenth century was compared to
the tenth. There would be no factories, no railroads, no electric
power, no great cities with millions of inhabitants—even more,
there would be no proletariat and no socialism. Socialists not
only admit all this; they insist on it as the key to understanding
the world we live in. How then, it may be asked, can they propose to abolish capitalism and with it the profit motive? How
can they hope to do without this powerful engine of economic
efficiency and progress?

In order to answer these questions it is necessary to remember
that the development of capitalism has brought with it basic
changes in the significance and functioning of the profit motive.
Until roughly the last quarter of the nineteenth century the typical capitalist enterprise—typical, that is, in the sense of being
decisive for the operation of the system as a whole—was under
the immediate control of an entrepreneur, who concentrated in
his own person an extraordinary variety of functions and responsibilities. (Nothing essential in the argument is changed if, as
often happened, the entrepreneur consisted of a small group of
partners; hence it is legitimate to speak in terms of a single individual. It should also be noted that the mere fact of legal incor-
poration, unless accompanied by other changes which will be discussed presently, is without economic significance.) He was an
owner of capital, an employer of labor, an organizer of production, and a salesman of commodities. It was his energy, skill,
shrewdness, and luck that decided the success or failure of the
enterprise. Moreover, and this is the crucial point, he carried out
his numerous functions and exercised whatever faculties he possessed in direct response to the profit motive. Success meant, *to
him personally*, the amassing of a fortune, security for himself
and family, social advancement. Failure meant poverty, frustra-

tion of ambition, social degradation. Under these conditions the making of profits not only furnished the criteria by which all important economic decisions were made—in the nature of the case capitalism knows no other criteria—but also exerted a direct and powerful pressure on the entrepreneur who both made the decisions and saw to it that they were carried out.

The basic change which occurred during the late nineteenth and early twentieth centuries can be briefly described by saying that the typical capitalist enterprise outgrew the personal entrepreneur. His functions and responsibilities were now split up among a number of more or less separate groups. The function of the capitalist—to provide capital—was assumed by shareholders whose only concern was the state of the corporation's profit-and-loss account and the price of its shares. The functions of employer of labor, organizer of production, and salesman of commodities were taken over by a hierarchy of salaried officials, engineers, and accountants, who became increasingly specialized and expert in their respective spheres of activity. Final authority in a corporation of this sort lies with a board of directors, nominally elected by the body of shareholders but actually chosen by a complex process in which not only those who exercise capitalist and entrepreneurial functions but also outside groups (such as bankers or important customers) normally play a part. The role of the board of directors is that of coordinator and arbitrator; it has to see that the various parties at interest do not work at cross purposes and to settle disputes which may arise among them.

What of the profit motive in a system dominated by large-scale corporate enterprise? We must be clear on one point: the making of profits remains the objective of the corporation as such. Within the economic and legal framework of capitalism there is no other possible goal for a business unit to pursue, whatever its form may be. In order to convince ourselves that this is the case, it is necessary only to reflect that if the officials of a corporation were deliberately to set out to pursue some other objective—say, the maximum welfare of the community in which its factories happened to be located—a shareholder would be able to go into court and get an injunction restraining them from following this course on the ground that they were failing in their legal obligation to manage his property with reasonable diligence and prudence. In other words, the law imposes on corporation officials a positive obligation to make profits; and it is obvious that if they fail to do so over a considerable period of time, the business will have to be liquidated and they will be out of a job. But this is a very different thing from saying that the corporation officials are activated by the profit motive in the same sense as the old-fashioned entrepreneur. Let us examine this question more closely; it is crucial to the socialist contention that socialism can do without the profit motive.

We have seen that in the single-man enterprise there is a direct and powerful relation between the profit goal and the performance of the entrepreneurial function. In the large corporation this relation no longer exists. Corporation officials, like government officials, work for salaries. Profits go directly or indirectly to shareholders. It is true that some corporations have a bonus scheme for rewarding leading officials in proportion to profits earned, but the fact that many corporations do not pay bonuses proves them to be far from an essential feature of the corporate system. It is also true that there are large corporations in which the leading officials are at the same time large shareholders and therefore benefit directly in proportion to the profits of their firms. But, as in the case of bonuses, there is ample evidence that this partial identification of shareholders and corporate officials is incidental rather than essential to the functioning of the corporate system. The corporations in which officials hold only negligible quantities of stock are generally as successful as those in which the officials are large stockholders. *In principle,* the development of the large corporation has separated the receiving of profits from the performance of entrepreneurial functions; the fact that the principle is not always completely realized in practice should not be allowed to obscure the fundamental nature of the change that has taken place.

What is the significance of this change? If it were true, as many defenders of capitalism maintain, that the tasks of economic leadership can be effectively performed only under the spur of the profit motive, it would follow logically that the last 50 years must have witnessed a deterioration of capitalism's capacity to manage, organize, and innovate. But, of course, nothing of the sort has happened. The modern large corporation is both more efficient and technologically more progressive than the one-man enterprise ever was. The reason for this is clearly that training and specialization are economically more important than personal interest. Professor Schumpeter, who has probably done more than any other contemporary economist to bring out the creative role of the individual entrepreneur in the development of capitalism, puts his finger on the crucial point when he writes:

> Technological progress is increasingly becoming the business of teams of trained specialists who turn out what is required and make it work in predictable ways. The romance of earlier commercial adventure is rapidly wearing away, because so many more things can be strictly calculated that had of old to be visualized in a flash of genius.[8]

Nor does Professor Schumpeter balk at drawing the logical inference: "Since capitalist enterprise," he writes, "by its very achievements, tends to automatize progress, we conclude that it ends by making itself superfluous."[9] The socialist need claim no more.

It may be objected that all this has to do with capitalism and does not provide any solution to the problem of economic leadership under socialism. But surely with respect to forms and methods, though not with respect to aims, socialism has simply to take

[8] J. A. Schumpeter, *Capitalism, Socialism, and Democracy* (1942), p. 132.
[9] *Ibid.*, p. 134.

over where big business leaves off. Economic units under socialism will be rationalized versions of the large corporation, with
salaried executives and qualified specialists occupying the decisive managerial positions, and with the functions of the board of
directors in the hands of duly constituted public authorities.
The crucial difference, of course, will be that the objective of the
socialist unit will be fulfillment of its share of the general plan,
where the objective of the capitalist firm is the maximization of
the profit of the corporation. So far as either of these objectives
provides an incentive to the various persons concerned, it would
seem that fulfilling the plan, since it is both more intelligible
and more obviously related to the welfare of the community,
would be the more stimulating. The socialist, however, does not
need to insist on this in order to refute the contention that socialism would bog down in a morass of inefficiency and technological backwardness. If it is agreed that big-business capitalism
is efficient and technologically progressive, then it is sufficient
to know that socialism could do at least as well.

Further Considerations on the Problem of Efficiency

There are certain further considerations bearing on the relative efficiency of capitalism and socialism which do not properly
fall under either of the headings so far discussed but which arise
instead from the differing structures of the two systems.

First, there is the problem of the growing scale and complexity
of technological research. About the turn of the last century it
became apparent that neither the individual inventor nor the relatively small one-man business enterprise could undertake the
research and experimentation required to exploit the possibilities of science and technology which were then opening up. It
was necessary for the big corporation, with its well-equipped
laboratories and staffs of trained scientists, to step into the picture. But today we can already see that the requirements of further progress are beginning to outgrow the resources of even the

largest corporation. The most dramatic illustration of this, of course, is the atomic bomb, which is said to have involved an outlay of 2 billion dollars, certainly much more than the largest corporation could ever afford to spend on a research and development program. The capitalist state is capable of carrying out such projects for military purposes, but it cannot be expected to supersede private industry in so far as research into methods of increasing and improving peacetime production is concerned. The reason for this is inherent in the structure of capitalist industry: each firm or industry seeks competitive advantage through research and can neither relinquish responsibility to the government nor pool resources with its rivals. Hence it is inevitable that under capitalism work of this kind should be undertaken on a comparatively limited scale and in an uncoordinated fashion. The advantages enjoyed by socialism in this respect are too obvious to require elaboration.

Second, there is the problem of the waste which results from depressions and unemployment. We have already seen in Chapter 7 how Marxian theory relates these phenomena to the structure of capitalism. But one need not be a Marxist to agree that capitalism inevitably gives rise to booms and slumps; in this respect the conclusions reached by Marxists are not essentially very different from those of the outstanding modern bourgeois theorists (for example, Keynes and Schumpeter). Moreover, there is almost equally wide agreement that a planned socialist economy would be able to maintain a steady rate of economic advance and thus avoid the periodic waste of idle resources and underproduction. Thus, to take several representative authorities, Professor Schumpeter holds that the planning of progress "would eliminate the cause of the cyclical ups and downs whereas in the capitalist order it is only possible to mitigate them." [10] Professor Pigou, dean of the Cambridge school of economists, concludes, after a careful analysis of the problem, that there is "little doubt

[10] *Ibid.*, p. 195.

that, for tackling the problem of unemployment, a socialist system, with central planning, has definite advantages over a capitalist one." [11] And Dr. Klein, one of the younger Keynesians, expresses a view which would probably be accepted by most of the followers of the late Lord Keynes when he says: "Proper policy by socialist planners can always lead to full employment." [12] If one takes into account the magnitude of the losses of income from depressions—the total figure for the years 1930–1938 in the United States has been estimated at 133 billion dollars [13]—one may well conclude that the ability of socialism to avoid these wastes is its greatest single economic advantage.

Third, there is the problem of the waste involved in selling commodities under capitalism. We are not, of course, referring to the necessary costs of transportation, stocking, display, delivery, and the like, which are common to both capitalism and socialism, but rather to the costs of advertising and salesmanship which are incurred by profit-seeking producers and merchants in an effort to get customers to buy *their* products instead of some other seller's products. No exact estimate can be made of the amount of socially futile effort that is expended in this way, but many persons (especially socialists) are likely to put the total high. Needless to say, a centrally planned system would by its very nature eliminate the problem of competitive salesmanship.

Fourth, there is the related problem of the waste of resources and manpower, especially high-grade managerial talent, which is involved in coping with the all-pervading uncertainties of the capitalist system. As Professor Schumpeter has well said,

> one of the most important difficulties of running a business —the difficulty which absorbs most of the energy of the successful business leader—consists in the uncertainties surrounding every decision. . . . The managements of social-

[11] A. C. Pigou, *Socialism versus Capitalism* (1937), p. 67.
[12] L. R. Klein, *The Keynesian Revolution* (1947), p. 79.
[13] Temporary National Economic Committee, *Hearings,* Part I, p. 16.

ized industries and plants would be in a position to know exactly what the other fellows proposed to do and nothing would prevent them from getting together for concerted action. The central board could, and to a certain extent would unavoidably, act as a clearing house of information and as a coordinator of decisions. . . . This would immensely reduce the amount of work to be done in the workshops of managerial brains and much less intelligence would be necessary to run such a system than is required to steer a concern of any importance through the waves and breakers of the capitalist sea.[14]

Fifth, there are what Professor Schumpeter has called the "costs and losses incident to the struggle" between private business and public authority.[15] For a variety of reasons as capitalism matures, the state plays a more and more active part in the economic process; and this activity, though it is frequently in the interests of the system as a whole (as in the regulation of railroad and public-utility rates), necessarily appears to the private corporations as "interference," which has to be countered and if possible rendered ineffectual. The result is that there is a tendency for two bureaucracies, each swollen by the necessity of fighting the other, to be built up where one would be sufficient to do all that is required from a strictly eonomic point of view. Here again the expansion of the public sphere and the contraction of the private sphere which socialism brings about would largely eliminate this problem. As Professor Pigou puts the issue: "Would it not obviate expense, overlapping and, above all, friction, if, instead of there being a controlling authority *plus* a controlled one, control and operation were united, as under socialism they would be, in the same hand?"[16]

Finally, as an offset to the foregoing advantages enjoyed by

[14] Schumpeter, *op. cit.*, p. 186.
[15] *Ibid.*, p. 197.
[16] Pigou, *op. cit.*, pp. 45–46.

socialism, there are the costs and losses incident to setting up and operating a system of central economic planning. These involve not only the staffing of the planning agencies as such but also the wastes resulting from the mistakes which are bound to occur in formulating and carrying out anything so vast and complicated as a central economic plan. No quantitative estimate of this factor is possible, and analysts will certainly differ widely in their judgment of its importance. Defenders of capitalism are likely to assume that the wastes of central planning are more than enough to offset the advantages of socialism, while socialists are likely to assume that all serious difficulties will be overcome as experience and "know-how" are accumulated. We may cite Professor Pigou's view as one that falls somewhere between these extremes:

> How nearly complete success will be approached [in solving the practical problem facing a central planning authority] depends, of course, on the degree of skill and probity of the controlling authority itself, and of the subordinate bodies through which it works. But except in a world of supermen, many and grave lapses are certain to occur. In any country where socialism as an ideal is being weighed against capitalism as a fact, this truth must be borne in mind.[17]

The Lessons of Soviet Experience

We cannot leave the subject of the relative efficiency and progressiveness of capitalism and socialism without saying something about the lessons of Soviet experience. It might be argued that the simplest way to settle the whole issue would be to compare the actual situation in the Soviet Union with that in one of the advanced capitalist countries, say the United States. But the fallacy of this suggestion is obvious. Capitalism has been developing in the United States for more than 150 years under the

[17] *Ibid.*, pp. 119–120.

most favorable conditions in the world, while socialism has been developing in the Soviet Union for only about 25 years under conditions which have been in many respects very unfavorable. To judge the systems by comparing their respective performances in the two countries would be like judging the effectiveness of two educational systems by giving the same test to a college graduate of one and a grammar-school graduate of the other. Nor would it be easy to find a capitalist country that is fairly comparable to the Soviet Union in the respects which now interest us. This does not mean that nothing can be learned from the experience of the world's first socialist country; it only means that one must study that experience in its historical context and exercise both caution and restraint in generalizing from it.

With this in mind, we may reproduce the relevant conclusions of the late Sidney and Beatrice Webb in their monumental study, *Soviet Communism*.[18] The Webbs are valuable witnesses for two reasons: they spent the better part of their lives in studying the institutional development of British capitalism and hence have a good sense of historical perspective against which to view Soviet developments; and, as the intellectual parents (along with George Bernard Shaw) of British Fabianism, they came to the study of the Soviet Union without any particular sympathy for either capitalism or the Bolshevik regime in Russia. Here is what the Webbs wrote in summing up their study of the subject before us:

> To end this chapter on the communist incentives "in place of profit" we may be permitted to draw the student's attention to its strangely ironic conclusion. The one striking superiority of the capitalist organization of industry over that of Soviet Communism is not found in the profit-makers' control and direction of production and distribution. . . . Nor does any such superiority manifest itself in the capitalists' capacity to evoke, from the mass of the manual workers,

[18] First edition 1935, second edition 1937. The passage quoted is from the one-volume edition of 1944, pp. 651–652.

either that universal continuous participation in the work of production, or that assiduity and inventiveness, which are both indispensable to the maximum output of the community as a whole. Alike in directing industry so as to satisfy the needs and desires of the entire community, and in obtaining from the whole mass of manual workers the utmost useful production, Soviet Communism bids fair actually to surpass the achievement of profit-making capitalism. Yet, as we have suggested, there is one part of the structure of wealth-production in which the organization of capitalist industry has so far shown itself superior in efficiency to that of Soviet Communism. This is in the zeal, honesty, punctuality and loyalty to be counted on in Great Britain and some other countries of western Europe in the large and heterogeneous category of salaried workers who fill the intermediate positions between the directors and controllers of policy on the one hand, and the manual workers engaged in direct production on the other. It is in this middle section of the organization, comprising the clerical and accounting staffs, the foremen and overseers who combine high craftsmanship with managerial capacity, the chiefs of railway depots and local repair shops, the train conductors, the multitude of store managers, shop assistants and cashiers—the human links between those few who plan and direct and the many who actually produce—that the capitalists' industry at present shows its greatest superiority. It is owing to the manifest shortcomings of this intermediate section in the USSR that the aggregate results of soviet industry have not been all that might have been expected; that there has been in so many soviet enterprises such a terrifying wearing out and breaking of machinery, such a waste of material and components, and such an amount of production of inferior quality. In the industrial organization of Great Britain, we venture to say, this intermediate section is markedly superior to the corresponding section in the USSR. And yet it is exactly this salaried "lower middle class" that has been, under modern capitalism, most assiduously excluded from the incentive of profit-making!

These findings are quite consistent with the analysis of this chapter. They emphasize the capacity of socialism to evoke an enthusiastic response from the mass of the workers and the relative unimportance of the profit motive under modern conditions of large-scale industry. Nor are the Webbs' observations on the comparative merits of the British and Soviet "middle sections" surprising when viewed in terms of the history of the two countries. British capitalism set out well over a century ago to provide itself with an adequate supply of literate and reliable workers for the intermediate jobs; this was one of the strongest forces making for the spread of popular education. Pre-Revolutionary Russia, on the other hand, had made only feeble beginnings in this direction. The Bolsheviks have accomplished a great deal, but it could hardly be expected that they would catch up with Britain in two or three decades. What is important from the point of view of the problem of this chapter is that the deficiencies of the Soviet middle section are an inheritance from the Russian past and have nothing to do with the nature of socialism. Indeed, the rapid progress of the period since the Revolution suggests that socialism is at least as capable as capitalism of molding a largely feudal population to the requirements of modern industry and science.

CHAPTER 11

Can Socialism Utilize Resources Rationally?

IT WAS POINTED OUT in the introduction to the last chapter that there are those who deny that socialism can achieve a rational utilization of productive resources and that the well-known publicist Walter Lippmann believes that "an acquaintance with this school of socialist criticism is indispensable to all who would now discuss the problem of collectivism." What, then, is this school and what are its main doctrines?

The Viennese School of Antisocialism

Leading socialist thinkers, at least since the time of Marx and Engels, have been aware of the fact that socialism, like every other form of society, would have to develop a mechanism for allocating resources among different branches of production and for distributing goods and services to consumers. As Marx himself said,

> Every child knows that the mass of products corresponding to the different needs require different and quantitatively determined masses of the total labour of society. That this necessity of distributing social labour in definite proportions cannot be done away with by the *particular form* of social production, but can only change the *form it assumes,* is self-evident.[1]

But Marx and Engels declined "to write recipes for the cookshops of the future." Their job was to hasten the coming of socialism,

[1] Karl Marx and Friedrich Engels, *Correspondence, 1846–1895: A Selection with Commentary and Notes* (1935), p. 246. Italics in original.

not to tell future generations how to run it; and this self-imposed limitation was generally observed by their followers.

For a long time the attitude taken by Marxists on this issue was accepted as reasonable by socialists and antisocialists alike. True, in the early years of the present century the problem was discussed by a few continental economists, some of whom doubted the capacity of socialism to solve it, while others presented what they regarded as satisfactory socialist solutions.[2] It would be an exaggeration to speak of a debate in this connection, however; and when the late Professor Taussig wrote his *Principles of Economics* in 1911, he merely referred to the argument "that goods could not be valued" under socialism—in other words, that no rational allocation of resources could be achieved—as one of the objections to socialism that "are of little weight." And this is where the matter stood until after the First World War.

In the years immediately after the Russian Revolution and the war, however, the peoples of several European countries were more or less obliged to take a stand on the question of socialism whether they wanted to or not; and under these circumstances every argument for and against socialism was brought out and dressed up as attractively as possible. Naturally the argument "that goods could not be valued" was not neglected. It now reappeared almost simultaneously in the writings of the Russian economist Boris Brutzkus, the German sociologist Max Weber, and the Austrian economist Ludwig Mises. Among these three versions by far the most emphatic, elaborate, and in the long run influential was that of Mises, himself a follower of the famous Austrian school of economics, which had been founded by Menger, Böhm-Bawerk, and Wieser in the late nineteenth century. Owing almost entirely to the efforts of Mises, the doctrine

[2] F. A. Hayek (ed.), *Collectivist Economic Planning* (1935). This book contains some account of these early discussions, together with translations of articles by the Dutch economist Pierson and the Italian economist Barone, written in 1902 and 1908 respectively, which typify the two attitudes mentioned in the text.

in question became closely identified with the postwar Viennese group; and when the members of this group moved to England and America as the fortunes of Austria declined, they brought the doctrine with them. It is for this reason that we are justified in speaking of the Viennese school of antisocialism.

The argument of Mises is extremely simple.[3] Reduced to essentials, it consists of the following steps: (1) under capitalism resources are allocated to various industries and the appropriate methods of production are determined through the medium of a price system, which in turn is regulated by the market competition of independent owners of the means of production (with this proposition, incidentally, socialist as well as bourgeois economists are in agreement); (2) under socialism all means of production are the property of the community as a whole; (3) since, therefore, there are no independent owners to compete on the market, it follows that there can be no pricing of the means of production under socialism; (4) without prices for the means of production rational economic calculation is impossible; (5) hence, finally, socialism is bound to fail.

It must be remembered that the article in which Mises first stated this position came out in 1920, at a time when the Soviet Union was in the midst of its so-called War Communism phase of development,[4] and when many loose and ill-thought-out socialist schemes were being freely bandied about. Not a few of these schemes envisaged the abandonment of money and prices under socialism and included glowing descriptions of the advantages of a purely "natural" economy. Considered as an attack on such fantasies, Mises' argument was undoubtedly justified and served

---

[3] Mises' article "Economic Calculation in the Socialist Commonwealth," in *ibid.,* contains all that is necessary for an understanding of his position. His larger work, published in English under the title *Socialism: An Economic and Sociological Analysis* (1936), adds nothing so far as the problem here under discussion is concerned.

[4] See pp. 16–17.

the valuable purpose of cutting the ground from under the feet of some of the more imaginative Utopia builders.

But Mises made the mistake of identifying those schemes which were open to legitimate attack with socialism in general. Time and again he asserted, flatly and with no supporting evidence, that in the absence of private ownership of the means of production there can be no pricing of the means of production. If this is granted, the rest of the argument follows; if it is disproved, the whole case collapses. His opponents, therefore, had only to demonstrate that rational pricing of the means of production is consistent with common ownership of the means of production to dispose of Mises once and for all.

There is no general agreement as to who should be given credit for first presenting such a demonstration, but in any case there is no doubt that the task was adequately performed by the late Professor F. M. Taylor in his presidential address to the American Economic Association in 1928.[5] Taylor took the position that the right way for a socialist state to allocate resources would be to distribute income to its citizens in the form of money to be spent in a free market for consumers' goods. The state should then be guided by consumers' demand in the sense that the various goods and services should be produced in such quantities as could be sold at prices equal to costs of production. Taylor recognized that this would involve imputing values to the factors of production and—perhaps with Mises and his followers in mind—that "it is not unlikely that more than one economist would question the possibility of solving that problem at all under the conditions necessarily prevailing in a socialist state." [6]

Taylor brushed these doubts aside as quite unfounded. The socialist state, he argued, could solve the problem of imputation by a process of trial and error. It would assign values to factors of production on the basis of a careful study of available data,

[5] This address is reprinted in Benjamin Lippincott (ed.), *On the Economic Theory of Socialism* (1938).
[6] *Ibid.*, p. 51.

and it would then proceed to act as though these provisional values were correct. Errors would show up in unmistakable ways: where values had been set too high, there would be undue parsimony in the use of the factor in question and a surplus would appear; where too low, there would be undue liberality in the use of the factor and a deficit would appear. "Surplus or deficit—one or the other would result from every wrong valuation of a factor." [7] The job of the authorities would then be to change the valuations in the indicated directions until finally the correct figures had been discovered. On the basis of this reasoning, Taylor concluded:

> I find myself disposed to affirm rather dogmatically that, if the economic authorities of a socialist state would recognize equality between cost of production on the one hand and the demand price of the buyer on the other as being the adequate and the only adequate proof that the commodity in question ought to be produced, they could, under all ordinary conditions, perform their duties, as the persons who were immediately responsible for the guidance of production, with well-founded confidence that they would never make any other than the right use of the economic resources placed at their disposal. [8]

Taylor's argument was unquestionably sound as far as it went, and it should have been sufficient to settle the issue. But Mises and his followers seem to have misunderstood Taylor. They assumed that he, in common with certain other writers who took up the problem a little later, had only tried

> to show that on the assumption of a complete knowledge of all relevant data, the values and the quantities of the different commodities to be produced might be determined

[7] *Ibid.,* p. 53.
[8] *Ibid.,* p. 54.

by the application of the apparatus by which theoretical economics explains the formation of prices and the direction of production in a competitive system.[9]

As we have seen, however, Taylor actually pointed out how the socialist state could make use of a trial-and-error method (not at all the apparatus of theoretical economics) to find the right valuations and quantities. By ignoring this demonstration, Professors Hayek and Robbins,[10] both of the London School of Economics and both under the influence of Mises, were able to carry on the debate and to reach influential persons in Britain and the United States who would have otherwise probably never heard of Mises.

Hayek and Robbins took a considerably less dogmatic position than Mises. They did not maintain, as the latter had, that without private property in the means of production it would be *theoretically* impossible to assign rational valuations to the means of production; they asserted rather that, while such a procedure might be logically conceivable, it was *practically* impossible. The gist of their position can be most easily conveyed by quoting a passage from Robbins:

> On paper we can conceive this problem to be solved by a series of mathematical calculations. We can imagine tables to be drawn up expressing the consumers' demand for all the different commodities, which could be produced by each of the various possible combinations of the factors of production. On such a basis a system of simultaneous equations could be constructed whose solution would show the equilibrium distribution of factors and the equilibrium production of commodities.
>
> But in practice this solution is quite unworkable. It would necessitate the drawing up of millions of equations on the

---

[9] F. A. Hayek, "The Present State of the Debate," in Hayek, *op. cit.*, p. 207.

[10] For Robbins's contribution, see Lionel Robbins, *The Great Depression* (1934), pp. 148–156.

basis of millions of statistical tables based on many more millions of individual computations. By the time the equations were solved, the information on which they were based would have become obsolete and they would need to be calculated anew. . . . There is no hope in this direction of discovering the relative sacrifices of alternative kinds of investment. There is no hope here of a means of adjusting production to meet the preferences of consumers.[11]

This argument is perhaps intellectually less satisfying than the logical certitudes of Mises, but its political implications are exactly the same; and this explains its ready acceptance by considerable sections of antisocialist opinion in Britain and America.

Lange's Refutation of the Viennese School

It is difficult to estimate how many nonsocialist economists accepted either the Mises or the Hayek-Robbins case against socialism; probably relatively fewer economists than publicists and editorial writers. But it is clear at any rate that a comprehensive answer from the socialist side was called for, and this was finally supplied by Dr. Oscar Lange in a paper entitled "On the Economic Theory of Socialism." [12] Lange's presentation is so concise and clear that it will be more useful to summarize the relevant parts than to attempt an independent appraisal of the doctrines of the Viennese school.

Lange begins with a tribute to Mises for having insistently called attention to the importance of a rational system of economic accounting to guide the allocation of resources in a socialist society. He points out, however, that Mises' denial of the possibility of such a rational system is based on a confusion regarding

[11] *Ibid.,* p. 151.

[12] First published in the *Review of Economic Studies,* October, 1936, and February, 1937; reprinted in Lippincott, *op. cit.* Quotations are from this volume.

the nature of prices. A price may be a concrete market fact between independent buyers and sellers or it may simply be what Lange calls "an index of terms on which alternatives are offered." In either case it can serve as the basis of a rational costing system. Mises' error was quite simply to assume that prices can exist and have meaning only in the former sense. Once it is recognized that this is not the case—and, of course, the experience of large capitalist concerns, which are always assigning "prices" for interdepartmental transactions, proves that it is not—Mises' argument collapses.

Lange next takes up the Hayek-Robbins modification of the Mises position. They admit the possibility of prices in the second sense but deny that in the absence of a market there is any practical method of discovering the right ones. Lange notes that this objection has already been answered in principle by Taylor but sees the need for further elaboration.

Lange then proceeds to a brief and lucid exposition of "the determination of equilibrium on a competitive market." The conditions of equilibrium are threefold: (1) each consumer and producer must so adjust his buying and selling that he cannot add to either his income or his satisfactions—this is called the "subjective condition"; (2) each price must be such that total supply of, and demand for, the commodity in question are in balance—this is called the "objective condition"; and (3) the incomes of consumers must be equal to their receipts from selling productive services plus profits. If these three conditions are fulfilled, resources are being utilized in a way which is rational from the point of view of the capitalist system with its unequal distribution of the ownership of means of production.

But the question arises as to how such an equilibrium could ever be arrived at in practice. There is no all-wise providence to establish the right system of prices, and the various individuals are concerned only with their own affairs. The answer, according to Lange, is that equilibrium is reached through a process of trial and error.

Let us start with a set of prices given *at random*. . . . On the basis of this *random* set of prices . . . the individuals fulfill their subjective equilibrium conditions and attain their maximum positions. For each commodity a quantity demanded and a quantity supplied is established. Now the objective equilibrium condition comes into play. If the quantity demanded and the quantity supplied happen to be equal, the entire situation is settled and the prices are the equilibrium prices. If, however, the quantities demanded and the quantities supplied diverge, the competition of the buyers and sellers will alter the prices. . . . As a result we get a *new* set of prices, which serves as a new base for the individuals' striving to satisfy their subjective equilibrium conditions. . . . And so the process goes on until the objective equilibrium condition is satisfied and equilibrium finally reached. Actually it is the *historically given* prices which serve as a basis for the process of successive trials.[13]

Lange next turns his attention to a socialist society in which the means of production are publicly owned but in which freedom of choice of consumption and freedom of choice of occupation are maintained. (This, incidentally, has been the normal peacetime situation in the Soviet Union.) In such a society markets for consumption goods and for labor exist, but there are no markets for capital goods and intermediate products. Goods which fall in the last two categories must be assigned a price for accounting purposes by the Central Planning Board. What are the equilibrium conditions for this case corresponding to those for the capitalist case analyzed above? (1) The subjective condition is in part the same and in part different. Workers will still maximize their incomes and their satisfactions, but plant managers will no longer be out to maximize their profits. Instead, they will regulate their "buying" and "selling" according to certain principles laid down by the Central Planning Board. These principles will

[13] *Ibid.*, pp. 72–73. Italics in original.

be considered presently; for the moment it is sufficient to know that they will be no less determinate than the principle of profit maximization. (2) The objective condition is the same in both cases: prices (whether market or accounting) must be such that the quantity of each commodity supplied is equal to the quantity demanded. (3) The final condition is different, since no consumers' incomes are derived from the ownership of means of production. Here again it is necessary that certain definite principles of income formation be laid down by the Central Planning Board. Lange solves this problem by assuming that each consumer will receive his wages plus a social dividend constituting his share of the income accruing to society because of its ownership of the means of production.

Lange next inquires into the rules which the Central Planning Board should prescribe for the conduct of plant managers and concludes that they should be two in number. First, each manager should be instructed to combine productive goods and services in such a way that average cost of production for any given output is a minimum. This will guarantee that no factor of production is used in such a way that its relative effectiveness might be greater in some other employment. Second, each manager should choose that scale of output which equates marginal cost to price. It is not sufficient, however, to address this second rule to plant managers alone; it must also be addressed to the managers of whole industries (for example, the National Coal Trust) so that they will know when to add new plants or to refrain from replacing old ones as they wear out. If these two rules are followed, the output of each industry and plant as well as the total demand for the various factors of production are determined, as they are when all entrepreneurs attempt to maximize their profits.

The question now arises as to what means are open to the Central Planning Board to find the equilibrium market and accounting prices. (In practice, though Lange does not say this, the Planning Board must set both kinds of prices; it does not matter in this respect whether they are used as a basis for actual market transactions or merely for accounting purposes.) The answer is formally analogous to that given in the case of the competitive system. The Planning Board makes the best estimate it can of the correct prices—in practice it would undoubtedly start from the historically given price system—and instructs all managers to act as though they were in fact the correct prices. Errors will then show up through the emergence of surpluses or shortages; price readjustments will be made; mistakes will again be observed; and so on until the equilibrium position has been reached. From this, Lange concludes as follows:

> As we have seen, there is not the slightest reason why a trial and error procedure, similar to that in a competitive market, could not work in a socialist economy to determine the accounting prices of capital goods and of the productive resources in public ownership. Indeed, it seems that this trial and error procedure would, or at least could, work *much better* in a socialist economy than in a competitive market. For the Central Planning Board has a much wider knowledge of what is going on in the whole economic system than any private entrepreneur can ever have, and, consequently, may be able to reach the right equilibrium prices by a *much shorter* series of successive trials than a competitive market actually does. The argument that in a socialist economy the accounting prices of capital goods and of productive services in public ownership cannot be determined objectively, either because this is theoretically impossible, or because there is no adequate trial and error procedure available, cannot be maintained.[14]

Lange thus not only refutes the antisocialist case of Mises and his followers but actually turns the tables on them by showing that socialism possesses definite advantages where they regard it as most vulnerable.

[14] *Ibid.,* pp. 89–90. Italics in original.

Finally, Lange shows that neither the possibility of rational accounting nor the use of the trial-and-error method is dependent on the special assumptions underlying the particular type of socialist society which he chooses for purposes of illustration. Freedom of choice of consumption and freedom of occupation can both be absent without making it impossible for the Central Planning Board to achieve a rational allocation of resources; the only difference is that in this case the valuation scales of the Planning Board are substituted for those of the individual citizens. This is significant not because there is any considerable body of socialist opinion which wants to abolish these freedoms, but because there are considerable sectors of consumption where individual freedom of choice either does not work at all or works very unsatisfactorily. This is true, for example, of highways, fire protection, health services, and national defence (if security from external aggression can be classified as a consumers' good). In providing goods and services of this kind, the valuations of the Planning Board, or of some other public agency, must be substituted for those of the individual consumers. Lange's analysis shows that this necessity in no way interferes with the possibility of establishing a rational allocation and costing system.

Planning and the Utilization of Resources

As far as the economics profession is concerned, Lange's paper may be regarded as having finally removed any doubts about the capacity of socialism to utilize resources rationally. Professor Schumpeter probably expresses the opinion of the great majority of competent economists—socialist and nonsocialist alike—when he says not only that socialism passes the test of "logical definiteness and consistency" but also that it is "eminently operational." [15] Even Professor Hayek seems to have retreated from his earlier position; at any rate there are hardly any traces in *The Road to*

[15] *Capitalism, Socialism, and Democracy,* pp. 184, 185.

Serfdom of the antisocialist arguments which we have been examining in this chapter. In this work Hayek builds his case against socialism on the ground that it is incompatible with freedom, the contention which will be examined in the next chapter. There are, of course, still many who believe that socialism is impossible for economic reasons, but with their chief intellectual arsenal out of production it seems reasonable to suppose that they will gradually run out of ammunition and either give up the fight or resort to other weapons.

It would, however, be a mistake to assume that the debate which we have been reviewing exhausts the problems of resource utilization under socialism. All it really does is to dispose of certain preliminaries and prepare the ground for consideration of the substantive problems of socialist planning. It is impossible in the space available to discuss these problems in detail, but it is desirable to indicate their general character. This is particularly important since the reader might otherwise get the impression that real-life socialism would have to, or in some sense ought to, conform to Lange's model, forgetting that the latter was designed to serve a definite and relatively restricted theoretical purpose.

Perhaps the most striking feature of Lange's model is that the function of the Central Planning Board is virtually confined to providing a substitute for the market as the coordinator of the activities of the various plants and industries. The truth is that Lange's Board is not a *planning* agency at all but rather a *price-fixing* agency; in his model production decisions are left to a myriad of essentially independent units, just as they are under capitalism.

Such a system is certainly conceivable, but most socialists will probably feel that it reproduces some of the worst features of capitalism and fails to take advantage of the constructive possibilities of economic planning. Moreover, as H. D. Dickinson has pointed out, an "unplanned collectivism" is most unlikely in practice.

It is easy to see [he writes] that it would almost inevitably slide into a planned system. The separateness of the various enterprises and the mutual blindness of those who conduct them, while natural under private ownership, would be a highly artificial state of affairs under public ownership. The organs of public economy would have every reason for mutual consultation and publicity, none for separateness and secrecy. In particular, the organs responsible for the investment of savings and the creation of new capital would, by the very nature of their functions, tend to envisage their task from the viewpoint of the social economy as a whole, and thus become, whether they would or not, planning organs. Thus, unplanned collectivism, although logically thinkable, is unlikely to occur in practice.[16]

As this statement suggests, the management of investment is the crux of the whole problem. Investment is forward-looking activity. It must be based on assumptions about the future; it also helps to shape the future. And by its effect on the current utilization of resources it is likewise one of the decisive factors determining the size and composition of present consumable income. In an unplanned economy—whether capitalist or collectivist—investment decisions are made by many independent units, each of which is obliged to operate on its own forecasts and estimates. Since the probability that all these forecasts and estimates will be consistent is so small as to be negligible, it follows that any individual will be right only by the sheerest accident. The result is that no one knows where such an economy is headed; and in it the practice of economic rationality on any but the most restricted plane is out of the question. It is this circumstance that accounts for the irrational behavior of an unplanned economy: the alternation of booms and slumps, the coexistence of gluts and shortages, the paradox of unemployed workers with unsatisfied wants. These are the unwanted products of a system which makes independent

[16] H. D. Dickinson, *The Economics of Socialism* (1939), p. 17.

units responsible for investment decisions and then leaves it to the market to coordinate them regardless of the consequences.

Since the means of production are publicly owned in a socialist society, it follows that responsibility for investment decisions necessarily falls on the state as the representative of the public. As Dickinson indicates, it is scarcely conceivable that the socialist state will so decentralize the making of investment decisions as to recreate the blindness and uncertainty of unplanned capitalism. Moreover, it is not hard to see that the centralization of investment decisions makes comprehensive economic planning all but inevitable. Assume, for example, that the government of a socialist society makes a basic policy decision to invest a certain percentage of the national income over a period of, say, five or ten years and lays down certain general goals such as the building up of heavy industry, the rehousing of a specified proportion of the population, and the development of hitherto backward regions. The next step would naturally be to charge the Central Planning Board with the task of drawing up an investment plan for carrying out these decisions. This investment plan will begin by translating the general goals laid down by the government into quantitative terms: so many new factories, railroads, power plants, mines, apartment houses, schools, hospitals, theaters, and so forth. The dates at which these various construction projects are to be started and finished will then be specified. From these data it will be possible to draw up schedules of the different kinds of materials and labor which will be required. At this point the investment plan may be said to be complete. But would it be sensible for the Central Planning Board to stop here and to rely on price and income controls to ensure that what is needed will be ready at the right time, at the right place, and in the right quantities?

The answer is surely that it would not be. When the needs of the investment plan have been determined, the Central Planning Board will, almost as a matter of course, take steps to see that they are met; and this can be done only by extending the scope of the plan to include the various sectors of the economy which are directly concerned. Such an extension is not possible, however, if only the requirements of investment are taken into account, since materials and manpower are needed for both consumption and investment purposes. Hence the Central Planning Board will find it necessary to estimate consumer demand for all products which compete for resources with the investment plan and to draw up a second set of schedules showing the different kinds of materials and labor which will be required. It should now be possible, by consolidating the investment and consumption schedules and by comparing them with current and prospective supplies, to work out a general plan for the development of the economy over the period in question.

When this is done, it may be found that the investment plan is overambitious and would entail excessive cuts in certain types of consumption, perhaps even necessitating rationing in some lines; or it may be found that the general level of consumption which has been allowed will permit an even more extensive development of investment in some directions. If discrepancies of this sort are discovered, the Central Planning Board will have to seek new directives from the government as a basis for revising the plan and bringing it into line with objective possibilities. When a consistent and practical plan has finally been adopted, it cannot be left to the discretion of individual industry and plant managers whether or not they will conform to it; rather it must be their first duty, imposed by law, to carry out their part of the plan to the best of their ability—just as, for example, it is the duty of corporate managers under capitalism to make profits for the owners.

It must be said at once that the argument of the preceding paragraph will admit of certain qualifications. The plan, in the sense of a coordinated set of directives to the managers of production, does not need to be all-inclusive. For example, a considerable sector of private ownership in agriculture and handicrafts may be retained in a predominantly socialist society, and it may be perfectly possible to coordinate this private sector with the general development of the economy by means of indirect financial controls and incentives. But this is possible only if the socialized sector is predominant, and it should not obscure the general principle that there is a very strong tendency for partial planning to become comprehensive planning.

It is hard to say whether the experience of the Soviet Union can be fairly taken as an illustration of the working of this principle. It is true that planning in the Soviet Union started in particular branches of the national economy and developed only gradually into the comprehensive system which functions today. As Baykov has expressed it, "the Control Figures gradually grew from a *series* of figures and measures taken in separate industries into a *system* of figures knitting more closely together the planned measures to be taken in various branches of the national economy in the ensuing year." [17] But since the Bolsheviks were from the outset aiming at a comprehensively planned system, it could be argued that events would have followed the same course whether or not there is an immanent tendency for partial planning to become comprehensive.

This argument, however, could not be applied to the war economies of capitalist countries. Here it is normal for planning to begin with military requirements and gradually to spread to other sectors of the economy; and the reason is clearly not attachment to planning as such but rather the empirical discovery that the interdependence of the various sectors forces the authorities to assume an increasingly direct and comprehensive control over the utilization of resources. While there are, of course, fundamental differences between a socialist economy and a wartime capitalist economy, there is no reason to suppose that the forces which drive the latter to more and more comprehensive planning would not also operate in the former. *In this respect,* the main

[17] A. Baykov, *The Development of the Soviet Economic System* (1946), p. 440.

difference seems to be that these forces would meet with fewer ideological and practical barriers in the socialist economy.

We may, then, regard it as established by both theoretical reasoning and practical experience that a socialist economy will be centrally planned in a sense very different from that in which Lange's model may be said to be centrally planned. Lange's Central Planning Board is primarily a price-fixing agency, whereas in any actual socialist society it must be expected that the function of the Central Planning Board will be to lay down concrete directives which will be binding on the managers of socialized industries and plants.

This conclusion raises an important question which must be answered before our discussion of the utilization of resources under socialism can be considered complete. We have already seen that the possibility of rational accounting and allocation of resources exists in Lange's model. Is this also true of a comprehensively planned economy? Is it possible that in going from one to the other we have unwittingly fallen into the clutches of Mises and his followers? The answer is that rational accounting and allocation are still possible under comprehensive planning. The only quarry which Mises and his followers can hope to bag is the now nearly extinct breed of socialist who wants to do away with all money and prices and to calculate everything in physical quantities. As the experience of the Soviet Union proves, there is no conflict between comprehensive planning and money calculation; once this is admitted, it is not difficult to show that rationality in Lange's sense is quite compatible with comprehensive planning.

The crucial difference between Lange's model and the comprehensively planned economy lies in the location of the authority to make decisions about production. In the one these decisions are made by many independent units; in the other by the Central Planning Board. (This is, of course, oversimplified since in any case considerable latitude must be left to the managers on the spot, but the oversimplification serves to sharpen rather than obscure the issue.) The important thing, from our present point of view, is that this shift in the location of the authority to make production decisions in no way disturbs the logic of Lange's argument. In his model, managers of plants and industries are directed to make their decisions according to certain rules; it is obvious that the Central Planning Board—or rather those sections of it which devote their attention to production problems—can be directed to follow exactly the same rules. It follows that from a formal standpoint there is nothing to choose between the two systems. And since the whole problem of rational accounting and allocation is a formal one, this consideration alone is conclusive as far as any question of principle is involved.

This formal equivalence between the two systems does not mean that they would operate identically. In the unplanned system managers make their decisions in ignorance of what the others are going to do, and it is only through a step-by-step process that their actions are fitted together into a consistent pattern. In the planned system the Central Planning Board attempts in drawing up the plan to fit all the decisions together into a consistent pattern. If surrounding conditions were completely static—no changes in consumers' tastes, techniques of production, availability of natural resources, and so forth—the two systems would presumably arrive at the same end result, though by different paths. With surrounding conditions in a continuous state of change, however, there is no such thing as an end result; there are only paths of development, and there is no reason to suppose that the paths traced out by the two systems would ever cross.

Finally, in order to avoid misunderstanding, it is necessary to stress that the logical possibility of rational accounting and resource allocation by no means ensures that these goals will always be attained in practice. There will be areas of indeterminacy, miscalculations, errors of execution. But this is true of all systems, including competitive capitalism, monopolistic capitalism, unplanned collectivism, and planned socialism; and in this respect it seems safe to say that planned socialism need not fear comparison with its hypothetical and actual rivals.

CHAPTER 12

Are Socialism and Freedom Compatible?

IN THE UNITED STATES today most discussions of freedom or liberty (we shall use the two terms interchangeably) are confined to the relation between the individual and the state. Freedom is commonly assumed to exist to the extent that the state does not regulate or interfere with the lives of its citizens. The ideally free society, according to this criterion, would be anarchy, for anarchy is by definition a society in which there is no state and no government.

Let us provisionally adopt this conception of freedom and inquire how far it may be attainable in a socialist society. By following this course we do not, of course, commit ourselves to the view that this is either the only possible or even the most significant meaning of freedom. A church or an employer, no less than the state, may regulate and interfere with the lives of individuals; and in the larger sense the late Professor Whitehead was doubtless right in maintaining that "the essence of freedom is the practicability of purpose." [1] But before we approach the problem of freedom in this more comprehensive meaning of the term, we must examine some of the common arguments concerning the relation between the socialist state and the individual.

Planning and Economic Freedom

Historically, the first and most important of modern freedoms was economic freedom—freedom for the individual to buy and

[1] A. N. Whitehead, *Adventures of Ideas* (1935), p. 84.

sell subject only to the provisions of general laws which are
equally applicable to everyone. It is important to remember that
freedom to buy and sell, when it is defined so as to apply to both
goods and services, includes freedom to engage in any lawful occupation. It does not, of course, include freedom to violate the terms
of a contract once entered into.

There are those who regard economic freedom in this sense as
an evil. They include romantics who look back upon the ancient
or the medieval world as a lost paradise; they also include authori-
tarians and fascists who believe in the right of some to rule the
lives of others. But socialists are not to be found in this company.
Socialists look upon the attainment of economic freedom—and, of
course, of other individual liberties which will be considered
later—as a great historical advance. They believe that under capitalism economic freedom is used by the capitalist class for ultimately disastrous purposes. The socialist remedy, however, is not
to do away with freedom but rather to do away with classes. In
the socialist view the vast majority of mankind, far from having
too much economic freedom, does not have enough. It is therefore
one of the most telling of antisocialist arguments that comprehensive economic planning necessarily implies the abrogation of
the most cherished of economic freedoms, the freedom of the
consumer to spend his income as he sees fit and the freedom of
the worker to choose his own occupation. Let us examine this
argument as it is presented by such stalwart champions of old-
fashioned liberalism as Professor Hayek and Walter Lippmann.[2]

Neither Hayek nor Lippmann questions the genuineness of the
socialists' attachment to the ideal of freedom. They claim that the
tragedy of socialism is that the means which it adopts, economic
planning, must lead to the opposite of what it wants. The reasoning behind this claim is simple. An economic plan, they say, cannot be directed toward a goal so vague and undefined as "the

[2] F. A. Hayek, *The Road to Serfdom* (1944), and Walter Lippmann, *The
Good Society* (1937).

general welfare" or "the common good." Its objectives must be described in specific terms in order to determine a particular course of action.

> The welfare of a people cannot be adequately expressed as a single end, but only as a hierarchy of ends, a comprehensive scale of values in which every need of every person is given its place. To direct all of our activities according to a single plan presupposes that every one of our needs is given its rank in an order of values which must be complete enough to make it possible to decide between all the different courses between which the planner has to choose.[3]

Since no one is in a position to know "every one of our needs," it follows that the planners themselves must "impose their scale of preferences on the community for which they plan."[4] This scale of preferences, once embodied in the plan, necessarily supersedes the actual preferences of individuals; people must take what is planned for them, not what they would choose for themselves. Hence freedom of consumers' choice and planning are incompatible. In Lippmann's opinion "a planned production to meet a free demand is a contradiction in terms and as meaningless as a square circle."[5] But this is not all. To quote Lippmann again, "a plan of production is not only a plan of consumption, but a plan of how long, at what, and where the people shall work. . . . Therefore the inevitable and necessary complement of the rationing of consumption is the conscription of labor."[6]

What is wrong with this argument is not its logic but its basic premise. It assumes that a determinate and stable quantitative aggregate can exist only if each individual unit which goes to make up the aggregate is also determinate and stable. If this were the case, it would be quite true that the quantitative goals of a

[3] Hayek, *op. cit.,* pp. 42–43.
[4] *Ibid.,* p. 48.
[5] Lippmann, *op. cit.,* p. 102.
[6] *Ibid.*

production plan would have to be based on the summation of
the specific requirements of all the individuals making up society;
and it would also be true that the carrying out of the plan would
involve the regimentation of the individuals concerned. But in
reality it is one of the axioms of statistical science—with which
one would expect Professor Hayek, at any rate, to be familiar—
that determinateness and stability of aggregates are compatible
with indeterminateness and instability of the individual items
making up the aggregates. As John Neville Keynes said as long
ago as 1890 in his standard work, *The Scope and Method of
Political Economy,* "the manner in which, when a sufficient number of instances are taken, aggregate regularity is found to emerge
out of individual irregularity has been one of the most striking
results of statistical research." [7] When this fact is kept in mind,
it is easy to see that freedom of *individual* choice is quite compatible with planning of *social* production.

The Central Planning Board must have certain basic data if it
is to be able to plan production to meet a free consumers' demand.
These include (1) reliable population statistics, (2) total consumers' income, (3) the distribution of income by size, and (4) the
expenditure pattern of typical consuming units in each size class.
With these data in hand the Central Planning Board can estimate
with a high degree of accuracy the demand for the various commodities which must be produced. Is the Central Planning Board
in a position to obtain these data? The answer is certainly yes.
The case is obvious with respect to population statistics; total
consumers' income and its distribution by size form a part of the
plan and are therefore known; and the Central Planning Board
is in a specially favorable position to make comprehensive and
accurate budget studies. When demands have been estimated,
production can be planned accordingly.

There are, of course, bound to be errors in the estimates, but
there is no reason why these errors should upset the functioning

[7] P. 321.

of the system. It is only necessary to maintain adequate inventories at the various levels of production and to make more or less continuous adjustments in the production plan as these inventories fluctuate. It is important to understand not only the necessity but also the feasibility of such adjustments, because the anti-planners have attempted to bolster their case by stressing the supposed rigidity of an economic plan once it has been formulated and put into operation. For example, Lippmann argues that

> a plan subject to change from month to month or even from year to year is not a plan; if the decision has been taken to make ten million cars at $500 and one million suburban houses at $3000, the people cannot change their minds a year later, scrap the machinery to make the cars, abandon the houses when they are partly built, and decide to produce instead skyscraper apartment houses and underground railroads.[8]

The answer to this is that no people in their right minds would want to do what Lippmann here tells them they cannot do. But they might decide "a year later" that they want *some* fewer cars and suburban houses and *some* more skyscraper apartments and underground railroads. If the plan has been drawn up with the possibility of such marginal adjustments in mind, they can be made as a matter of routine. Lippmann tries to prove too much. He is fond of military analogies, and he believes that war and planning go together. Would he maintain that a military plan "which is subject to change . . . is not a plan?"

A related, but nevertheless distinct, problem has to do with changes in consumer-expenditure patterns. These may result from changes in incomes, from changes in tastes, from the introduction of new commodities, or from the invention of new and cheaper ways of producing existing commodities. For the most part such changes are gradual, can be observed in operation over a period

[8] Lippmann, *op. cit.*, p. 103.

of years, and can be planned for in advance on the basis of established trends. To the extent that this is so, they complicate the practical problem of planning but introduce no new questions of principle. This is particularly likely to be the case with changes which originate on the consumers' side. Changes in income are almost certain to be gradual and reasonably calculable, while sudden or far-reaching changes in tastes are nearly always a reflection of the availability of new or cheaper commodities.[9] Practically speaking, therefore, this problem boils down to the relation between planning and the invention of new commodities and new techniques of production. It is a well-known fact that under capitalism such inventions are capable of causing the most serious disturbances, and some writers have even attributed to them major responsibility for the business cycle. Would they not throw a monkey wrench into the mechanism of economic planning? And if so, would not a socialist society either have to give up planning or else suppress technological progress?

It would be foolish to deny that major technological discoveries will pose very serious problems for a planned as well as for an unplanned society. They will unquestionably introduce new sources of error into planning and will make the maintenance of flexibility even more important than it otherwise would be. But there is no justification for assuming that they would make planning impossible. On the contrary, it is only through planning that major technological discoveries can be rationally introduced and their undesirable secondary consequences minimized.

That this is so can best be seen by analyzing a particular case. Let us assume the invention of a really cheap and practical prefabricated house. Under capitalism such an invention would be fought by a multitude of vested interests (building-material manufacturers, contractors, and building trade unions, to mention

[9] We may omit the case of changes in taste deliberately induced by producers (e.g., women's fashions under capitalism). Not that a socialist society might not find merit in inducing such changes in taste, but only that if it does the Central Planning Board will certainly know about it in advance.

the most important). If successfully introduced, it would leave in its wake a mass of economic wreckage in the form of bankrupt firms, derelict communities, and unemployed workers with obsolete skills. In a socialist society, on the other hand, the new invention could be introduced in an orderly manner. The absence of vested property interests would obviously permit a more rapid pace to be set, while the necessity of providing for the conversion of communities to new production tasks and the training of workers to new skills would indicate the wisdom of a slower pace. Whether or not the resultant speed of introduction of the new houses would be faster or slower than under capitalism cannot be determined by general reasoning. But what can be said is that the speed under socialism could be deliberately regulated in such a way as to maximize the difference between the social advantages of the new invention and the social costs of its adoption. Moreover, those whose interests must necessarily be injured by the innovation—and even with the most skillful planning there will probably be some who fall into this category—can be compensated at the expense of the community as a whole. In other words, not only can the costs be minimized but what costs there are can be shouldered by everyone instead of by an unlucky minority.

At this point we may anticipate a query from the ranks of the socialists themselves. If the socialist society permits complete freedom of consumers' choice, they may ask, what function is left for the Central Planning Board but to anticipate what consumers want and plan production accordingly? How are we going to make over society and raise the level of consumers' tastes on this basis? The answer is very simple. To respect the freedom of consumers' choice does not mean to chase after the ideal of consumers' sovereignty, which some economists have set up as their *summum bonum*. The expenditure of a considerable proportion of the national income must be determined by the Central Planning Board (more accurately, by the government acting through the Central Planning Board) without any direct guidance from consumers. This applies, for example, to a large part of capital

investment and to all of what is sometimes called collective consumption, that is to say, the provision of free goods and services.

A little reflection will show that we have here a very wide sphere
for governmental initiative under socialism and that the opportunities which are thus offered for remaking society, and with it
the individual consumers themselves, should be extensive enough
to satisfy the most ambitious socialist. Three examples will illustrate the point. Planning of cities and towns—in other words, the
surroundings in which most people live—cannot be done in response to consumers' demands for particular types of houses; it
must be undertaken on the initiative of the government and by
people trained to see the problem as a whole. Health service, particularly the kind that helps to make people strong and well as
distinct from the kind that tries to cure them after they have fallen
ill, cannot be provided entirely in response to consumers' demands; it, too, must be largely a social responsibility. And finally,
education, if the socialist ideal of free education to all in proportion to their ability to benefit is to become a reality, must be
furnished by the community in response to social rather than
individual needs. It is surely obvious that the way to make people
over is to make over their surroundings, their bodies, and their
minds; and all these things can be done without interfering with
free consumers' choice in the usual sense of the term.[10]

So far we have said nothing about freedom of choice of occupation. After the discussion of consumption, however, this problem
can be dealt with very briefly. The contention of the antiplanners,
it will be remembered, is that a production plan necessarily implies a "plan of how long, at what, and where the people shall
work." In a sense this is certainly true. So many workers are
needed in coal mining, so many in manufacturing automobiles,
so many as doctors, and so on. But this does not mean that the
Central Planning Board has to decide that John Jones must

[10] This *principle* is, of course, fully recognized in the social welfare programs of the more advanced capitalist countries.

become a miner, or James Smith an auto worker, or Tom Brown a doctor. Once again the critics of socialism overlook the difference between individual units and statistical aggregates. It is quite possible to control the latter without controlling the former. An individual may decide to become an artist, come what may; but most people choose an occupation after considering such matters as opportunities for training, relative pay scales and working conditions, and possibilities of advancement. In a centrally planned economy these are all variables subject to the control of the Central Planning Board; if they are adjusted carefully and in accordance with the requirements of the plan there is no reason to suppose that satisfactory results cannot be obtained. The techniques as such are, after all, pretty much the same as those which operate in a capitalist society to direct the flow of workers into various occupations; and even under capitalism, where there is no coordination and planning and hence much confusion and waste, they do work. The burden of proof surely rests on those who maintain that they would cease to work if they were used in a planned and coordinated fashion.

Civil Liberties

Antisocialists usually argue nowadays that socialism is incompatible with the establishment and maintenance of civil liberties of the kind that are enjoyed by Britons and by most white, and some colored, Americans—freedom from arbitrary arrest, freedom of conscience, freedom of assembly, freedom of speech, and so on. At the present time, indeed, this is probably the most common, and perhaps the most influential, of all antisocialist arguments. The reasoning behind it seems to take one or more of three forms.

First, it is asserted that the basis of all freedom is economic freedom. If you control what a person consumes and what he works at, you necessarily control every other aspect of his life. "To be controlled in our economic pursuits," says Professor

Hayek, "is to be . . . controlled in everything." [11] As we have already seen, Hayek and Lippmann and other old-fashioned liberals hold that socialism and economic freedom are incompatible. They, therefore, require no new or independent grounds for concluding that socialism and civil liberties are incompatible. But, of course, the argument is no stronger than its foundation. If it is correct, as we attempted to show in the previous section, that socialism and economic freedom are compatible, then in this respect at any rate it follows that socialism and civil liberties are also compatible.

Second, it is asserted that socialism and civil liberties are incompatible for the reason, certainly persuasive if valid, that it is a part of the basic doctrine of socialism to suppress civil liberties. (Sometimes this argument is limited to "communism," though usually without any effort to define the term or to distinguish between communism and socialism.) This contention, however, is simply not true. Its credibility rests altogether on constant repetition and not at all on conformity to facts. No significant branch of the socialist movement has ever advocated the suppression of civil liberties. This applies as much to the Bolsheviks as it does to the British Labor Party or the German Social Democrats. As far as the Bolsheviks are concerned, this can be readily verified by consulting Chapter X of the Soviet Constitution, which deals with "Basic Rights and Duties of Citizens." All the usual civil liberties are guaranteed in terms which are entirely familiar to an English or American reader. Nor can it be maintained that the Soviet Constitution is mere window dressing. It is disseminated and studied inside the Soviet Union at least as extensively as the United States Constitution is in this country; and, like our constitution, it is generally accepted as a statement of the ideals which ought to guide the actions of both the state and the individual citizen. That these ideals are not always lived up to—either in the Soviet Union or in the United States—is certainly both true and important; but it does not mean that they do not exist

[11] Hayek, *op. cit.,* p. 68.

or that they can be ignored, still less that they can be transformed into their opposites.

Third, it is asserted that experience of socialism in the Soviet Union proves that socialism and civil liberties are incompatible. There need be no dispute about the facts of the case; all competent observers agree that in fact there are many restrictions on the civil liberties of the Soviet citizen. The only question is what interpretation the facts will bear. In its positive aspect this is a difficult question about which we shall have something to say in the final section of this chapter. Fortunately it is a simpler matter to show that the facts will not support the argument that socialism and civil liberties are incompatible. It is of the nature of a specific historical experience that it will support one type of generalization but not another. If something has actually happened, we are justified in concluding that it is possible and might happen again; we are not justified in concluding that something else is impossible. For example, Soviet experience justifies the conclusion that socialism is a workable social system; it also justifies the conclusion that socialism is compatible with restrictions on civil liberties. On the other hand, it does not justify the conclusion that a socialist state must take the form of a federation, or that it must organize agriculture on the basis of collective farms, or that socialism and civil liberties are necessarily incompatible.

Of course, a generalization of the latter type might be true, but it cannot be proved by the citation of one or more specific instances. There must be independent grounds for believing it to be true. If there are such independent grounds, the specific instances will certainly lend weight to the case. If there are no such independent grounds, the presumption is that the generalization is false and that the facts on which it is based must be interpreted in some other way. Consider, for example, another generalization: feudalism and civil liberties are incompatible. We shall certainly find that it is borne out by every historical instance of which we have a record. But what makes us sure that it is a valid generalization is our knowledge that the decisive social relation of feudalism is the *personal* relation of vassalage, which necessarily implies the right of some to govern the lives of others.

We have already seen that there is nothing in the structure or ideals of socialism which is incompatible with the existence of civil liberties. It follows that the restrictions on civil liberties which undoubtedly exist in the Soviet Union cannot be attributed to socialism as such; they must be explained in some other way.

New Freedoms under Socialism

So far we have confined our attention to the arguments of those who hold that socialism must necessarily do away with the kind of economic and civil liberties which have been won in some—though by no means all—of the more advanced capitalist countries. We have seen that none of these arguments stands up to analysis. As its adherents have always maintained, socialism is quite capable of preserving the advances of human freedom which have characterized the centuries since the Renaissance and the Reformation.

No socialist, however, would be content to let the matter drop there. Socialists hold that in two crucial respects the freedoms of capitalism are incomplete and that this is a situation which capitalism, by its very nature, is incapable of remedying. First, they maintain that capitalist society can never generalize the freedoms which, under certain conditions, it brings to a favored section of its members. And second, they maintain that capitalist society does not and cannot transcend an essentially negative conception of freedom. Socialism, on the other hand, they argue, can extend traditional freedoms to all its citizens and eventually, taking them for granted, can consciously move toward the goal of endowing everyone with positive freedom to live life to the full. Let us examine these two contentions in turn.

That capitalism has failed to generalize the freedoms which its spokesmen extol is an indisputable fact. Great Britain, for example, has never extended to its dependent empire the economic freedom and the civil liberties which are enjoyed by the inhabitants of the British Isles. And in the United States there are millions whose citizenship is but second-class—Negroes, Mexicans, and members of other minority groups—whose supposed constitutional rights are being constantly trampled on in ways which are sometimes open and obvious, sometimes hidden and obscure. Even the most free capitalist society, in short, practices forms of discrimination which inevitably involve curtailment of the liberties of some of its members or dependents. Is there reason to believe that this discrimination arises from the nature of the capitalist system itself, or must it be accounted for in some other way?

Socialists argue that discrimination is indeed rooted in the most fundamental characteristic of the capitalist system, the economic primacy of profit making. From a business point of view discrimination pays; and since this is the case, it survives and reappears despite all efforts which may be made to abolish it. There is no space here to present a generalized version of the economic theory of discrimination, but a couple of illustrations should suffice to make clear the nature of the reasoning involved. If Negroes can be excluded from a wide range of occupations, they must necessarily crowd into those which remain open to them and in this way drive wages down below levels which would otherwise be set. This is directly beneficial to the employers of Negro labor; and, what is perhaps more important, it is indirectly beneficial to capitalists in general since it creates a division in the working class and enables employers to play the two groups off against each other. It may be to the temporary advantage of the white workers in the occupations from which Negroes are excluded, but in the long run even the white workers probably lose more through weakened bargaining power than they gain from the absence of Negro competition. Or, to take a case of a different kind, if Negroes in a city can be forced to live in a certain restricted area, the result will be not only overcrowding but also excessively high rents and real-estate prices, which accrue to the benefit of land-lords in the district concerned.

Much the same forces are at work to maintain discrimination in colonial empires, though here their scope is normally even wider. In certain parts of Africa, for example, white settlers ac-complish a double purpose by reserving the best lands for them-selves: they monopolize the most lucrative economic opportuni-ties, and they force natives to become wage workers because the land which the natives are free to cultivate is insufficient to pro-vide a minimum livelihood. Capitalists in the mother country who invest in the colonies have similar motives for obstructing the full development of native economies; by so doing they fortify their own control over the most valuable natural resources and assure an ample supply of cheap labor. In all these cases, more-over, the denial or restriction of economic freedom is almost inevitably accompanied by a comparable denial or restriction of political and civil liberties. In arguing that the latter cannot exist without the former, the socialist is at one with the old-fashioned liberal. Political and civil liberties will sooner or later be used to fight against economic unfreedom, and in the ensuing struggle the one or the other must go under. The socialist has no doubt as to which side the forces of capitalist society will be on.

But what reason, it may be asked, is there to suppose that social-ism could abolish discrimination? The socialist answer is simple. Discrimination is never economically beneficial to a community as a whole. On the contrary, since it stunts the development of some members of the community and creates unnecessary conflict and friction, it inevitably impairs the productive powers of the community as a whole. Discrimination is practiced under capital-ism because the interests of a class, and often of particular groups within that class, are decisive for the functioning of the system. But socialism abolishes classes and substitutes the interest of the entire community as the guiding star of policy. Under these con-ditions it is clear that what pays is not discrimination but the abolition of discrimination. The principle of equal treatment for all is as deeply rooted in socialist economics as the principle of unequal treatment is in capitalist economics.

The experience of the Soviet Union does not prove that socialism and discrimination are incompatible—we have already seen that a particular historical experience cannot prove a generalization of this type—but it lends strong supporting evidence. Pre-Revolutionary Russia was the scene of every kind of discrimination in its most virulent form. The word "pogrom" is of Russian origin, and no colonial peoples in the world were worse treated than some of the nomadic tribes of Central Asia. And yet even the severest critics of the Soviet regime admit that within the space of two decades it effectively abolished discrimination from all the territories under its control. To do so was, of course, in keeping with the ideology of the Bolsheviks, but it was also a vital step in building up an economically productive and politically stable community. That antidiscrimination really has paid in the Soviet Union was dramatically illustrated during the Second World War, when soldiers of dozens of different nationalities fought with equal determination and courage against the foreign invaders. By way of contrast, during the First World War several of the nationalities of Central Asia were in bitter rebellion against the Czarist regime and could be subdued only by punitive expeditions, which drew strength away from the fighting fronts.

Let us turn now to the second socialist contention mentioned at the beginning of this section. Socialists do not, as is sometimes implied, deny the importance of freedom in the liberal sense of absence of arbitrary coercion; but they do maintain that this is not the only kind of freedom that counts or even, for the vast majority of mankind, the most important kind. Of what use is freedom from coercion to a starving man? What does it matter to people whose lives are lived on a level little above that of beasts? Can one even seriously speak of freedom when the range of alternatives open to a person is so limited as to be virtually nonexistent? Faced with questions of this sort—and they can scarcely be avoided by anyone who observes the world around him—the socialist concludes that there is another kind of freedom which the liberal tends to overlook or chooses to ignore, the positive freedom to do things, to know variety, to develop personality, in short to live a life worthy of human beings.[12]

Freedom in this sense is a compound of security and leisure on the one hand and of the material means to their enjoyment on the other. Hitherto it has for all practical purposes been the prerogative of the property-owning classes. Socialists concede that until very recent times this was inevitable. The productivity of human labor was so low that the vast majority of mankind was condemned to a life of toil and drudgery; only through the concentration of the surplus product in the hands of a small minority was it possible for civilization to rise and develop. Thus the class division of society and the exploitation of man by man, with their attendant limitation of positive freedom to the few, have had a common origin and a common justification in the low level of human productivity.

Socialists maintain that capitalism has changed all that. Capitalism, in the words of the *Communist Manifesto,* "has created more massive and more colossal productive forces than all preceding generations together." Thanks to "the immense increase of the productive forces attained through large-scale industry," Engels wrote, it is now possible

> to distribute labour over all members of society without exception, and thereby to limit the labour time of each individual member to such an extent that all have enough free time left to take part in the general—both theoretical and practical—affairs of society. It is only now, therefore, that any ruling and exploiting class has become superfluous. . . .[13]

[12] Professor Hayek holds that in talking this way, socialists are guilty of confusing freedom with wealth or power (*ibid.,* p. 19). But is it not really Professor Hayek who is guilty of confusion? Socialists certainly do not deny that wealth and power have usually been the source of freedom to do things, but it hardly clarifies the issue to identify the cause with the effect.

[13] *Anti-Dühring,* p. 207.

One might be tempted to argue that a system which has released such mighty productive forces should also be able to solve the problem of creating leisure, security, and abundance for all its members. The reasons why socialists reject this argument have been given in Chapter 7 and need not be repeated here. They can be summed up in statements of Marx and Lenin.

> It is the fact [Marx wrote] that capital and its self-expansion appear as the starting and closing point, as the motive and aim of production; that production is merely production for *capital,* and not vice versa, the means of production mere means for an ever expanding system of the life process for the benefit of the *society* of producers. . . . Thus, while the capitalist mode of production is one of the historical means by which the material forces of production are developed and the world-market required for them created, it is at the same time in continual conflict with this historical task and the conditions of social production corresponding to it.[14]

And Lenin made essentially the same point when he said that "the historical mission of capitalism . . . consists in the development of society's productive forces; its structure prevents the useful application of these technical achievements for the benefit of the masses of the people." [15]

Socialism suffers from no such inherent limitations. By abolishing classes and by introducing economic planning in the interests of the whole community, socialism overcomes the contradictions of capitalism and lays the basis for a continuous rise in living standards. Socialists do not maintain that this will bring the highest type of freedom—the freedom to live life to the full—to everyone overnight. Even in the most advanced countries the process will necessarily be slow, while at the other extreme, in

[14] *Capital,* Vol. III, p. 293.
[15] *Sämtliche Werke,* Vol. III, pp. 20–21.

the overpopulated and poverty-ridden countries of Asia, the time required to reach the goal may well be measured in centuries. But socialists hold that the question of how long it will take is not the real issue; no one denies that the task is huge and the difficulties many. The important thing is that mankind is at last in a position to tackle the task and to overcome the difficulties. The mission of capitalism was one of preparation; the mission of socialism will be one of fulfillment.

Freedom in Historical Perspective

It is a commonplace of liberal thought that the period from the fifteenth to the nineteenth centuries was a period of "stupendous liberation of the minds and spirits and conduct of men." [16] And socialists, while insisting that the vast majority of mankind was affected much less than such sweeping language would suggest, are not disposed to deny the direction or the importance of the change which occurred.[17] But then, sometime during the second half of the nineteenth century, the tide turned. What Lippmann calls "the method of freedom" was abandoned, and

> the world moved into an era of intensified national rivalry . . . and of intensified domestic struggle which has racked all nations and reduced some to a condition where there are assassination, massacre, persecution, and the ravaging of armed bands such as have not been known in the western world for at least two centuries.[18]

How explain this sudden turn of events, so unexpected by the nineteenth-century prophets of liberalism? Their modern descendants can only reply that someone made a mistake. Lipp-

[16] Lippmann, op. cit., p. 20.

[17] For an excellent statement of the socialist position on this issue, see Harold Laski, The Rise of European Liberalism (1936).

[18] Lippmann, op. cit., pp. 20–21.

mann thinks it was the liberals themselves who erred and is inclined to see in Herbert Spencer the archoffender. Hayek blames the Germans, and especially the German socialist thinkers. But none of this really explains anything. From some points of view history is doubtless nothing but a series of mistakes; but this does not absolve us from the task of discovering why people in general, or particular groups of people, make the mistakes they do when they do.

If this book has succeeded at all in accomplishing what it set out to accomplish, it will have demonstrated that socialists at any rate have a rational explanation of the phenomena which the liberals describe and deplore. For the whole body of Marxian economics leads to the conclusion that capitalism must pass through a transformation like that which took place during the last third of the nineteenth century. And if we follow up the implications of this analysis, we shall find it easy to understand why capitalism in its latest phase is unable to support the degree of liberty which it achieved in an earlier phase.

Put in its simplest terms, the essential change in the capitalist economy was from competition and free trade to monopoly and imperialism. Under the regime of competition and free trade the social and international conflicts of capitalist society were confined within narrow limits; moderate forces tended to dominate political life; the social order itself seemed to rest on secure foundations; the ruling classes could afford to practice the methods of concession and conciliation. A steady widening of popular liberties was a natural consequence of these conditions. In the period of monopoly and imperialism, on the other hand, capitalist society became increasingly geared to the methods of violence and warfare, and this fact exerted a profound influence on almost every phase of social existence. As the German Social Democrat Rudolf Hilferding wrote several years before the First World War, "the bourgeoisie ceases to be peaceful and humanitarian. . . . As an ideal there now appears the conquest of world mastery for one's own nation. . . . In place of the democratic ideal of equality steps an oligarchical ideal of mastery." [19] Under these changed conditions a centuries-long trend to greater freedom was reversed in the relatively brief span of a few decades.

The form which this reversal of trend took, of course, was not everywhere the same; what happened in each country was conditioned by previous history and existing circumstances. Thus, in those regions like western Europe and America where liberty was most firmly entrenched, it showed itself most resistant to attacks; in those regions like central and eastern Europe where it was new and superficially rooted, it gave way more easily; while in those regions like Asia and Africa where it had never really established a foothold, there was now no opportunity for it to do so.

The actual course of events is well known, and the reader need only be reminded of certain salient features. Under the tremendous strain of the First World War the chain of capitalist society broke in its weakest link, the Russian Empire. Socialism thus came into the world, amid conditions of economic chaos and civil war, in a vast country which had earned for itself the reputation of being "the prison of the peoples." The new society was fiercely combated by the former Russian ruling classes and by the capitalist world in general; at one time there were, in addition to innumerable White armies and bands, soldiers of more than a dozen foreign nations on Soviet soil. The task of building socialism in Russia would have been enormously difficult even under the most favorable conditions; in the beleaguered-fortress atmosphere of the years after 1917 it was a task of almost unimaginable difficulty. No regime which was serious about carrying it through to successful completion could afford to be guided by the comfort or convenience, to say nothing of the liberty, of the individual citizen. And the Bolsheviks were serious.

It is true that there was a period of relative stabilization in the capitalist world during the twenties; and as the Soviet Union

[19] See the passage from Hilferding's *Das Finanzkapital* (1910), translated and published under the title "The Ideology of Imperialism" as Appendix B in P. M. Sweezy, *The Theory of Capitalist Development* (1942).

recovered from the effects of war, revolution, and civil strife, some easing of the tension between and within European countries took place. But the respite was short-lived; close on the heels of the Great Depression came German fascism and feverish preparations for a new war.

The requirements of successful coalition warfare produced a brief period of *rapprochement* between the Soviet Union and the major capitalist powers during and immediately after the Second World War. The underlying trends, however, were not affected and, once the pressure of military necessity was removed, began to reassert themselves more insistently than ever. At the present time capitalism as a world system is riddled with contradictions and conflicts; socialism is wrestling with the problems left by vast material damage suffered during the war; and the two systems are struggling in dead earnest for the minds and souls of men, with no one able to say whether or how long the struggle will remain peaceful.

What conclusion do we reach from viewing our own epoch in retrospect? Surely that the ebb tide of liberty, which began to flow some three-quarters of a century ago, has not yet run its course. For while it has been clear ever since 1917 that socialism has been fighting for its life, it is now no less evident that capitalism is facing a mortal danger of collapse and disintegration. And, as Laski has well said, "when a system is fighting for its life, it has no time for the habits of a debating society." [20] The restrictions on liberty which are characteristic of Soviet Russia are far less symptomatic of the times than the crisis of liberty in the United States. Russia, after all, never knew liberty, while the United States was built up largely through the efforts of those who sought a haven from oppression and injustice. The lesson is all too clear: regardless of the nature of the social system, liberty does not and cannot thrive in an atmosphere of social crisis and international conflict.

[20] Laski, *op. cit.*, p. 247.

"So," in the words of Professor Laski, "mankind seemed to enter upon a long period of winter. We can comfort ourselves only with the hope that a later generation will detect in its rigours the grim prelude to a brighter spring." [21] Is the hope justified? Socialists believe that it is. They believe that the present period of crisis and struggle can come to an end only with the general triumph of socialism. And they believe that socialism, when it no longer has to fight for its life, will usher in a period of unprecedented economic advance and social peace. Under these conditions liberty may once more come into its own, but on a higher level and in a fuller sense than any previous epoch has been privileged to know. It is these beliefs that constitute the ultimate driving force of socialism in the world today.

[21] *Ibid.*, p. 264.

Bibliography of Works Cited

BARKER, ERNEST (ed.): *The Politics of Aristotle,* Oxford University Press, New York, 1946.

BAROU, N. (ed.): *The Co-operative Movement in Labour Britain,* Victor Gollancz, Ltd., London, 1948.

BAYKOV, ALEXANDER: *The Development of the Soviet Economic System,* Cambridge University Press, London, 1946.

BONAR, JAMES: "Socialism," *Encyclopaedia Britannica,* 13th ed.

BRAUNTHAL, JULIUS: *In Search of the Millennium,* Victor Gollancz, Ltd., London, 1945.

British Labour Party: *Let Us Face the Future,* London, 1945.

CARR, E. H.: *The Soviet Impact on the Western World,* The Macmillan Company, New York, 1947.

DICKINSON, H. D.: *The Economics of Socialism,* Oxford University Press, New York, 1939.

DIMITROV, GEORGI: "The Communists and the Fatherland Front," *Political Affairs,* August, 1946.

Economic Survey for 1947, Cmd. 7046, His Majesty's Stationery Office, London, 1947. (Reprinted in *Federal Reserve Bulletin,* April, 1947.)

ENGELS, FRIEDRICH: *Herr Eugen Dühring's Revolution in Science [Anti-Dühring],* International Publishers Co., New York, no date.

———: *The Origin of the Family, Private Property, and the State,* Charles Kerr & Co., Chicago, 1902.

——— and KARL MARX: *see* Marx, Karl, and Friedrich Engels.

GOMULKA, WLADYSLAW: "People's Democracy: The Way to the Peaceful Development of Poland," *Political Affairs,* April, 1947.

GRAY, ALEXANDER: *The Socialist Tradition: Moses to Lenin,* Longmans, Green & Co., Inc., New York, 1946.

HANSEN, A. H.: *Full Recovery or Stagnation?*, W. W. Norton & Company, New York, 1938.

HARRIS, S. E. (ed.): *The New Economics*, Alfred A. Knopf, Inc., New York, 1947.

HAYEK, F. A.: *The Road to Serfdom*, The University of Chicago Press, Chicago, 1945.

—— (ed.): *Collectivist Economic Planning*, George Routledge & Sons, Ltd., and Kegan, Paul, Trench, Trubner & Co., Ltd., London, 1935.

HILFERDING, RUDOLF: *Das Finanzkapital*, Wiener Volksbuchhandlung, Vienna, 1923.

KAUTSKY, KARL: *Die materialistische Geschichtsauffassung*, 2d ed., 2 vols., J. H. W. Dietz, Berlin, 1929.

KEYNES, J. N.: *The Scope and Method of Political Economy*, Macmillan & Co., Ltd., London, 1891.

KLEIN, L. R.: *The Keynesian Revolution*, The Macmillan Company, New York, 1947.

The Land of Socialism Today and Tomorrow, Reports and speeches at the Eighteenth Congress of the Communist Party of the Soviet Union (Bolsheviks), March 10–21, 1939, Foreign Languages Publishing House, Moscow, 1939.

LASKI, H. J.: *The Rise of European Liberalism: An Essay in Interpretation*, George Allen & Unwin, Ltd., London, 1936.

LENIN, V. I.: *The State and Revolution*, International Publishers Co., New York, 1932.

LIPPINCOTT, BENJAMIN (ed.): *On the Economic Theory of Socialism*, University of Minnesota Press, Minneapolis, 1938.

LIPPMANN, WALTER: *The Good Society*, 2d ed., Little, Brown & Company, Boston, 1943.

LOCKE, JOHN: *Two Treatises of Government*, edited with an introduction by Thomas I. Cook, Hafner Publishing Co., New York, 1947.

LOUIS, PAUL: *Histoire du socialisme en France, 1789–1945*, Librairie Marcel Rivière et cie., Paris, 1946.

MARKHAM, S. F., *A History of Socialism,* The Macmillan Company, New York, 1931.

MARX, KARL: *Capital,* Charles Kerr & Co., Chicago, Vol. I, 1906; Vols. II and III, 1909.

——: *Critique of the Gotha Programme,* International Publishers Co., New York, 1933.

——: *The Eighteenth Brumaire of Louis Bonaparte,* International Publishers Co., New York, no date.

——: *The Poverty of Philosophy,* International Publishers Co., New York, no date.

—— and FRIEDRICH ENGELS: The *Communist Manifesto,* with an introduction and explanatory notes by D. Ryazanoff, Martin Lawrence, Ltd., London, 1930.

——: *Correspondence, 1846–1895: A Selection with Commentary and Notes,* International Publishers Co., New York, 1935.

——: *The German Ideology* (Parts I and III), International Publishers Co., New York, 1939.

——: *Gesamtausgabe,* Marx-Engels-Lenin Institute, Moscow, 1927——. (This is the authoritative edition of the works of Marx and Engels. Many volumes are still to be published. Certain works, such as Part II of *The German Ideology,* are available only in the *Gesamtausgabe.*)

MEHRING, FRANZ: *Karl Marx,* Covici, Friede, Inc., New York, 1935.

MINC, HILARY: *The Nationalization of Industry in Poland: Speech by the Minister of Industry, Hilary Minc, at the Ninth Session of the National Council of the Homeland,* The State Publishing Institute, Warsaw, 1946.

——: "Plan for Poland's Economic Reconstruction," *Poland of Today* (monthly bulletin of the Polish Research and Information Service, New York), November, 1946.

——: "Poland and the U.S.S.R.—Economic Cooperation," *Poland of Today* (monthly bulletin of the Polish Research and Information Service, New York), August, 1946.

Mises, Ludwig: *Socialism: An Economic and Sociological Analysis,* The Macmillan Company, New York, 1936.

More, Thomas: *Utopia* (Everyman's Library), J. M. Dent & Sons, Ltd., London and Toronto, 1928.

Page, C. H.: *Class and American Sociology: From Ward to Ross,* Dial Press, Inc., New York, 1940.

Petegorsky, D. W.: *Left-Wing Democracy in the English Civil War,* Victor Gollancz, Ltd., London, 1940.

Pigou, A. C.: *Socialism Versus Capitalism,* Macmillan & Co., Ltd., London, 1937.

Pirenne, Henri: *Economic and Social History of Medieval Europe,* Harcourt, Brace & Company, Inc., New York, no date.

Polish National Economic Plan, Central Board of Planning, Warsaw, 1946.

Reinhold, Meyer: "Historian of the Classic World: A Critique of Rostovtzeff," *Science and Society,* Fall, 1946.

Robbins, Lionel: *The Great Depression,* Macmillan & Co., Ltd., London, 1934.

Rothstein, Theodore: *From Chartism to Labourism,* Martin Lawrence, Ltd., London, 1929.

Sabine, G. H. (ed.): *The Works of Gerrard Winstanley,* Cornell University Press, Ithaca, New York, 1941.

Schlesinger, Rudolf: *Soviet Legal Theory,* Oxford University Press, New York, 1945.

Schuman, F. L.: *Soviet Politics at Home and Abroad,* Alfred A. Knopf, Inc., New York, 1946.

Schumpeter, J. A.: *Capitalism, Socialism, and Democracy,* Harper & Brothers, New York, 1942.

Smith, Adam: *The Wealth of Nations,* 2 vols., Methuen & Co., Ltd., London, 1930.

Strachey, John: *Socialism Looks Forward,* Philosophical Library, Inc., New York, 1945.

Sumner, B. H.: *A Short History of Russia,* Reynal & Hitchcock, Inc., New York, 1943.

SWEEZY, P. M.: *The Theory of Capitalist Development,* Oxford University Press, New York, 1942.

TAUSSIG, F. W.: *Principles of Economics,* 2 vols., The Macmillan Company, New York, 1911.

TAWNEY, R. H.: *The Acquisitive Society,* Harcourt, Brace & Company, New York, 1920.

Temporary National Economic Committee, *Hearings,* Part I, U.S. Government Printing Office, Washington, D. C., 1938.

WEBB, SIDNEY and BEATRICE: *Soviet Communism: A New Civilization,* 3d ed., Longmans, Green & Co., Inc., New York, 1944.

WHITEHEAD, A. N.: *Adventures of Ideas,* The Macmillan Company, New York, 1935.

WINSTANLEY, GERRARD: *see* Sabine, G. H.

Index

A

Accumulation of capital, 144*ff.*
  and consumption, 144, 149
  and crises, 146
  long-run effects of, 147*ff.*
  and wages, 145–146
Adler, Friedrich, 187
Albania, 61, 62
Anglo-Iranian Oil Company, 50*n.*
Atomic energy, 120

B

Babeuf, F. N., 100–101, 106
Barker, Ernest, 92–93
Barone, Enrico, 222*n.*
Baykov, Alexander, 30, 31, 33, 237
Bebel, August, 162, 169
Bentham, Jeremy, 198
Bernstein, Eduard, 99, 168, 169, 185
Bohemia, 61
Bolsheviks, 169, 171, 174, 176–181,
  219, 237, 250, 255, 260
Bonar, James, 7
Braunthal, Julius, 187–188
Brutzkus, Boris, 222
Bulgaria, 61, 62, 64
Burke, Edmond, 200

C

Capital, 124
  (*See also Das Kapital*)
Capital, centralization of, 150

Capital, constant, 143, 145
  organic composition of, 143
  variable, 143, 145
    (*See also* Accumulation of capi-
    tal)
Capitalism, contradictions of, 147*ff.*,
  152
  defined, 4
  and discrimination, 253–254
  duplication of effort under, 215
  economic leadership under, 207*ff.*
  incentives to work under, 202*ff.*
  nature cf, 135–138
  place in history of, 111–112, 257
  and selling costs, 214
  and technology, 214
  and uncertainty, 214–215
Carr, E. H., 66
Chartism, 104–106
Christianity, 92
Civil liberties, 249*ff.*
Class struggles, in history, 110–111,
  121
  and the state, 127, 133–134
Classes, 121, 133–134
  abolition of, 130–131
  and the state, 127–129
Clynes, J. R., 36
C–M–C, 137–138
Collectivization of agriculture, in
  eastern Europe, 68–69
  in Poland, 87
  in Soviet Union, 20–23
    (*See also* Land reform)